Tales from the Captain's Log

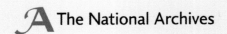

Adlard Coles Nautical

An imprint of Bloomsbury Publishing Plc

50 Bedford Square	1385 Broadway
London New	York
WC1B 3DP	NY 10018
UK	USA

www.bloomsbury.com

www.adlardcoles.com

British Library Cataloguing-in-Publication Data

A catalogue record for this book is available from the British Library.

Library of Congress Cataloguing-in-Publication data has been applied for.

ISBN: HB: 978-1-4729-4866-3
         ePDF: 978-1-4729-4867-0
         ePub: 978-1-4729-4868-7

2 4 6 8 10 9 7 5 3 1

Design by Nicola Liddiard, Nimbus Design

Printed in China by RRD Asia Printing Solutions Limited

To find out more about our authors and books visit www.bloomsbury.com.

Here you will find extracts, author interviews, details of forthcoming
events and the option to sign up for our newsletters.

Tales from the
Captain's Log

From *Captain Cook* to
Charles Darwin, *Blackbeard*
and *Nelson* – accounts of great events
at sea from those who were there

 The National Archives

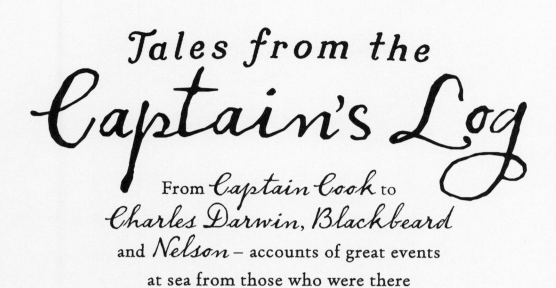

ADLARD COLES NAUTICAL

BLOOMSBURY
LONDON · NEW DELHI · NEW YORK · SYDNEY

Contents

East end of Tahiti.

In the Age of Sail, people took to the seas for many reasons. For some, serving the Royal Navy and defending British interests on the water was a vocation. For others, great voyages opened up opportunities for new discoveries, be they map-makers charting miles of previously unknown coastlines or botanists collecting specimens of exotic plants and animals. And for others still, long passages at sea were something to be endured, with the prospect of a better life waiting for them in another land. The late seventeenth and early eighteenth centuries were the golden age of piracy, where lawless bandits of the sea capitalised on the large number of vessels on the water by pillaging and plundering vulnerable ships, and then selling off their ill-gotten gains for huge profits. Other disreputable characters were also to be found at sea in the form of convicts who, instead of being sentenced to the death penalty, were leaving family and friends behind for good as they were transported to Australia.

The challenges of life at sea were numerous. Not only was there the danger posed by lurking pirates, threatening to ransack any passing ship, there were other life-threatening hazards as well, such as gale-force winds, not to mention the rampant spread of diseases such as cholera. In addition, provisioning a ship with sufficient food and drinking water for long stints at sea was a huge and difficult task, with unpredictable weather conditions meaning that journeys often took longer than expected. As a result, food had to be rationed carefully. However, fresh fruit could not last for long periods, and the resulting deficiency in Vitamin C among many crew and passengers on long sea journeys led them to suffer from scurvy. All of these factors, alongside the common complaint of sea sickness, meant that travel by sea could be a real trial.

The opening chapter of this book, covering exploration and discovery, examines the ships' logs taken from botanical and cartographical missions. In 1851, the eminent nineteenth-century botanist Richard Spruce wrote: 'The greatest pleasure of naturalists (understated by certain utilitarians) is to discover new species, to point to new islands on the map of nature, and to populate continents that seem to be deserts.'

The exquisitely detailed watercolours in sketchbooks and the first-hand reactions of intrepid individuals as they ventured into new and unfamiliar lands make for compelling reading, and shine the spotlight on an amazing era

Sea coast charts taken from John Sellar's *Atlas Maritimus* first published in 1698.
RIGHT

of invention and discovery. Among the explorations covered in this chapter is Captain Cook's voyage on HMS *Endeavour*, his first contact with the indigenous people of Eastern Australia at Botany Bay in April 1770, the collection of many new species by the botanists on board, and the charting of over 5,000 miles of previously unmapped coastline, literally changing the view of the world.

The struggle for authority on the waves is the subject of the second chapter, on pirates and mutiny. It draws on a rich array of swashbuckling characters, giving valuable insights into the struggle to combat unlawful pillaging at sea. Edward Thatch was a pirate of terrifying repute with a large untamed beard covering his entire face up to his eyes, earning him the nickname Blackbeard. Though his pirating career spanned no more than three years, he cultivated such a fearsome reputation that his name was enough for many ship's captains to surrender to him without a fight. At the height of his dominance he had amassed a formidable flotilla of ships, but his demise came when he boarded HMS *Jane* in 1718, and was surrounded by crew from below deck and beheaded. In other cases, the distinction between supposedly lawful privateering and illegal piracy was less clear, and the stories of the infamous Captain Kidd and Henry Morgan attest to this. Mutiny was also an ever present danger. The events on board the *Bounty* are recounted in Captain Bligh's own words, as well as his truly remarkable 4,000 mile voyage to safety in a small boat. Less well-known is the uprising on HMS *Hermione* in September 1797 – the bloodiest mutiny in the history of the Royal Navy.

Chapter Three focuses on science and medicine at sea. We join Charles Darwin on one of the most important scientific expeditions in history: the five-year voyage of HMS *Beagle* across the southern hemisphere, during which Darwin gathered the findings that formed the basis of his famous tome *On the Origin of Species* (1859). While Darwin may have been in seventh heaven as a naturalist, enthusing about the amazing bird life on the Galapagos, he was not a natural sailor and he struggled with seasickness in between studying the local flora and fauna of the region. The experiences of surgeons at sea were integral to the progress of medicine in the eighteenth and nineteenth centuries. The gruesome and realistic illustrations drawn by ship surgeons depict the injuries and diseases that often blighted ships' crews, such as scurvy.

Focusing on a number of key sea battles, Chapter Four looks at naval conflict in the eighteenth and nineteenth centuries. 'England expects that every man will do his duty,' Admiral Lord Nelson signalled to his fleet before the Battle of Trafalgar commenced on 21 October 1805. In a minute-by-minute account of the battle, the log of HMS *Victory* offers fascinating insights into the reality of naval conflict. With victory at Trafalgar, the Royal Navy established mastery at sea, and although it would last for over a century, it was overshadowed at the time by the death of Nelson, a hugely popular British national hero. As well as Trafalgar, this chapter covers other significant battles during the Age of Sail such as the Battle of Quiberon Bay in 1759 and the Battle of the Nile in 1798.

Finally, Chapter Five takes as its subject sea passengers who left Britain for new lives abroad. Emigration to the New World in the eighteenth century and to Australia in the nineteenth was driven by the opportunities these unexplored territories offered to start over, seek wealth and expand boundaries. On the other hand, this era also saw the transportation of convicted criminals to penal colonies in Australia. Indeed, between 1787 and 1867 as many as 160,000 convicts were sent there.

Bringing together history, science and adventure, *Tales from the Captain's Log* delves into original logs, letters and journals of great expeditions, voyages and sea battles, all of which have been selected from the 126 shelf-miles of documents held within The National Archives' extensive collection. Brought together, they uncover remarkable and often long-forgotten stories of enormous courage, spirit and endurance at sea.

Dr Hester Vaizey

1

Exploration & Discovery

Spying in the Mediterranean

GRENVILLE COLLINS ... 1676

In the annals of seafaring, Captain Grenville Collins has perhaps undeservedly been overlooked, for he was the first Englishman to chart the British coast systematically, and he recorded his work in *Great Britain's Coasting Pilot*. This was no mean feat: the modern British coastline has been measured at 7,723 miles and would have been full of hazards for a seventeenth-century wooden vessel.

Collins' early naval career as an officer and hydrographer saw him touring the South Seas and the coast of South America from 1669 to 1671, but his most intriguing assignment was to the Mediterranean in 1676, on the orders of none other than Samuel Pepys, the Secretary to the Admiralty. Collins' logs on a succession of Royal Navy vessels – *Charles*, *James*, *Newcastle*, *Plymouth* and *Lark* – record the journeys of his vessels, the places they visited, the navigation, instances of piracy and the weather each day. His hydrography mission was ostensibly innocuous, yet the covert aim of the voyage to the Mediterranean was espionage.

The journey began in Falmouth in January 1677, and from there Collins sailed through the Bay of Biscay to the coast of Portugal and on to Tangier, recording his arrival there in the log of the *Charles* frigate on Sunday 11 February 1677, as well as providing a drawing of the town and bay:

> '… and at five in the morning made sayle the wind blowing hard out of the straits mouth we made several boards to turn into Tangier Bay, where we anchored at twelve at noon in 19 ffathom water the easternmost point bearing ENE ¼ N, Old Tangier SE ½ S, Peterborough Tower SW ¼ W, the westernmost point W ½ S, and the ffountains just open of the mould head. Our Lieut went a shoare to waite on our Capt and to carry him his commission and deliver the ship to his command, all night the Lieut returned on board bringing word that Capt Hambleton our comander was in good health, and likewise all the garrison.'

DOC. 1 The first page of Grenville Collins' *Journal* from 1676.

This book bought off a Stall on Moorfields
the Year 1774 for 6 Shillings, and presented
to Rear Adm.l Man. Left by him to Captain
Robert Man ――

Received this book from Robert Man Esq.r Commander of H.M.S. Bedford
through the hands of my friend George Stone Esq.r of Plymouth at Plymouth
April 1.st 1788. William

*Journal in his Maj.ts Rowing Fryggot
the*

Charles

*By Grenvill Collins Master of y.e said Fryggot
1676*

Began Rigging wages at Woolwich
the 16.th Octo.r 1676)

DOC. 2

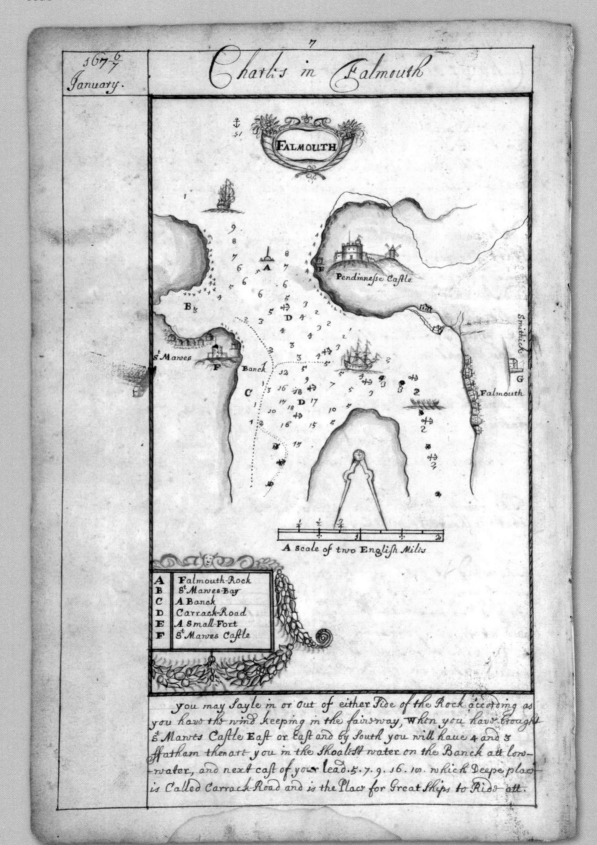

1676/7
January.

FALMOUTH

Pendinnesse Castle

Smithick

St Mawes

Banck

Falmouth

A scale of two English Miles

A	Falmouth-Rock
B	St Mawes-Bay
C	A Banck
D	Carrack-Road
E	A Small-Fort
F	St Mawes Castle

You may Sayle in or out of either side of the Rock according as you have the wind keeping in the fairway, when you have brought St Mawes Castle East or East and by South you will have 4 and 3 ffathem then art you in the shoalest water on the Banck att low-water, and next cast of your lead 5. 7. 9. 16. 10. which Deepe place is Called Carrack-Road and is the Place for Great Ships to Ride att.

On Monday 12 February he recorded the skirmishes with the Moors in Tangier:

> *'The wind at E a fresh gale, Capt Hamble[ton] came on board bringing severall*
> *gentlemen of Tangier with him, Tangier is at present at warr with the moores our*
> *English have taken in a new spott of ground and set stockades round it, soe that the*
> *moores have drawn down a great army against Tangier, and in the night time intrench*
> *themselves neere the stockadoes and pull many of them downe and cary them away to*
> *there loss of many men, and some of ours, every day and night there are some small*
> *skirmishes with the moores.'*

Collins followed the coast, reaching Alicante. He proceeded to sketch out
the topography of the port and recorded the fortifications for the benefit of
the Admiralty.

On 16 March 1678 Collins, on board the frigate *Newcastle*, arrived in the
Bay of Naples having sailed via Livorno on the Tuscan coast of Italy. He set to
work recording the coastline on a set of charts, incorporating information which
would be of use to the Admiralty, such as anchorages, rocks and other hazards.
This was supplemented with a fairly florid description of Naples, recording not
only its impressive buildings and the dress worn by the inhabitants, but also the
military installations and garrison of the city – information that would be useful,
as Naples was controlled by the Spanish Empire:

> *'Discription of Naples*
> *This most ffamos and butifull citty lyeth on the side of a mountaine, by a good and*
> *convenient haven, in a rich and ffleurishing soyle. Bounded on the SE side with a bay*
> *of the Tyrrhen Sea, unacquainted with tempests; alongst which she stretcheth; and*
> *is backt by mountaines enriched with most excellent viniards, she enjoyeth the delicate*
> *prospect of Vesuvius, Surrentum, Caprea, Misenus, Prochita, and Enaria, Her beauty*
> *is most glorious. The private buildings being gracefull, and the publick stately: adorned*
> *with staues, the workes of exellent workemen, and sundry preserved antiquities.*
>
> *As for her strength, the hand of art hath joyined with nature to make her*
> *invincible. For, besides the being almost surrounded with the sea, and mountaines not*
> *to be transcended without much difficulty and disadvantage; she is strongly walled and*

DOC. 2 The start of the journey in
Falmouth, January 1677.

DOC. 3 & 4 The journal's record of the
skirmishes with the Moors in Tangier.

167 6/7 February	*Charl's Frygg. in Tangier.*
Sunday 11th	

167 6/7 February	Charl's Frygg. in Tangier.
Sunday 11th +3 In Tangier	wee lay By, and at five in the morning made Sayle the wind Blowing hard out of the Straits mouth, wee made Severall Boards to Turn into Tangier Bay, where we Anchored at twelve at Noone in 19 fathom Water the Eastermost point bearing ENE 2/4 N, Old Tangier S 8 1/2 S, Peterbourough Tower SW 1/4 W, the Westermost point W 1/2 S, and the Fountaine Just open of the Mould head Our Lieu^t went ashoare to waib on our Capt and to Cary him his Commission and Deliver the Ship to his Command, all Night the Lieu^t Returnd onboard bringing word that Capt Hambleton our Comander was in good health, and likewise all the Garrison

Munday 12th.

The wind at S afresh Gale, Capt Hamble^t came on Board bringing Severall Gentlemen of Tangier with him, Tangier is at Prisant at warr with the moores our English have takenin a new Spott of ground and Set Stockadoes Round it, Soo that the moores have drawne downe a great Army against Tangier, and in the Night time Intrench them Selves neere the Stockadoes and pull many of them downe and Cary them away to there loss of many men, and some of ours, Every Day and Night there are Some Small Skermishes with the moores.

Tuesday 13th.

The James Frygot Sayled for Cadiz, to attend Sr Robt Robinson in the Assurance, The Swan Frygott Capt Carter Arrived heare with three English Ships Under his Convoy they haveing now passes, the wind att ENE afresh Gale

Wednesday 14th

The wind att ENE afresh Gale, wee tooke in water and Ballass, and our Cap^{ts} Goods

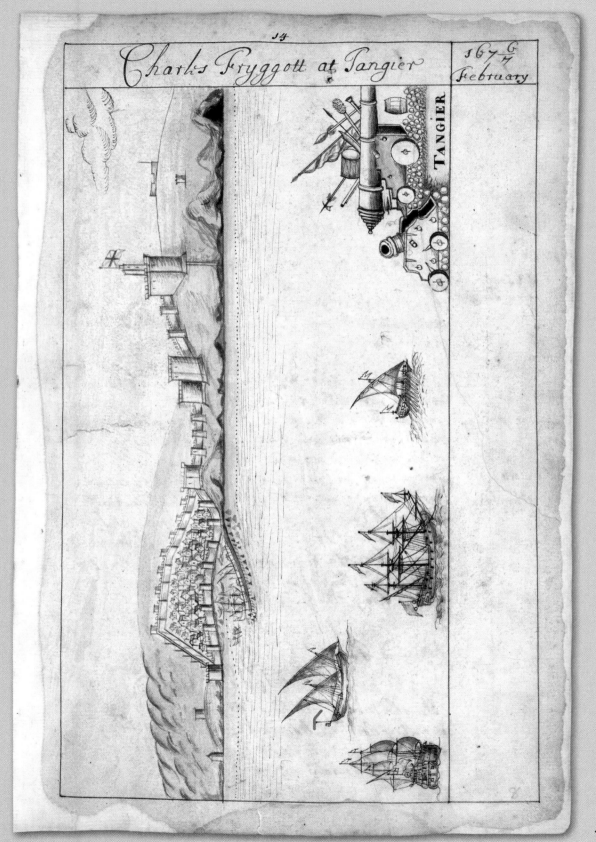

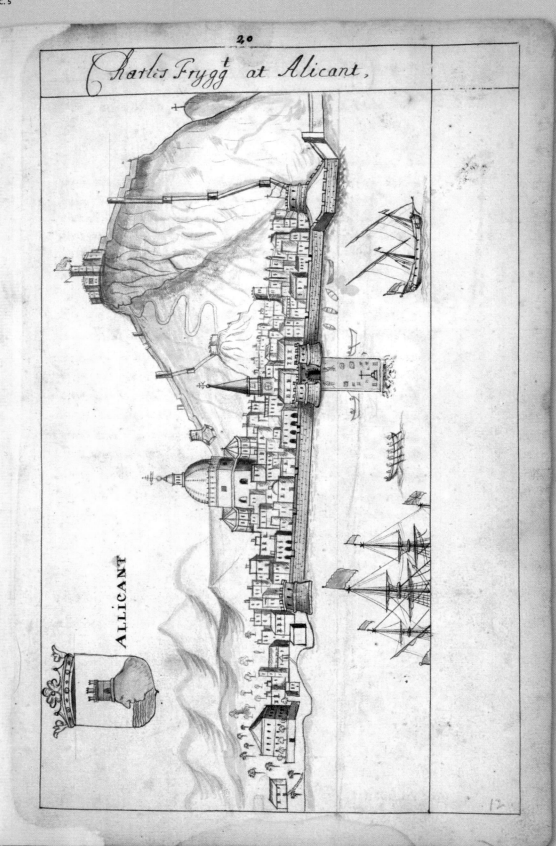

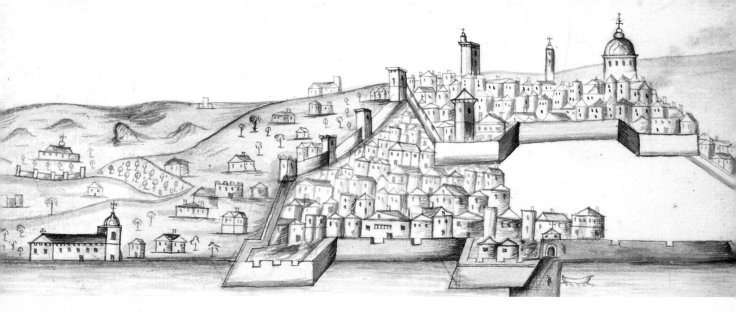

further strengthened with three strong castles the one of which is impregnable and standeth aloft, and is a defence to the adjoyning countrey: a safeguard and a curb to the citty. For it overlooketh it all: and hath both sea and land a large survey, and noe narrow comand. Charles the fifth did strongly rebuild it according to the moderne ffortification. The souldiers have goodly orchards about it to the increase of their entertainment. A pleasant place, and pleasantly they live there: arrivering at the extremity of old age through the excellency of aire. Within the citty, neare to the sea, there standeth an other castle, named the New-Castle, which may stand in comparison with the principall ffortifies of Italy…

The king doth keep in this kingdome a regiment of fouer thousand Spaniards, besides 18 hundred in the maritime townes, the battalion consists of two hundd thousand, five hundred threescore and 13, these are not in pay, but in time of service, and then raised in part according to location. For every hundred ssires are charged with footmen, and there are four millions eleven thousand fouer hundred and 54 ssires in the kingdome. Their strength at sea consisteth in gallyes.

Naples is the pleasantest of cittys, if not the most butifull: the buildings are ffreestone & marble, and are commonly ye ones stories high, the streets are broad & well paved, and watered with many stately ffountaines and water workes, her pallaces are exceedingly ffaire, but her temples stately, and gorgeously ffurnished, whereof adding chappels and monasteries within her walls and without, (for the suburbs do squell the citty in magnitude) she containeth 3000. It is supposed that there are in her 300000 men; besides women and children, their habit is generally Spanish; the gentry delight much in horses, the number of coaches is incredible, and likewise sedans, they are richly clothed and silk is a worke day ware for the wife of the moarish tradesman…'

DOC. 5 The arrival of the frigate *Charles* into Alicante.

A view of the city of Livorno. ABOVE

Collins also climbed Mount Vesuvius and left a fascinating account of the volcano, which had recently erupted twice with great force, first in 1631, and then again in 1660. By the time Collins reached Naples it was still active and billowing smoke:

> *'Thus showeth Mount Vesuvius, as you ride at anchor in Naples Bay.*
> *Thus showeth the concave or mouth of Mount Vesuvius where fire and smoke cometh out.*
> *A The top of the mountain*
> *B/C the way to the top*
> *D A monument erected about 30 years ago, for so far the fires came tumbling down the mountain about 32 years since, and belch out fire and brimstone for three days time, ejecting millions of tons of great and small stones, throwing some of them as far the monument, which is three English miles from the tip, consuming many brave villages and pleasant vineyards and gardens, for three miles around, so that now there is nothing to be seen, but stones, cinders and ashes, of which the ground is covered, which maketh the way very difficult to get up; we rid up on mules as far as C and there left the mules and with much trouble & pains ascended to the top, where we looked down into the concave, which showed as in the figure H.I.K. the circumference I judge to be three miles round and at the brims at H, and the depth from H to I I judge to be 200 yards, in the middle of the pit there was a small hill as IK out of the top of which cometh out the fire and smoke, in the daytime you can see nothing but the smoke, the descent is perpendicular and in many ways small places smoaksth.'*

DOC. 6 A sketch map of the Bay of Naples.

DOCS. 7 & 8 A record of the arrival in Naples in March 1678.

DOC. 10 & 11 Views of the still-active volcanoes, Vesuvius and Stromboli.

Setting sail towards the north coast of Sicily, Collins produced sketches of Stromboli - another active volcano which he described thus: '….*in the night little wind soe that we could not see any spark of ffire blow out, but when the winds blow hard breaketh much out in fflames….*'

Collins' expedition to the Mediterranean continued until 1679, when he returned to England along with his logs.

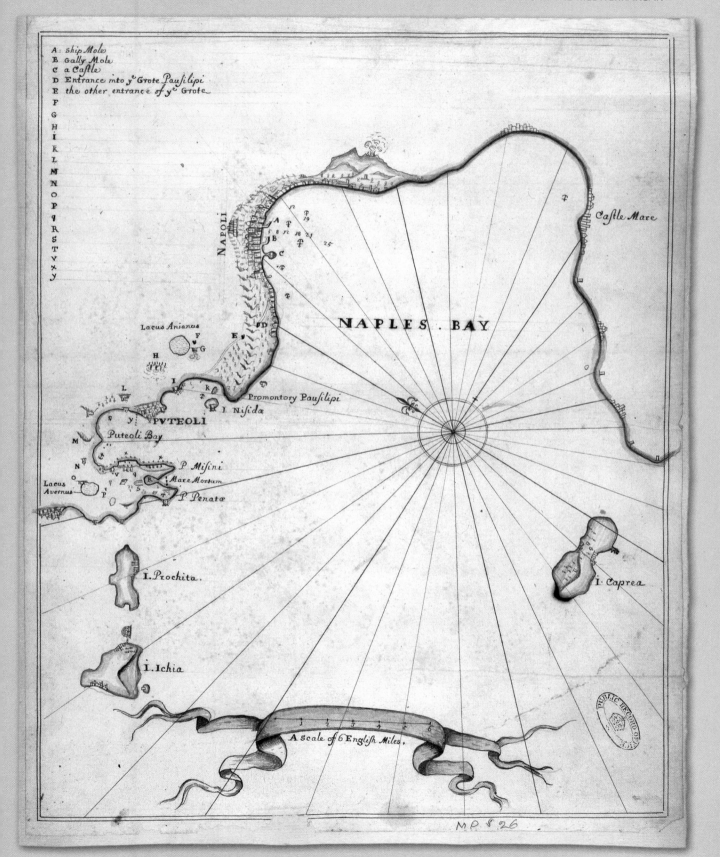

A: Ship Mole
B: Gally Mole
C: a Castle
D: Entrance into y.e Grote Pausilipi
E: the other entrance of y.e Grote
F
G
H
I
K
L
M
N
O
P
Q
R
S
T
V
X
Y

NAPOLI

Castle Mare

NAPLES . BAY

Lacus Anianus
F
G
H
I

Promontory Pausilipi

I. Nisidæ

PVTEOLI

Puteoli Bay

P. Mifini
Mare Mortam
P. Penatæ

Lacus Avernus

I. Prochita.

I. Caprea

I. Ichia

A Scale of 6 English Miles.

PVBLIC RECORD OFFICE

MP 8 26

Livorno to Naples,

At Six at Night Anchor'd in the Bay of
Naples Right against the Citty in 19 fatham
water about three quarters of a Mile of: the
Castle on the hill over the Citty boare NNbW

Discription of Naples,

This most ffamos and Butifull Citty lyeth vn
the Side of a Mountaine, by a good and Convenient
Haven, in a Rich and fflorishing Soyle. Bounded on
the: SE Side with a Bay of the Tyrrhen Sa, vnacqainted
with Tempsts; alongst which She Strecheth; and is
bacht by mountains Enriched with most Excellent
Viniards, She enjoyeth the delicate prospect of
Vesuvius, Surrentum, Caprea, Misenus, Prochita, and
Enaria, Her Beauty is most Glorious. The private
Buildings being gracefull, and the Publick Stately:
adorned with Statues, the works of Excellent work-
=men, and Sundry preserued Antiquities

  As for her Strength, the hand of Art hath
joyned with Nature to make her inuincible. For,
besides the being almost Surrounded with the Sa, and
mountains not to be transcended without much
difficulty and disadvantage; She is Strongly walld
and further Strengthened with three Strong Castles
the one of wch is Inpregnable and Standeth aloft, and
is a defence to the adjoyning Countty: a Safegaurd
and a Curb to the Citty. For it over looketh it all: and
hath both Sea and land a large Survey, and noe
nattow comand. Charles the fifth did Strongly rebuild
it according to the Moderne ffortification. The Souldiers
haue goodly Orchards about it to the incrdse of their
entertainment. A pleasant place, and pleasantly they
liue there: arriueing at the extremity of old age
through the excellency of elire. Within the Citty,
neare to the Sa, there Standeth an other Castle, Named
the New Castle, which may Stand in comparison with
the principall ffortifices of Italy, wherein is a

74

At Naplis,

with Princes, Noble-men and Gentry: her Streets with
Rich Citizens and fforrainers, in pursuite of their delight and profitt, Soe that she seemeth at this day
to affoord you all things but her former vacancy.
Being the first the receptable of Phylosophie, then
of musis, and lastly of the Souldiery,

The king doth keep in this kingdome a Regiment
of foure thousand Spaniards, besides 16 hundred in the
maritime Townis, The Battalion consists of two hund
thousand, fiue hundred threescore and 13, these are not
in pay, but in time of Service, and then raised in part
according to occation. For euery hundred ffirs are
charged with 5 foot-men. and there are foure millions
eleven thousand foure hundred and 54 ffires in the
kingdome: Their Strength at Sea consisteth in Gallyes

This kingdom is divided into 13 Provinces: wherein
are 1563 Cittyes and Townes, (twenty of them are of
Seats of Archbishops, and an hundred & Seuen of
Bishops). The Taxes that are imposed vpon Silky, as
well wrought as vn wrought, hath Soe inhanced the
Price, that fforram merchants Neglect to Trade, to
the great impoverishment of the Citizens, whose
especiall commodity doth consist in the working
& quick Sale thereof. And what Rates are imposed
vpon Victualy & winis may be gathered from this,
that the Cystomes of Herbs Spent yearly in Naplis
amounteth to 4000 pounds of our English money,
and of winis they haue such quantity, that 12000
Butts are euery Seson Transparted out of this
Kingdome, — Naplis is the pleasantest of Cittyes,
if not the most Butifull: the buildings are ffree-
Stone & marble, and are commonly 7 or 8 Stories high, the Streets are broad & well paued,
and watered with many Stately ffountaines and
water workes, Her Pallaces are exceeding ffaire, but
her Temples Stately, and Gorgeously ffurnished, where of.

60

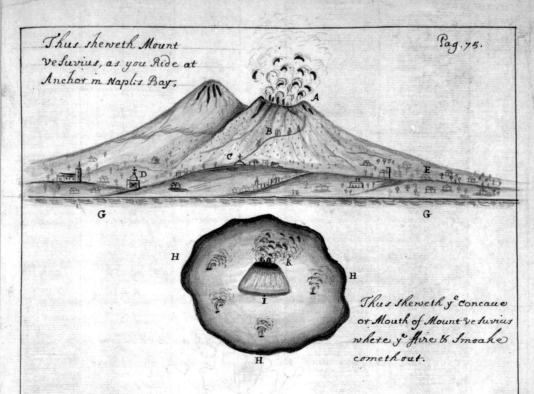

Thus sheweth Mount
Vesuvius, as you Ride at
Anchor in Naples Bay.

Pag. 75.

Thus sheweth y e Concaue
or Mouth of Mount Vesuvius
where y e ffire & Smoake
cometh out.

A the top of y e Mountaine

B c the way vp to y e top

D a Monument erected about 30 yeares agoe, for soe far the ffire came
tumbling downe the Mountaine about 32 yeares since, and Belcht out
ffire & Brimstone for three dayes time, Ejecting Millions of Tunny
of Great and Small Stones, throwing some of them as far as the
monument, w ch is three English miles from the top, consuming
many Braue Villidges, and pleasant Vineards and Gardens, for 3 miles
round, Soe that now there is nothing to be seene, but Stones Sindery
and Ashes, of which the ground is couered, which maketh the way
very difficult to get vp; We Rid vp on mules as far as c, and there
left the mules, and with much trouble & paine Ascended to the top,
where we lookt downe into the Concaue, which shewed as in the
ffigure H I K. the Circumfrence J Judg'd to be 5 miles round at y e times
a H, and the depth from H to I J Judged to be 200 yards, in the middle
of w ch Pitt there was a Small hill as I k. out of the top of w ch com:th out
the ffire and Smoake, in the day time you can see nothing but the
Smoake, the descent is perpendicular, and in many Small places
Smoaketh

79

1670 March	New-castle Frygg.t from

SW and NE, about 3 leagues off, in the Evening we
Saw two fires on the South Side of Strombelo, wch
are made by the Sicillian fisher men who come
to fish amongst these Islands,

Strombelo.

Thus sheweth Strombelo when it beareth E¼S°
about 3 miles off,

Thus sheweth Strombelo when it beareth N¼E
about 3 miles off, this Island is Round and about
7 miles Circumference, in the Night little wind
So that we could not See any Spark of fire
blow out, but when the winds blow hard it
breaketh much out in flames, the Vari: of Messina
beareth from this Island S&bS° there are
Islands that ly to the Southard of Strombelo
two of which Smoke the one is called Volkin and
the other Volkinello

the 20: All the forenoon little wind and variable
with Calms, At noon we gott within a mile of the
Vari: at wch time Sprung up a gale at SW, we

Voyages around the Pacific
CAPTAIN SAMUEL WALLIS ON HMS *DOLPHIN* … 1766–68

The end of the Seven Years War in 1763 saw a revitalisation of British interest in the Pacific. As the mariner John Byron passed the Tuamotus in 1765, he speculated that these might be outliers of a southern continent, hitherto posited as *terra australis incognita*. In 1766 the Admiralty instructed Captain Samuel Wallis of HMS *Dolphin* to find these lands. Accompanying Wallis was George Robertson, the chief mate. His journal provides a rich account of the voyage, as well as of the customs of the people of Tahiti.

Portrait of Samuel Wallis, 1728–95.

Giants of Patagonia

Wallis left Plymouth on 21 August 1766, accompanied by HMS *Swallow* under the command of Captain Philip Carteret. The plan was to cross the Atlantic, negotiate the Straits of Magellan and then explore the Pacific at as southern a latitude as possible. The Atlantic crossing was uneventful but the *Swallow*, which was a much slower ship, had trouble keeping up. December 1766 found the expedition off the coast of Patagonia. Wallis and Robertson were intrigued by myths of giants there and soon had a chance to investigate. As the ship anchored near the Straits of Magellan, the crew saw hundreds of men on horseback riding down the Cape. Adventurously, and armed to the teeth, Wallis and his companions went ashore. The two groups exchanged friendly greetings and gifts, but Wallis, keen to test the myth, had also brought a measuring rod. Wallis found that although the tallest among the group of Patagonians was six feet seven, most adult men were between five feet ten inches and six feet tall, with robust physiques. They were certainly big, but hardly giants:

> 'These people had every one his horse, with a decent saddle and stirrups and bridle. These men wore wooden stirrups, except one who had a large pair of Spanish spurs, brass stirrups and a Spanish scimitar without a scabbard. He did not seem to be of any greater authority than the rest. Having two measuring rods with we went round &

measured the tallest of them and found one that was six feet seven inches high, several
that were six feet five and six inches, but the majority of them were from five feet ten
inches to six feet. They were very well made, their hands and feet small...'

Navigating the Straits of Magellan

The next day, the *Dolphin* began navigating the Straits of Magellan. The passage
took three months of struggle against gales and the narrow channels presented
many hazards. The crew saw the fires of Tierra del Fuego and traded with local
inhabitants. Robertson noted the latter's poverty and the primitiveness of their
clothing, and speculated about their apparent indifference to the outside world:

> *'They have canoes to coast along shore with to get their provisions such as mussels and*
> *limpets which, with seals, is their Principal Food. They eat it raw and seem to be fond*
> *of the fattest part, which suck and hand to each other and offered some to our people*

Wallis' map of Good Luck Bay and the
Magellan Strait from the Journal. **BELOW**

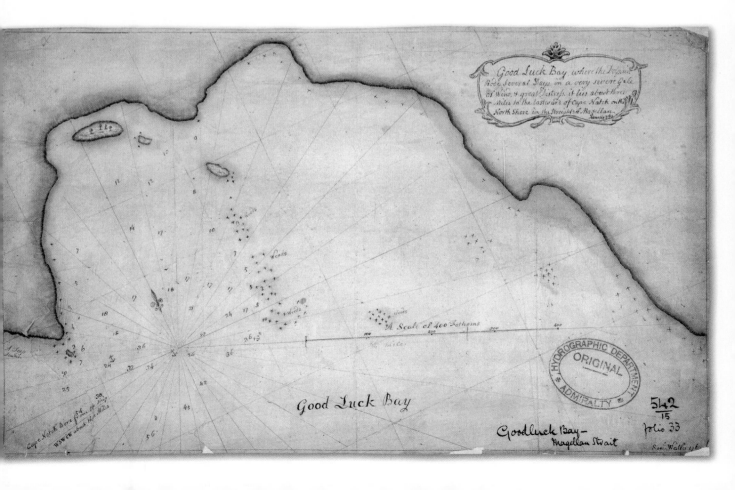

who did not think proper to deprive them of so delicious a morsel. Their bodies were covered with skins and they carry their children in them. Their arms are bows and arrows and slings with stones in them their bows have very little force…'

Into the Pacific

On 11 April 1767, as the *Dolphin* cleared Cape Pillar, contact was lost with the *Swallow*. As it set off across the Pacific, the *Dolphin* encountered unfavourable winds and storms, which forced it north of its intended southern trajectory. Provisions were running low and an epidemic of colds ensued, as well as cases of scurvy. By June, the *Dolphin* was in dire need of provisions. As they reached inhabited islands near the Tuamotu Archipelago, Wallis and the crew hoped to trade, but their early encounters with islanders were marked by violence. At Queen Charlotte's Island (Nukutavake), Robertson recorded the threatening posture of the islanders gathered on shore as the crew tried to find a safe landing place for their rowing boats:

> *'… saw several of the Indians gathering together amongst the Houses soon after our Boats rowd in nearer the Shoar which the Indians Obsd, and all came down to the shoar side resolved not to let our Men Land — they were in Number about fifty Men Women and Children, and all the Men and Women Armd with long picks or Spears Shod with some sort of Bone, their Spears was from then to fourteen foot long — Our men Made Signs that they wanted to land, and the Indians made signs for them to keep off and return to the Ship, at the same time the Men Advanced some steps nearer out Boats shaking their picks and pointing them towards the Boats — Meantime our people made all the friendly signs they Could think off, and the Lieut showed them Trinkets such as Beads, Ribbons, knives, Shears Nails &c But they still kept shaking their picks and Advanced a few steps in to the Water, where they stood in a threatening posture, but kept their Eyes fixt of they trinkets, at the same time some of the oldest men and the Women was very busey lighting fires in different places where there was any possibility of landing — this made our people supose they Worship fire…'*

Once they had managed to land, Robertson recorded what they found in the 'Indian' house they searched:

DOCS. 1 & 2 Page from George Robertson's log describing the people of Queen Charlotte Island (Nukutavake) and a deserted village on a neighbouring island; an account of conflict on Tahiti.

28

(67)

June 8th Continued there which our people saw full of fruit last Night was now intirely striped, which makes us suppose the Indians had resolved to Desert the Island before our Boats Landed, at Noon our Boats returned onto the Ship with as many Cocoa Nuts and palm Nuts as they could conveniently Carie — the Boats was immediately unloaded and sent Ashoar again for More Cocoa Nuts —

The Natives of this Island was a Middle Sized people, and a dark Coppper Colour with long Black hair, hainging low round their Shoulders, there Cloathing was some sort of Cloath or Matt tied round their Middles, but non of them had any kind of Shoues stocking or head Dress, except one who had a Curious plum of feathers — I suppose this man was some Chieff amongst them by haveing this head Ornaments, but non in the Boat could say they saw any kind of respect shewn him more than the rest —

June 9th The wind was Variable from East to WSW a fine Moderate Gale and Clear weather, at 6 PM our Boats returned full of Cocoa Nuts, but no palm Nuts as our people seem'd not to like them — the Officer in the Boat informed us that he had the Good Luck to Discover three smale pondes of Good water about a hundred yards to the Eastward of the Indian Town — this was more than we expected in this low Small Island, therefore gave us all the greater Joy, Especially as that Article was now turning short — and we was resolved to go to Short alloweance of Water the Day we left this Island, had we not found a Small Supply here, which gave us hopes of finding More on the Next Island, where the Indians Steere for — at Night we made Sail and Stood off and on all Night with a fine Brisk Gale — at Day Light we hoisted out the Barge and Cutter, and Sent Mr Gore with twenty Men all Armed to fill Water, they had provision for a Week and orders to lay Ashoar all Night in one of the Indian Houses, they were Ordered to keep a Strick looky out all Night for fear of being Surprized by any Body of Indians that might be Conceal'd in the Island or Land on it in the Night time — this forenoon all the Men was Imployed Cutting down Lows of palm and Cocoa Nut Trees, to lay on the Corale Rocks to make a proper place for rolling the water Casks on, I this day landed and went round a great part of the Island in order to see if their was any thing Curious to be found upon it — In the first place I found about twenty Houses in the Town built after the Indian manner and thatched with palm & Cocoa Tree Leaves as nett as any Farmers office house in England as for their furneture if they had any it was all Caried away in the Canoes, the only thing that I saw here worth notice, was three Large Craft upon the Stocks building, two of them about Eight or Ten Tuns, and one about twelve tun which was only framed but no planks upon her — what Trade they Carie on with this large Craft I know not, but am Certain they are not for fishing round this Island, but built in purpos for Carieing on a Trade to some distant Shoar thats of Greater Extent nor this Island, as a proof of this I found a great Number of turtle Backs all over the Island, and non of them can come Ashoar here, as the whole of the Island is Surrounded with Sharp pickd Corral Rocks, Wherefore think they are brought from some Sandy Shoar not far distant from this, all the Turtle Backs had been roasted with fire which had Spoil'd a great Quantity of very fine Tortous Shell, which was all Burnt on the Backs some of our Men found about Eight or ten pound of very fine thick Tortous Shell in one of the Houses which I supos they intended for Making small fish hooks, as we saw some Made of that sort — our people that Landed first on this Island, and on Whitsunday Island, got a great Many very fine Pearl Oyster Shells, they Canont be found about eather, of this Islands as there is no bottom to be found with forty and fifty fathom line all round them —

'...found neather men Women nor children in them – nor no living creature but a
great Number of Ratts running about every House, our Men began to load the Boats
with Cocoa and palm Nuts but found the Cocoa trees mostly stript of their fruit...
The Natives of this island was a Middle Sized people and a dark copper colour with
long Black hair hanging lose round their Shoulders, there Cloathing was some fort
of Cloath or Matt tied round their Middles, but non of them hade any kind Showes
stocking or head Dress, except one who hade a curious plum of feathers – I suppose this
Man was some chief amongst them by having his head ornamented...'

The 'Southern Continent' and the 'Discovery' of Tahiti

On 19 June, the *Dolphin*'s crew sighted what appeared to be extensive lands and
mountains to the south. The officers speculated that this must be the southern
continent and headed for the nearest land. At daybreak they found themselves
confronted by over a hundred and fifty canoes – the *Dolphin* had actually arrived
at the island of Tahiti, which Wallis named King George's Island.

This initial encounter seemed friendly and one of the islanders came on
board. However, the officers thought that the islanders were suspicious of them
and were determined to take control of the ship. Robertson was in one of the
Dolphin's boats taking soundings when he was surrounded by Tahitian canoes.
He ordered the marines to shoot, the resulting fusillade killing two islanders. In
another incident, the *Dolphin*'s guns fired on a flotilla of canoes attacking the ship,
and destroyed a Tahitian 'Great Canoe', killing many oarsmen. The violence
troubled Robertson, who was hoping to establish good relations:

'While this skirmish lasted all the Bay and tops of the Hills round was full of Men
Women and children to behould the onset and I daresay in great hopes of sheering
all our nails and Toys, beside the pleasure of calling our great Canoe their own, and
having all of us at their mercy, to ill or well use us as they thought most proper – but in
place of that, when they came all running doun to receive their Victorious friends, who
terrible must they be shockd to see their nearest and dearest of friends dead, and toar to
peces in such a manner as I am certain they neaver beheald before – to Attempt to say
what this poor Ignorant creatures thought of us, would be taking more upon me than I
am able to perform.'

(86)

25 June Continued Makeing some long talk in order to make peace with us when the ceremony was over the two men carried the two Hogs in to a Canoe and brought them off to the ship, their Canoe was allmost full of Green bows, and they both made a long speech and throwd some Green bows in to the sea, and some they threw on board the ship, then made signs for a rope to hall the two Hogs on b., when we got in the two fine fatt Hogs of about fifty pound Each, we offered them toys for them and some Nails, but they would receive nothing from us — but still kept talking and pointing to the pendant, Meaning as we afterwards found to give the Hogs for Liberty to Hoist the pendant — while this two old men was allong side, some of our people observed two men throw some stones at the pendant, and drive off all their Country Men from it, that was laying down plantein tree bows, and useing the same Ceremony as the others did, but this I saw not, however the very instant that the old men Landed they went and struck the pendant and Carried it Clean off — all this Night we had fine pleasant weather with some refreshing Showers, we heard no noise all this Night, but saw several large fires on the sides of the Hills allong shore — which I suppose was a signal to call the people of the Country together, from the River to the W end of the Island their was several very great fires —

At day light we Made and Armd all the Boats the same as yesterday, and Carryd a few water Casks ashore to fill, with some spear hands beside the thirty armd men, in two hours time we got off three Tun of exceeding good Water, and filld About three tun more, which we intended to bring off, But at ½ past 7 AM. we observed a great number of large Canoes, Coming towards the ships from the SW side of the Bay, and all full of Men, at same time we saw several thousands of Men Comming allong shore toward the River, the first great body of Men came over the tops of a Hill in the Bottom of the Bay, with our pendant flying at the end of a long pole, amongst the Middle of them, he that Carryd the pendant Appeared to be a tall brisk young Man, and the most of them Appeared to be Armd with Spears and Sticks or some such thing, this sight Alarmd us all and we soon Expected another Skirmish, therefor the Capt Orderd the Jolly Boat to go and order off Mr. Furneaux with all our men from the Shore — by the time our men imbark't their was several hundreds of the Natives within Gun shot of them, and several thousands comming through the Woods towards the Watering place, their was a great Many of them that had no sort of Arms, but we supposed they were for throwing of Stones, as we saw great Numbers of Stones piled up like shoat all Allong the River side, when our men was fairly imbarkt the Capt gave orders to fire a few random shot in to the Woods, in order to frighten them and Make them disperse — but this had not the Desired Effect, untill we was obliged to fire a few round and Grape shot amongst the thickest of them — then they began to run to the tops of the Hill, where they supposed they were safe, this we called Skirmish Hill, by this time about a hundred large Canoes, lay by abreast of the North end of Skirmish Hill, and sent some of their party Ashoar to get information how those on Shore went on, we observed some of them return from the Shoar and hold some sort of Council, soon after they began to paddle towards us but at a very slow rate, we supposed they were waiting a great Number of More Canoes, which was paddling up from the SW point of the Bay to join them, before they Attacked us, when we observed their intention we let them come within a short Mile of us, then fired a round shot amongst them in hopes they would give over their Designe — but they still persisted as the Shot hurt none of them, we therefor fired some round and Grape shot amongst them this soon put them to the flight, and the Most of them run their Canoes ashore, and run in to the Woods thinking themselves safe their, but we soon Convinced them that the Woods was not able to protect them from our round and Double headed Shot, as the Shot bent down several of the trees, and great Numbers of the Branches about their Heads, which they afterwards showd us when we became good friends, this so terrifyed them that they all fled to the top of Skirmish Hill, their a great Number of them sit down and thought themselves very safe and all the Canoes that was Comming up from the W end of the Bay put Ashoar, but about five or six which pulld up Close in shore, untill they got amongst those who put Ashoar at the N end of Skirmish Hill — we then fired one Gun Loaded with round and Grape shot at them, that soon sent them after their friends to the top of the Hill, by that time there was upward of Seventy or Eighty large Canoes at the North End of Skirmish Hill —

On 26 June, this unrest culminated in a small battle, the destruction of the islanders' canoes and the bombardment of a crowd on what became known to the crew as 'Skirmish Hill':

> 'When we observed their intention we let them come within a short mile of us, then fired a round shot amongs them in hopes they would give over their Design – but they still persisted as the short hurt non of them, we therefore fired some round and Grape shot amongst them this soon put them to the flight, and the most of them run their canoes ashore, and run into the Woods thinking themselves safe their, but we soon convinced them that the woods was not able to protect them from our round and Double headed shot, as the shot brout down several of the trees, and great number of the branches about their Heads, which they afterwards showd us when we became good friends, this so terrified them that they all fled to the top of Skirmish Hill, their a great number of them sit doun and thought them selves very safe...'

Onshore in Tahiti

After this decisive event, *Dolphin* was safely anchored in Matavai Bay. The crew were soon exploring the island and mixing with the Tahitians, with whom they had established friendly relations, and who were keen to trade for metal, generally in the form of iron nails. *Dolphin*'s stores were soon replenished with '*hogs and fowls*'. But a different type of trade soon emerged after Robertson and his companions, while exploring the island, met three young women who made a peculiar gesture towards them. As Robertson tells it:

> 'In returning back to the boats, three very fine Young Girls accosted us, and one of them made a Signal and smild in my face this made me stop to enquire what the Young Lady wanted and supposing the Young Gentlemen better acquainted nor me who had neaver seen any of the Young Ladys before, but at a great distance, I desired one of them to Explain the meaning of the Signal, they both put on a very Grave look and tould me they did not understand her Signs, I then supposed she hade something for sell, made signs for her to show her goods, but his seemd to displease her...'

Afterwards it was explained to the mate that the crew were exchanging ironware for sex and that the price of the 'old trade' was now 'fixt at a thirty penny nail each time'. This raised a dilemma for the officers, who feared the exchange would introduce venereal disease to a healthy population. The ship's doctor, however, believed that the crew were healthy – 'No venereal', Robertson recorded in red ink in his journal for 9 July. Nevertheless, Cook reported syphilis among the Tahitians when he arrived at Tahiti a couple of years later, blaming it on a recent French expedition. Worse, from the officers' point of view, was that the sailors were taking away metal from the ship to the extent that it threatened the vessel's viability. On 21 July, Robertson reported that crew members had stolen nails and cleats used to suspend the hammocks.

The Queen of Tahiti

In mid-July, Richard Pickersgill, a young officer, was walking on the island when he 'fell in with a great number assembled at a very long House'. A feast was being prepared in honour of an imposing woman, whom Pickersgill and his companions thought was the 'Queen of the Country'. She was in fact Purea, a chieftainess. Pickersgill was invited to the feast, and reported back:

> 'Trade now goes on very peaceable and quiet and our Liberty men ventured into the woods near a mile from the Gard that protects the traders. This day two of our men walkt near two mile from the watering place, where they fell in with a great number of the Natives assembled together at a very Long House, where the Queen of the Island lives, the Queen make signs for our gentlemen to sit down and dine with here which they complyed with. All the natives made a large ring and the Queen sat down in the middle...'

Wallis invited Purea to visit the *Dolphin* and established cordial relations with her and her people. Several visits to the ship and exchanges of gifts followed, with the Tahitians greatly interested in the *Dolphin*'s interior and decoration. When Wallis decided to leave Tahiti towards the end of July, he wrote that Purea did her best to persuade them to stay, to which he assigned purely innocent motives:

(47)

4.th July 1767
Continued

In returning back to the boats, three very fine young Girls accosted us, and one of them made a signal and smiled in my face, this made me stop to enquire what the young Lady wanted, and supposing the young Gentlemen better Acquainted nor one, who trade neaver seen any of the young Ladys before, but at a great distance, I desird one of them to Explain the meaning of the signal, they both put on a very Grave look and tould me they did not understand her Signs, I then supposed she had something for sell, made signs for her to show her goods, but this seemd to displeas her, and another repeated the same signal, which was this, she heeld up her right hand and first finger of the right hand streight, then laid hould of her right wrist with the left hand, and held the Right hand and first finger up streight and smiled, then Crooked all her fingers and kept playing with them, and Laughed very hearty, which sett my young freinds a Laughing as hearty as the young Girls, this made me insist upon their Explaining the Sign, and they tould me the young Girls only wanted a Long Naile each, but they neaver before saw them make a sign for one longer nor their fingers, but they supposd the young girls thought I carryed longer Nails nor the rest, because I was drest in a different mannar, I would⟨e⟩ them to explain the other part of the signal, that I might understand the whole, but the young men begd to be excused, I therefor gave the young Girls a Nail each, and parted good freinds, then walkt down to see how the traders went on, and tould the Gunner what trade happend betwixt us and the young Girls, and he Explaind the whole matter in few words, and tould me my young freinds was not so very Ignorant as they pretended to be, he likeways tould me that the price of the old trade, is now fixt to a thirty penny Naile each time, and he tould me that the Liberty men dealt so largely in that way — that he was much afraid of loseing his trade of Hogs, Pigs fowls and fruit — he said the people of this Country dealt very Cunningly, if they bring down three or four different things to sell, they always indeavour to sell the worst first, and if they get what they want for any trifling thing that they can easily spear, they carry back their Hogs pigs and fowls — he likeways says he has often seen them Conceal their best things, untill he purchased the other things of less Value, this made him afraid that the Natives would purchase all the Nails and toys by means of the old trade, and of Course bring no other Goods to Market, therefor Adviced me to indeavour to put a stop to it, when I went Onb,d by, preventing the Liberty men from comeing Ashore, this I tould him was out of my power, as the most of them was in the Sick list, he then tould me the healest of them traded a little, therefor could not be so very bad, as they pretended Onb,d, I then promised to represent the case to the Commanding Officer Onb,d, and the Surgeon, he then said my young freinds dealt a little, which might likeways be prevented, if I represented it properly Onb,d, but they excused themselves by affirming that he dealt more largely nor any one of them, therefor was the greatest spoiler of the trade him selfe —
I then saw how trade went on, and Adviced them to agree, and all deal moderately for fear of loseing the fresh broth and other Good things — When I returnd onb,d I acquainted the Secon,d Leiut.t who was then Commanding officer, the Capt,n and first Leiut.t then being Sick, I then let him and the Docter, and our your Merry freind the purser knows how trade went on Ashore — we then Consulted what was best to be done, some was of Oppinion it would be best to detain the Liberty men some days, others said it would be ruining all trade to keep them onb,d, and the Docter who was Certainly a man, that took the greatest care of his Gratuent — Affaird that the keeping the Liberty men, Confined onb,d the Ship, would ruin their health and Constitution for said he, any thing that depresses the mind and Spirit of men must Sertainly hurt them, we sent for a few which was in the Sick list, and Examend them, and threatned to Stop their Liberty for spoileing the Gunners trade, this effected the poor unthinking fellows so much, that we immediately sees a Visable Change in their Countinance, which pleanly Confirmd what the Docter said was very Just — we therefor agreed to prevent them as much as was possible, from takeing nails and toys Ashore with them —
we likeways put a very necessary Question to the Docter, who Affaird upon his Honour, that no man onb,d was Afflicted with any sort of disorder, that they would Communicate to the Natives of this beautifull Island —

no Venereal disorder

'...all this I think is a very clear proof that they have not treatcherous designe against us, in place of having a treatcherous designe, the Great Woman shaked hand with us, and when she found all her tears and intreatys could not prevail with us to stay two days longer — we indeavourd to make her understand that we would soon return again to her beautifull Island — this Seemd to please her a little...'

The officers feared that the islanders might make a last attempt to seize the ship, but the *Dolphin* was allowed to leave safely, having taken on board fresh food and water and gifts from the Purea and Tahitians. It reached London in May 1768.

DOC. 3 An encounter between sailors and Tahitian women.

Chart of Matavai Bay in Tahiti, drawn in 1792 and clearly showing the shoals off the harbours. **BELOW**

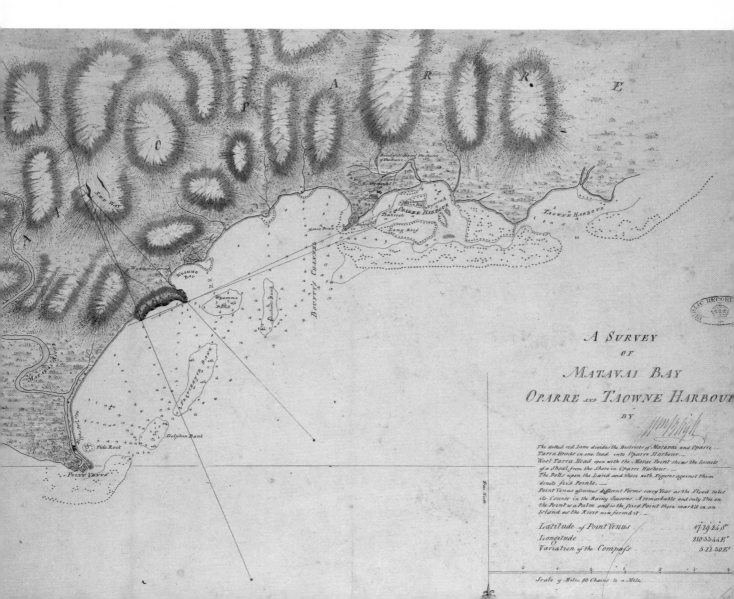

Exploring Botany Bay
CAPTAIN COOK ON HMS *ENDEAVOUR* ... 1768–71

Exploration of the Pacific was not a new trend in the eighteenth century. Since the sixteenth century, and perhaps even earlier, investigation and mapping of this part of the world had been the object of many ships' voyages. However, little reliable mapping had been achieved, and so the Pacific remained largely unknown. After peace was restored between Britain and France in the mid-eighteenth century following decades of hostility between the two countries, there was renewed interest in the Pacific and its tantalising potential of undiscovered resources.

In August 1768 Captain Cook set sail from Plymouth in HMS *Endeavour Bark* [Barque] bound for the recently discovered island of Tahiti. The Admiralty had issued Cook with instructions for the voyage that were in two parts. The first part was grounded in science and was influenced by the Royal Society. It instructed Cook to sail to Tahiti and observe the Transit of Venus, a

Captain James Cook, 1728–79. **ABOVE**

Contemporary engraving of Cook and some of his crew meeting the Tahitians. **LEFT**

DOC. 1 Captain Cook's journal for arrival at Botany Bay, Australia 1770

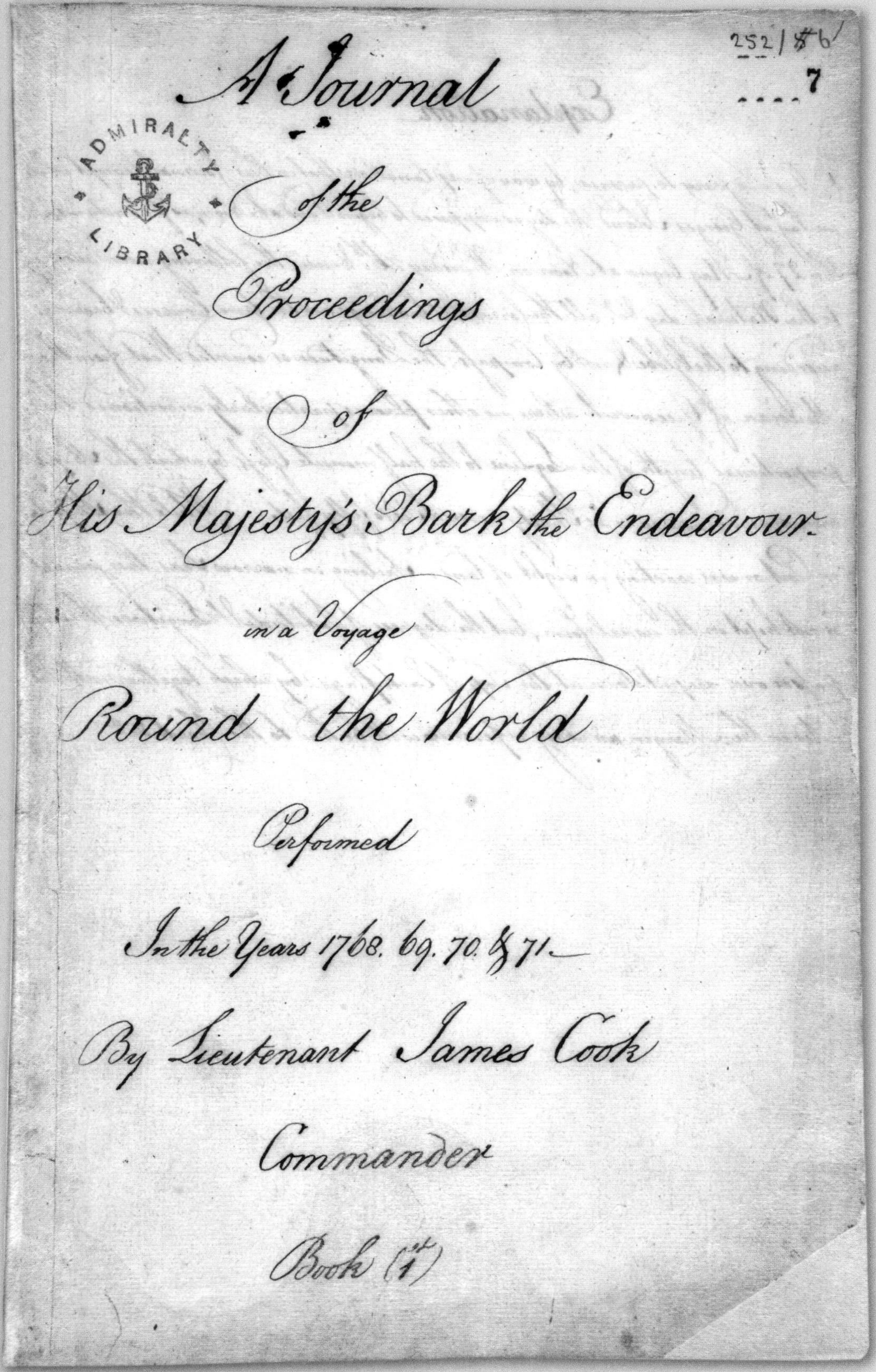

252/86

..... 7

A Journal

of the

Proceedings

of

His Majesty's Bark the Endeavour

in a Voyage

Round the World

Performed

In the Years 1768. 69. 70. & 71.

By Lieutenant James Cook

Commander

Book (1st)

phenomenon that would not recur for another century. The second part ordered Cook to sail south, and then west, in search of a rumoured southern continent, a task similar to those of previous voyages whose mission had been to increase geographical knowledge and develop new trade routes. If he failed to find the southern continent he was to sail westwards until he arrived at New Zealand and then return to England via the route he thought most appropriate.

Cook duly followed these instructions. Upon finding no evidence of the existence of the southern continent, he made for New Zealand. The *Endeavour* anchored at Poverty Bay on the north-east coast of New Zealand in early October 1769. Over the next six months Cook and his crew would survey all 2,400 miles of the New Zealand coastline, confirming that it consisted of two islands, neither of which was connected to a southern continent.

A decision now had to be made as to the best way to return to England. The most promising route for finding the southern continent lay to the east, but the worsening condition of the ship made this a risky venture. Instead Cook sailed west, which offered the possibility of new discoveries, or at least the chance to give the map of the Pacific greater clarity.

Cook is often wrongly credited with discovering Australia. In fact, Dutch explorers had charted western Australia and parts of the country's southern and northern coasts in the first half of the seventeenth century. The British explorer William Dampier had also visited western Australia in the early eighteenth century. All that remained to be explored and charted was the eastern coast, and the question of whether New Guinea was attached to Australia (or New Holland as it was then known) was still unanswered. Cook fulfilled both of these missions. On 28 April 1770 *Endeavour* anchored at Botany Bay, and Cook made the first recorded contact with the indigenous peoples of eastern Australia. However, the encounter was not entirely friendly, as Cook recorded in his log:

'[We] saw as we came in on both points of the bay several of the Natives & a few Hutts Men Women & Children on the south shore abreast of the ship to which place I went with the Boat accompanied by Mr Banks, Dr Solander and Tupia as we approached the shore they all made off except 2 men who seemed resolved to oppose our Landing as soon as I saw this I ordered the Boats to lay upon their Oars in order to

DOC. 2 Cook's chart of New Zealand c.1770. The peninsula to the south of present-day Christchurch was originally thought to be an island.

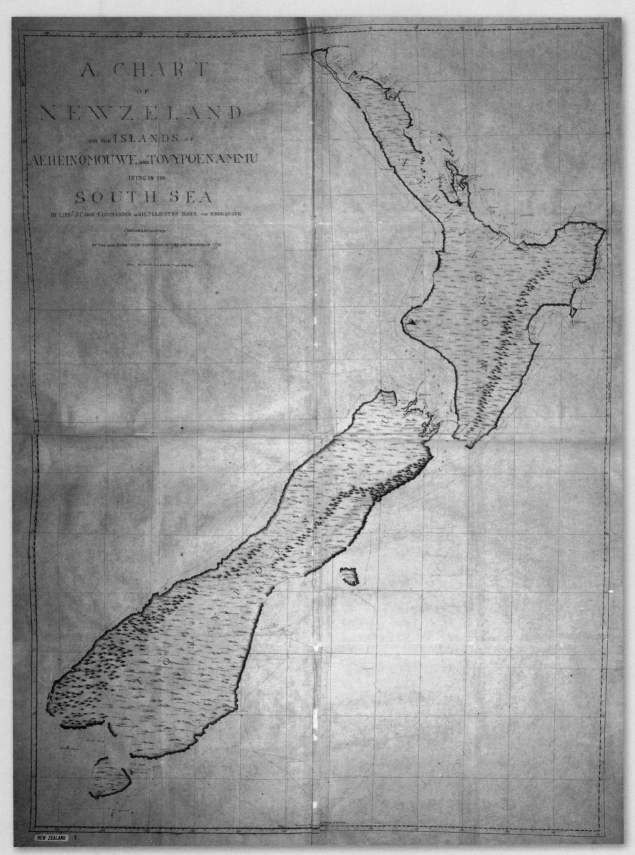

speak to them but this was to little purpose for neither us nor Tupia could understand one Word they said. We then threw them some Nails boards etc ashore which they took up & seemed not ill pleased in so much that I thought that they Beckoned to us to come ashore but in this we were Mistaken for as soon as We put the Boat in they again Came to oppose us upon which I fired a Musquet between the 2 which has no other effect than to make them retire back where bundles of their Darts lay & one of them took up a Stone & threw at us which caused my firing a Second Musquet load with Small shott & although some of the shott struck the Man yet it had no other Effect than to make him lay hold of a shield or Target to defend himself, immediately after this we landed which we had no sooner done than they throwed 2 Darts at us this obliged me to fire a third shot soon after which they both made off but not in such haste but what we might have taken one but Mr Bankes, being of Opinion that the Darts were poisoned made me courtious how I advanced into the woods we found here a few small Hutts made of the Bark of Trees, in one of which were 4 or 5 small children with whom we left some strings of beads etc. A Quantity of Darts lay about the Hutts which we took away with us, 3 Canoes lay upon the beach the worst I think I ever saw. They were about 12 or 14 feet long made of one piece of the Bark of a Tree drawn or tied up at each end & the Middle Kept open by means of pieces of sticks by way of thwarts, after searching for fresh water without success except a little in a small hole dug in the sand we Embarqued & went over to the north point of the bay were [where] in coming in we saw several people but when we now landed there were nobody to be seen, we found here some Fresh Water which came trinkling down & stood in pools among the Rocks.'

DOC. 3 Captain Cook's journal for arrival at Botany Bay, Australia 1770.

The bay where they landed was initially named Stingray Bay due to large numbers of this creature seen and caught there, which Cook noted: '*In the evening the yawl returned from fishing having caught 2 Sting Rays weighing near 600L.*' The crew spent a week exploring the bay. The botanists on board, Joseph Banks and Daniel Solander, collected specimens of many new plant species, which prompted Cook to rename the bay accordingly – '*the great quantity of new plants etc Mr Banks & Dr Solander Collected in this place occasioned my giving it the name of Botany Bay*'.

After exploring Botany Bay, Cook continued to sail north, eventually mapping the whole eastern side of Australia. This was not without its difficulties,

(234)

East Coast of New Holland

April 1770

Botany
Bay

morning Probably the Natives were afraid to take them away, after
breakfast we sent some Empty Casks ashore & a Party of men to cutt Wood
& I went my self in the Pinnace to Sound & explore the bay, in the doing of
which I saw several of the Natives but they all fled at my approach'd
land'd in 2 places one of which the People had but just left, as there were
Small fires & fresh Muscles broiling upon them here likewise large heaps
of the largest Oyster Shells I ever saw

Monday 30 As soon as the Wood'ers & Water'ers were come onb'd to Dinner 10 or
12 of the Natives came to the Watering Place & took away their Canoes that lay
there but did not offer to touch any one of our Casks that had been left ashore
& in the afternoon 16 or 18 of them came boldly up to within 100 Yards of our
People at the Watering Place & there made a Stand. M'r Hicks who was the
Officer ashore did all in his Power to intice them to him by offering them
Presents &c. but it was to no Purpose all they seem'd to want was for us
to be gone, after staying a short time they went away they were all
Arm'd with Darts & wooden swords, the Darts have each 4 prongs & pointed
with the fish bones, those we have seen seem to be intended more for
Striking fish than Offensive Weapons, neither are they poisoned as we
at first thought after I had return'd from Sounding the bay I went over to a
Cove on the N°. side, where in 3 or 4 Hauls with the Sean we caught about
300 pounds weight of fish which I caused to be equally divided among the
Ships Company In the AM I went in the Pinnace to sound & explore the
N°. side of the Bay where I neither met with inhabitants or any thing re-
-markable. M'r Green took the Suns Meridian Alt°. a little within the
S° Entrance of the Bay which gave the Lat°. 34:0 S

Monday 1 Gentle breezes Northerly In the AM 10 of the Natives again visited
the Watering Place I being onb'd at this time I went immediately ashore
but before I got there they were going away, I followed them alone & unarm'd
some distance along shore but they would not stop until they got farther
off than I chose to trust my self, these were Kind in the Same Manner
as those that came yesterday, In the evening I sent some hands to haul the
Sain but they caught but a very few fish, a little after sun rise I found
the Var'n to be 11D 3 E'. last Night Forby Sutherland Seaman departed
this Life in the AM his body was buried ashore at the Watering Place
which occasioned my calling the S° Point of this bay after his Name

This morning a Party of us went ashore to some Hutts not far from
the Watering Place were some of the Natives are daily Seen, here we
left several Articles such as Cloth, looking Glasses Combs beads &c.

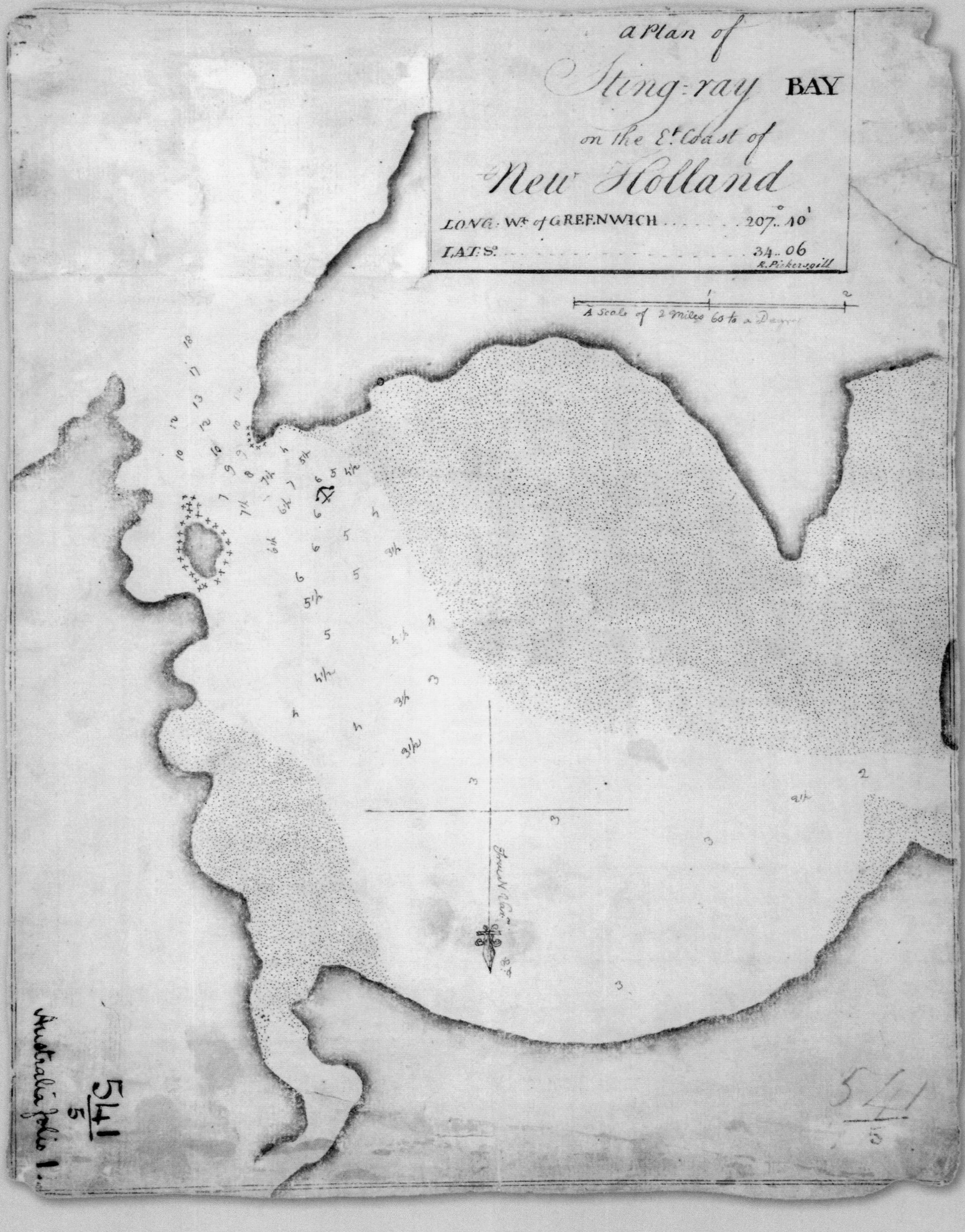

a Plan of

Sting=ray BAY

on the E.t Coast of

New Holland

LONG. W.t of GREENWICH . . . . 207° . 10'

LAT.S. . . . . 34 . 06

R. Pickersgill

A Scale of 2 Miles 60 to a Degree

541
5
Australia folio 1.

541
5

among them the fact that Cook and his crew had no prior knowledge of the Great Barrier Reef. On 10 June, *Endeavour* ran aground on a shoal just off the reef:

> '*The ship struck & stuck fast, immediately upon this we took in all our Sails hoisted out the boats & sounded round the ship & found that we had got upon the South East edge of a Reef of Coral rocks... we went to work to lighten her as fast as possible which seemed to be the only means we had left to get her off... [We] threw over board our Guns Irons & Stone ballast, Casks Hoops Stoves Oil Jarrs decayed stores ... all this time the Ship made little or no water.*'

Eventually *Endeavour* floated again and limped to the mouth of the Endeavour River, where the crew took stock of the considerable damage. The voyage was delayed by several weeks while Endeavour was repaired:

> '*[We] set up the Smith & Forge & set the Armourer & his Mate to work to make Nails & to repair the Ship ... a large piece of Coral Rock was sticking in one hole & several pieces of the fothering small stones [etc.] had made its way in & lodged between the Timbers which had stopped the water from forcing its way in in great Quantity.*'

While the ship underwent repair, Cook and his crew explored the surrounding area and he also records his first sighting of a kangaroo:

> '*I saw myself this morning, a little way from the Ship, one of the animals before spoken of. It was of a light mouse colour & the full size of a Grey Hound & shaped in every respect like one with a long tail which it carried like a Grey Hound. In short I should have taken it for a wild dog, but for its walking or running in which it jumps like a hare or deer. Another of them was seen today by some of our people who saw the first. They describe them as having very small legs and the point of the foot like that of a goat but this I could not see myself, because the ground the one I saw was upon was too hard and the length of the grass hindered my seeing its legs.*'

DOC. 4 A plan of Stingray Bay on the east coast of New Holland (near Botany Bay) drawn by Richard Pickersgill.

DOC. 5 The vicinity of Cape Flattery, drawn by Richard Pickersgill.

DOC. 6 Cook's journal, recording his first sighting of a kangaroo.

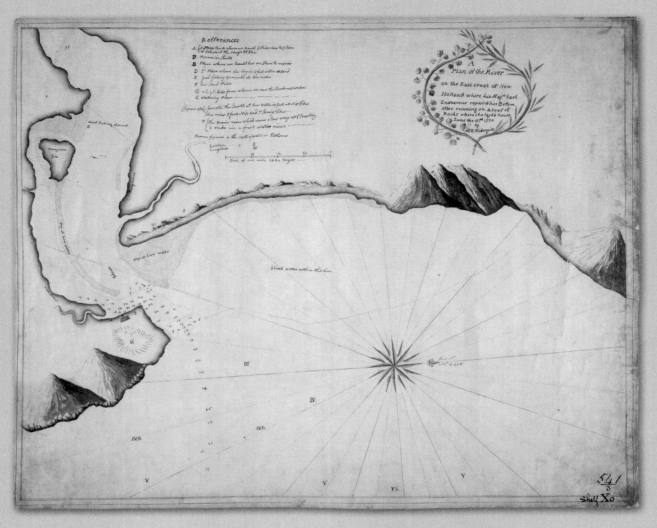

Lat 15: 26

(268)

New South Wales

1770

Endeavour River

under the Starboard side she being dry as far Aft as the After part of the
ForeChains, we could not find that she had received any other Damages
on this side but what hath been mentioned, In the morning I sent 3
Men into the Country to shoot Pidgeons as some few of these birds have been
seen flying about, in the Evening they returned with about ½ a Dozen
one of the Men saw an Animal something less than a grey hound
it was of a Mouse Colour very slender made & swift of foot, in the A M.
I sent a Boat to Haul the Seine who returned at Noon having made 3 Hauls
& caught only 3 Fish & yet we see plenty jumping about the Harbour
but can find no Method of Catching of them

23ᵈ   Sunday 24   Winds & wea, as yesterday in the P.M. the Carpenters fini=
-ished the Starboard side & at 9 Stock heels the Ship the other way & Hauld
her off about 2 feet for fear of Neeping. In the A M they went to Work
upon repairing the Sheathing under the larboard bow where we found
2 Planks Cut about ½ thro early in the Morning I sent a Party of Men
into the Country under the Direction of Mr Gore to seek for Refreshmentsᵈ
they returned about noon with a few Palm Cabages & a Bunch or 2 of Wild
Plantains, these last were much smaller than any I had ever seen & the
Pulp full of small Stones, otherwise they were well Tasted, I saw myself
this Morning a little way from the Ship One of the Animals before spoke
of it was of a light Mouse Colour & the full size of a grey hound & shaped
in every respect like one with a long Tail which it carried like a grey
hound in short, I should have taken it for a Wild Dog, but for its
Walking or running in which it Jumps like a Hare or Deer, another
of them was seen to day by some of our People who saw the first they de=
=scribe them as having very small Legs & the Prints of the foot like that
of a goat, but this I could not see my self, because the ground the one I saw
was upon was too Hard & the length of the Grass hindred my seeing its
legs.

24   Monday 25ᵗʰ   At low Water in the P.M. while the Carpenters were
buisey in repairing the Sheathing & Plank under the Starboard bow
I got People to go under the Ships bottom to examine all her larboard Side
she only being dry forward but abaft were 9 feet Water, they found a Part
of the Sheathing off abreast of the Main Mast about her Floor heads &
a part of one Plank a little Damaged there were 2 People who went
down who all agreed in the same Story, the Master was one who was
Positive that she had received no Material Damage besides the loss of

A month later, *Endeavour* was ready to sail again, though her condition was still fragile, so going in search of new discoveries was now out of the question. The difficulty of navigating the Great Barrier Reef remained, which Cook describes gravely in his log:

> *'I went myself upon the Hill which is over the South point to take a view of the sea at this time it was low water & I saw what gave me no small uneasiness, which was a number of Sand Banks or shoals laying all along the coast ... the outermost extended off to sea as far as I could see with my Glass ... the only hopes I have of getting clear of them is to the Northward where there Seems to be a passage for as the wind blows constantly from the South East we shall find it difficult if not impractical to return back to the southward.'*

Despite the perils and dangers of the voyage, *Endeavour* eventually anchored in the Downs, off the east Kent coast, on 12 July 1771, its mission successful on several counts. Throughout the journey Cook had insisted on the need for cleanliness and fresh food wherever possible, with the result, unprecedented for the time, that there were only a handful of scurvy cases, with no recorded fatalities from the disease. It had been one of the most notable botanical collecting expeditions of its time, and, moreover, Cook and his crew had charted over 5,000 miles of previously unknown coastline, so that there were now accurate charts. This voyage had literally changed the view of the world.

DOC. 7 The vicinity Cape Flattery to Cape Tribulation including the Great Barrier Reef by Richard Pickersgill.

An illustration, drawn c.1780 of a kangaroo found on the coast of New Holland. BELOW

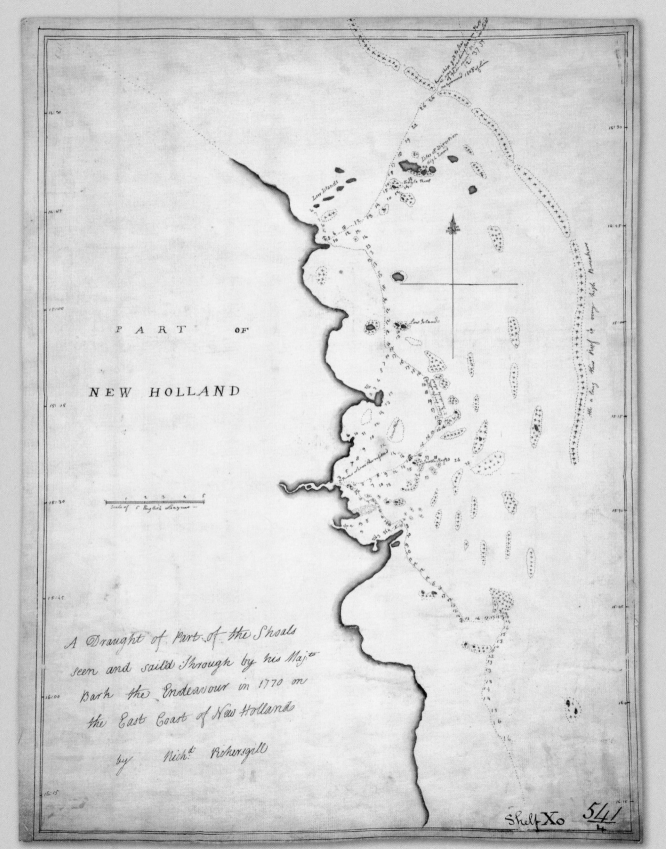

Expedition to the Northwest Passage

WILLIAM PARRY ON HMS *FURY* ... 1821–1823

The Northwest Passage is a route through the Arctic Ocean, via the
Canadian Arctic Archipelago, that enables vessels to sail from the Atlantic
Ocean to the Pacific, reducing maritime journeys by thousands of miles and
saving ships from undertaking a perilous trip through the wild seas at the tip
of South America. Now firmly established, for much of the nineteenth century,
in the days before the Panama Canal was constructed, its discovery was an
elusive goal.

In 1819–20, Rear Admiral Sir William Edward Parry made his first
voyage to the Arctic to discover the passage. There had been numerous previous
expeditions, including that of Captain Cook in 1776, all of which had failed
to find the Northwest Passage. In 1820, however, Parry managed to sail through
Lancaster Sound, which is pinpointed to the west of Baffin Bay on the map of
1856 shown here, and it was this initial success that led him to attempt a second
expedition in 1821.

Sir William Parry, 1790–1855.

Now a Fellow of the Royal Society thanks to his discoveries of 1820, Parry
once again set sail from Deptford in April 1821, in command of HMS *Fury* and
accompanied by HMS *Hecla*, in a renewed search for the passage. The timing
was crucial. His previous expedition had been successful partly because in the
summer of 1819 the Arctic had been unusually free of ice, and Parry hoped for
similar conditions this time around.

Parry opened his journal, kept between 8 May 1821 and 29 April 1822,
with a brief explanation of the expedition's purpose:

> 'The discoveries made by the expedition to the northwest in the years 1819–20 being
> such as to offer at least a presumptive proof of the existence of the desired passage from
> the Atlantic to the Pacific, while they served also to point out the most putative mode
> of its accomplishment, His Majesty, on the representation of Lord Viscount Melville,
> commanded another attempt to be made to affect that long-sought object, and the

Lords Commissioners of the Admiralty were pleased once more to honor me with the command of an expedition to be equipped at Deptford for that purpose.'

The expedition ships surrounded by icebergs – a sketch by Parry. **ABOVE**

'*Nothing of consequence*' happened during their Atlantic crossing, but during the evening of 3 July the vessels encountered impenetrable ice-packs which afforded an opportunity for the crew to practise firing at targets in the snow. On 16 July 1821 they broke their way through the ice, and on 21 July Parry and his crew made their first contact with the local Eskimo population, with whom they proceeded to barter for local products:

'The wind backed to the westward in the afternoon, and just as we were making fast to a large piece of ice, we heard voices inshore, which we soon knew to be those of Eskimaux coming off to us. Shortly after several canoes made their appearance between the pieces

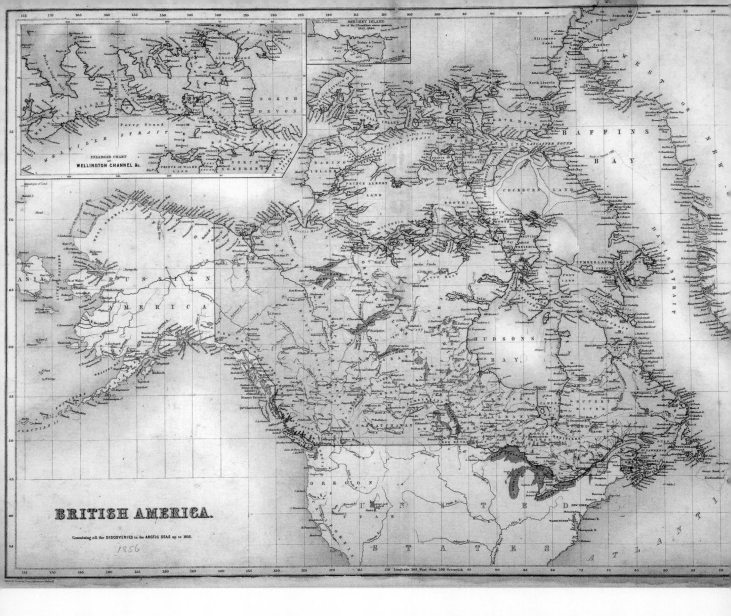

BRITISH AMERICA.

Containing all the DISCOVERIES in the ARCTIC SEAS up to 1856.

1856

of ice; at 6 some of them landed on the ice alongside of the Fury, hauled their kajaks upon the floe, and began to barter their commodities, consisting of seal and whale oil and blubber, whale bone, spears, lines, and the skins of the seal, bear, fox, dog etc etc. My first wish was to procure as much oil as possible, of which, we had been informed by the Hudson's Bay ships, that several tons are sometimes procured from these people. We soon had occasion to find that the Eskimaux had been well accustomed to the art of bargain-making, for it was with some difficulty that we could prevail upon them to sell the oil for anything of reasonable value. They frequently made signs that they wanted saws and harpoons in exchange for it, and as we could not spare these articles, it was not without trouble that we obtained in the course of the evening about two barrels of oil

Discoveries made in the seas of the Arctic up to 1856. **ABOVE**

for knives, large nails, pieces of iron hoops, and other things of that kind. If they saw more than one of these at a time, they would try hard to get the whole for the commodity they were about to sell, though, when we persisted in refusing, they would jump for joy in having already made so good a bargain. They always licked the article given them in exchange, and only in one instance did I notice the slightest inclination to break the contract, after this process had been gone through.'

At this stage, Parry had only made it as far as the entrance to Hudson Strait, the Atlantic opening of Hudson's Bay. On 1 August 1821 the expedition continued westwards, between Nottingham Island and the North Shore, and at this point Parry entered hitherto uncharted waters, which filled him with trepidation.

Leaving the ship on 15 August they made their way onto Southampton Island, possibly in boats similar to the one later sketched by Parry, reporting the presence of white whales, seals and narwhals. From there, they reached a vantage point where they could overlook the sea; a large expanse to the north

Drawings of a boat proposed for Parry's expedition, 1826. **BELOW**

DOCS. 1 & 2 Journal kept by Parry, 8 May 1821–29 April 1822, where he records his first contact with the local population.

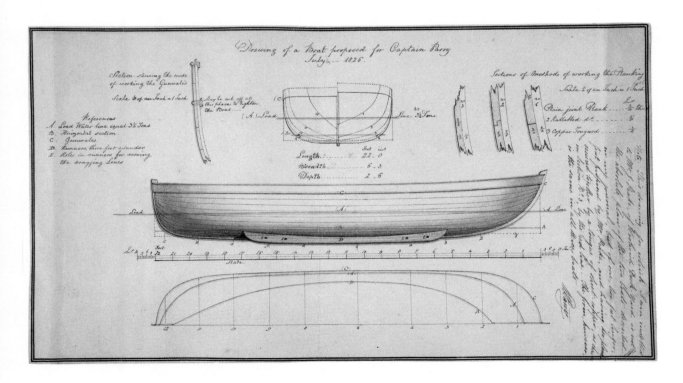

1821
July

enough to admit a ship between them, with a commanding breeze. The tides give us no trouble, nor indeed can we perceive how they set. The Hudson's Bay Ships were 4 or 5 miles to the Eastward of us. This day was very clear and the atmosphere extremely warm: the thermometer freely suspended in the sun, at 2 PM, stood at 74, and upon some black-painted lead on deck, at 116° — in the shade 45°.

Sat. 25th. Early on the 21st we made sail to the Westward, the ice being rather more slack, and, being favoured with an Easterly breeze, succeeded in making several miles of Westing. Our latitude at noon was 61.50.15, Long: by Chron.r 87.35.43. To the Westward of the Snowy Land before-mentioned, there appear to be several islands, and at noon we saw one which, from its appearance, we considered to be that called Saddle-back, and which bore N 38 W dist 5 leagues. The wind backed to the Westward in the afternoon, and just as we were making fast to a large piece of ice, we heard voices inshore, which we soon knew to be those of Eskimaux coming off to us. Shortly after several canoes made their appearance between the pieces of ice: at 6 some of them landed on the ice alongside of the Fury, hauled their kajaks upon the floe, and began to barter their commodities, consisting of seal and whale oil and blubber, whalebone, spears, lines, and the skins of the seal, bear, fox, dog &c &c. My first wish was to procure as much oil as possible, of which, we had been informed by the Hudson's Bay Ships, that several tons are sometimes procured from these people. We soon had occasion to find that the Eskimaux had been well accustomed to the art of bargain-making, for it was with some difficulty that we could prevail upon them to sell the oil for anything of reasonable value. They frequently made signs that they wanted saws and harpoons in exchange for it, and as we could not spare those articles, it was not without trouble that we obtained in the course of the evening about two barrels of oil for knives, large

20   27

1821
July

large nails, pieces of iron hoop, and other things of that kind. If they saw more than one of these at a time, they would try hard to get the whole for the commodity they were about to sell, though, when we persisted in refusing, they would jump for joy in having already made so good a bargain. They always licked the article given them in exchange, and only in one instance did I notice the slightest inclination to break the contract, after this proof had been gone through. Shortly after the first 17 canoes had landed, a large boat or *umiak* made her appearance, containing 6 or 7 women and 4 men: one of the latter, the oldest of the party, steered the boat with an oar. The women would not land, but held up little pieces of leather and other articles to exchange, vociferating loudly "pilletay" the whole time. There was a great quantity of oil in this boat, which I was very desirous to buy, but not even the knives which I offered in exchange would induce the old man to part with more than one skin of it, for what reason I cannot tell, except that they hoped to obtain, by perseverance, something more valuable. On my desiring our men to hand a second skin of oil out of the boat, for which I put into the old man's hand a second knife, he resisted very vehemently, and pushed our men aside with great violence. One of the younger men then interposed also, and was lifting the tiller of their boat to strike or push away our men, who only laughed at the old man's endeavour to master these all. As it would have been bad policy, however, to have allowed them to consider themselves in any way superior to us, I lifted up a boat-hook with which we held their boat to the ice, & pretended to be very angry with them. This cooled them at once, and I ordered our men out of the boat, to prevent further altercation. We had by this time bought nearly all the oil that was brought by the first canoes,

and

53

was '*unencumbered by ice*'. Rounding the northern end of Southampton Island in HMS *Fury*, Parry established that the southern part of Melville Peninsula blocked all access westward. By late September, as winter set in, the ice thickened and it was decided that they would weather the freezing conditions at Winter Island (Nunavut). In October, during the lengthy period when Parry's vessels were trapped in ice, the crew set up the Royal Arctic Theatre to keep themselves entertained, as well as a school and an observatory. Parry recorded in the log of HMS *Fury* both the extraordinary natural phenomena that he saw and two of the theatre productions that the crew staged:

> '*I, therefore, soon after arrival, proposed to Captn Lyon and the officers of both ships, once more to set on foot a series of theatrical entertainments, from which so much benefit in this way had before been derived. My proposal was immediately and unanimously acquiesced in. Captn Lyon obligingly consented to be our manager, and some preparations having been made, with this view, previous to our leaving England, every-thing was soon arranged for performing a play on board the Fury once a fortnight during the winter. In this, as in more important matters, our former experience stood us in good stead. Our theatre was now laid out on a larger and more commodious scale, its decorations much embellished, and what was no less important, both to actors and spectators, a more efficient plan adopted for warming it, whereby we hoped to keep our stage at a temperature somewhat above zero during the winter. To furnish rational and useful occupation to the men on the other evenings, a school was also established, under the voluntary superintendence of Mr. Halse, for the instruction of such of the men who were willing to take advantage of this opportunity of learning to read and write....*
>
> ....'*In the 26th, both in morning and evening, the Aurora Borealis appeared from SE to SW & West, the brightest part being about 10° above the horizon, and with rays shooting up towards the zenith. The compass was not at all affected. In almost every instance it is observable that the Aurora has that tendency to an arch-like form before observed so constantly. I do not know that we have ever yet seen any appearance of it in the northern quarter of the heavens. At ½ past one in the morning of the 27th, the Aurora Borealis which had been visible for several hours disappeared, & was again visible at 6, forming one distinct broad arch from East to West, passing nearly through the zenith: this evening the officers performed the*

*two farces of "Raising the Wind", and "the Mock-doctor", for the amusement of
the ships' companies. For several hours on the evening of the 28th, the Aurora was
seen in the SE, with rays shooting as high as the zenith. There is almost always one
stationary part, appearing, as it were, the source whence the shifting or variable part of
the phenomenon proceeds. In the two following days, it was also seen, the wind blowing
a fresh gale from the westward, but there was nothing remarkable in it, and the compass
was not affected. It was principally confined to a space between SW and SSE, and in
the brighter part not more than 10 degrees above the horizon.'*

DOCS. 3 & 4 Journal kept by Parry, 8 May
1821–29 April 1822, where he describes
the Royal Arctic Theatre.

Incredibly, it would not be until July 1822 that the ice was sufficiently thin for the
ships to break out and for Parry to be able to continue his expedition. Parry relied
on Toolemak, an Eskimo with whom they were by now well acquainted, in order
to help him find the elusive passage westward. This example is taken from Parry's
log entry of 9 August 1822:

*'[Toolemak] and his companions came on board the Fury, when I employed him
for a couple of hours in drawing a chart of the strait. Toolemak, though a sensible
and intelligent man, we soon found to be no draughtsman, so that his performance
in this way, if taken alone, was not a very intelligible delineation of the coast. By
dint, however, of a great deal of talking ... we at length obtained a copious verbal
illustration of his sketch, which confirmed all our former accounts respecting the
existence of a passage to the westward.'*

In the meantime, two sledging expeditions had been led by George Francis Lyon,
the commander of HMS *Hecla*, into the frozen interior of the landmass. That
summer, Parry reached the Fury and Hecla Strait but once again found his path
blocked by ice; a party was sent out under Lieutenant Reid which covered an
extraordinary 100 miles over land, and ended up in the Gulf of Boothia.

Spending the winter of 1822 at Igloolik, the Gulf of Boothia was as far
as Parry's 1821–1823 expedition would reach. As the ice closed in around them
once again in late summer 1823, Parry noted that on 1 August the ships were
securely confined with only a small pool of water around them, and he decided
that it would be prudent to escape while it was still possible. Franklin's later

prising manner the cure of this extraordinary disease, and those of an opposite nature to aggravate its fatal malignity. As a source of rational amusement to the men, I, therefore, soon after our arrival, proposed to Captn. Lyon and the officers of both ships, once more to set on foot a series of theatrical entertainments, from which so much benefit in this way had before been derived. My proposal was immediately and unanimously acquiesced in. Captn. Lyon obligingly consented to be our manager, and some preparations having been made, with this view, previous to our leaving England, every-thing was soon arranged for performing a play on board the Fury once a fortnight during the winter. In this, as in more important matters, our former experience stood us in good need. Our theatre was now laid out on a larger and more commodious scale, its decorations much embellished, and what was no less important, both to actors and spectators, a more efficient plan adopted for warming it, whereby we hoped to keep our stage at a temperature somewhat above zero during the winter.

To furnish rational and useful occupation to the men on the other evenings, a school was also established, under the voluntary superintendence of Mr. Halse, for the instruction of such of the men as were willing to take advantage of this opportunity of learning to read and write. The same plan was adopted on board the Hecla, Benjn. White, one of the seamen, who had been educated at Christ-Church school, volunteering to officiate as schoolmaster. Tables were set up in the middle part of the lower-deck, which was before unoccupied; some of the men who were already qualified for this purpose, readily undertook the task

of

count of the cold. I regret this, but am not in the least disappointed, as Mr. Fisher naturally is, because I know the difficulty too well to have expected it. Our bedding is aired once a week by hanging it upon lines on the lower deck, and the hammocks keep it in such comfortable order, that this is found quite sufficient. The reasons for not taking it on deck to "air" during the winter having been already fully detailed in the account of the last voyage, they need not here be repeated. There is, in my opinion, nothing more wonderful in nature, than the never-failing uniformity with which the same natural phenomena are exhibited at the same temperature of the atmosphere. We see this almost daily exemplified. Foxes are still caught occasionally at night. It is remarkable that one cold night killed two of those before caught, for without the means of burrowing in the snow, or of using proper exercise, they do not appear to be able to withstand very severe cold. Our dogs do not seem much inclined to hunt them; & a little white scotch terrier is little regarded by them, and would probably soon become quite familiar with them, if kept together.

In the 25th, both in morning and evening, the Aurora Borealis appeared from SE to SW & West, the brightest part being about 10° above the horizon, and with rays shooting up towards the zenith. Slater's compass was not at all affected. In almost every instance, it is observable that the Aurora has that tendency to an arch-like form before observed so constantly. I do not know that we have ever yet seen any appearance of it in the Northern quarter of the heavens.

At ½ past one on the morning of the 27th the Aurora Borealis, which had been visible for several hours disappeared, & was again visible at 6, forming one distinct broad arch from

expedition to the Northwest Passage in 1845, which vanished after becoming trapped in ice, would demonstrate the perils of the Arctic winter. Parry's solution, recorded in his log, was relatively simple:

> 'On the 4th, our sawing work commenced with the usual alacrity on the part of the officers and crew, and three hundred and fifty yards of ice were got out before night, the thickness being from one to four feet, but very irregular, on account of the numerous pools and holes. An equal length was accomplished on the following day, this not without much fatigue and wet to the men, several of whom fell into the water by the ice breaking under them... On the 6th the work was continued as before, and about four hundred yards of ice sawn through, and floated out, leaving a broad canal, eleven hundred yards in length, leading from the open water towards that formed by the gravelled space.'

Parry now had a decision to make: weather a third winter, or return to England. The advice of his surgeons – that a third winter would have an extremely adverse effect on the men – was unequivocal. It was fortunate that on 8 August 1823, the ice floes began to move and HMS *Fury* was directed into open waters by a strong breeze. While *Hecla* was freed from the ice, Parry took the opportunity to survey the state of the eastern mouth of the strait and soon realised that to continue his expedition would be futile. This realisation and his surgeons' advice led him to conclude, as he noted his log, that he should return to England with both vessels:

> 'It was the general opinion among the officers that this ice was more solid than at the same time and place the preceding year, but its situation did not, I believe, differ half as much from what it had then been. As the Sun went down nearly in the direction of the strait, we obtained from the masthead a clear view in that quarter, and it is impossible to conceive a more hopeless prospect than this now presented. One vast expanse of level solid ice occupied the whole space, and the eye wearied itself in vain to discover a single break upon its surface. Having finished the examination which at once set aside any hope respecting our passage through the strait which I had till lately never ceased to indulge, we again turned towards Igloolik, and, at 2 AM, saw the Hecla's masts over the island.'

The two vessels turned and crossed the Atlantic, reaching the Shetland Islands in October 1823. The expedition had not achieved its aim of discovering the Northwest Passage, but nonetheless Parry and his crew had endured two freezing winters, charted more of the Arctic waters and returned with both vessels intact. His third voyage the following year in 1824 would not be successful, and HMS *Fury* was abandoned and then sank off Somerset Island after it was damaged by ice. It would not be until 1906 that the Northwest Passage would finally be navigated by ship. Meanwhile, William Parry would go on to attempt to reach the North Pole in 1827; he did not manage to do so, but did set a record for the most northerly latitude explored – one that would last for forty-nine years. He was knighted, became a rear admiral in 1852 and has more recently had a crater on the Moon named after him.

Sketch by Parry showing the crew rowing to shore, 1824–25. **BELOW**

Antarctic exploration
CAPTAIN JAMES CLARK ROSS ... 1839–43

'Few people of the present day are capable of rightly appreciating this heroic deed, this brilliant proof of human courage and energy. With two ponderous craft — regular "tubs" according to our ideas — these men sailed right into the heart of the pack [ice], which all previous explorers had regarded as certain death... These men were heroes — heroes in the highest sense of the word.'

Captain James Clark Ross 1800–62.

Those words were written about Captain James Clark Ross's achievements by none other than Roald Amundsen, the first person ever to reach the South Pole in 1911. Ross succeeded in charting almost the entire Antarctic coastline, as well as in discovering the Ross Sea, Victoria Land and the two volcanoes, Mount Erebus and Mount Terror. These achievements were recognised in 1844 with a knighthood. When the Admiralty asked him to head an expedition to the polar continent in 1839, it was drawing on his very extensive experience as a sailor and explorer. He had joined the Navy in 1812 and served with his uncle Sir John Ross on his own expedition to find the Northwest Passage in 1818. Subsequently he followed Sir William Parry on four expeditions to the Arctic between 1819 and 1827, and then accompanied Sir John Ross on his second Arctic voyage between 1829 and 1833, when they located the North Magnetic Pole. By 1834 he was a captain, and it was his famous Antarctic expedition of 1839–43 that would seal his reputation as a great explorer.

The principal purpose of the expedition was to discover more about what was then termed 'terrestrial magnetism' – the phenomenon whereby the compass point direction would change at different points on the Earth's surface. Various theories were put forward to explain this, one attributing it to a magnetic cycle of several centuries depending on internal movements in the Earth, and another to the cycle of heat and cold produced by the annual movements of the Sun. In his book of 1847, *A voyage of discovery and research in the southern and Antarctic regions, during the years 1839–43*, Ross wrote that the British Association for the Advancement of Science considered it *'highly important that the deficiency, yet existing in our knowledge of terrestrial magnetism in the southern hemisphere, should be supplied by observations of the magnetic direction and intensity, especially in the high southern latitudes between the meridians of New Holland and Cape Horn; and they desire strongly to recommend to Her Majesty's government the appointment of a naval expedition expressly directed to that object.'*

Ross was also to lay down charts of any hitherto unexplored waters and coastlines and record what he saw there; a hydrographer was supplied to the expedition for this purpose. A botanist, Joseph Hooker, accompanied Ross to collect zoological and botanical specimens. The expedition was also furnished with extensive supplies, including tinned food, a recent innovation developed by Donkin, Hall and Gamble of Bermondsey, who specialised in packaging food:

'As opportunities might not occur of replenishing our stores and provisions, it was desirable to carry with us as much as we could possibly stow away. Preserved meats, according to Donkin's invention, in consequence of their portability and excellence, formed a large proportion of our provisions... I would, however, suggest to them and others engaged in this branch of trade, that for voyages of several years' duration it would be better that the canisters in which the meats are preserved, should be of a much stouter tin.'

Although Ross was concerned about the possibility of the tins rusting, their development was clearly a major step forward in supplying lengthy naval expeditions in the nineteenth century. In fact, when some of John Franklin's tinned supplies were discovered in 1857 during the search for his lost expedition, they were in a much better condition than was expected. In 1939, one of the tins was opened and the food inside found to be nutritious and edible.

So it was that in 1839 Ross set out for Antarctica in command of HMS *Terror* and accompanied by HMS *Erebus*, two heavy mortar vessels of the Royal Navy with strong hulls that were well suited to breaking through ice. They left Chatham on 25 August 1839, but it would be more than a year until the vessels departed from Tasmania for the Antarctic, on 21 November 1840. On the way, they stopped at Campbell Island in New Zealand where the magnetic dip and variation was promptly measured. Ross noted that the results were anomalous: *'for here we found a great amount of local attraction; the same instrument in different places giving widely different results, and proving how very liable to error all surveys made by compass must be, and especially so upon lands of volcanic formation'*. A set of colour sketches was also produced to record the impressive landscape of Campbell Island. On 27 January 1841, as Ross recorded, they finally sighted land:

> *'We proceeded at once therefore to take possession of the island in due form; and to the great satisfaction of every individual in the expedition, I named it "Franklin Island;" in compliment to His Excellency Captain Sir John Franklin of the Royal Navy, to whom, and his amiable lady, I have already had occasion to express the gratitude we all felt for the great kindness we received at their hands... Franklin Island is situate in lat. 76 degrees 8' S, long. 168 degrees 12' E. It is about twelve miles long and six miles broad, and is composed wholly of igneous rocks; the northern side presents a line of dark*

Campbell Island

precipitous cliffs, between five and six hundred feet high, exposing several longitudinal broad white, probably aluminous, bands of several feet thickness... We could not perceive the smallest trace of vegetation, not even a lichen or piece of sea-weed growing on the rocks; and I have no doubt from the total absence of it, that the vegetable kingdom has no representative in Antarctic lands.'

One of Ross's great discoveries was of two Antarctic volcanoes. In the meteorological logs for HMS *Erebus*, on the tenth hour of the morning of 28 January 1841, he recorded this moment as follows: '*Burning Mountain SE & S*'. His account of the voyage describes the volcanoes in more detail:

'We stood to the southward, close to some land which had not been in sight since the preceding noon, and which we then called the "High Island;" it proved to be a mountain twelve thousand four hundred feet of elevation above the level of the sea, emitting flame

A sketch of the Campbell Islands by I. E. Davies, 1840. **BELOW**

ar the Harbor N 34° E , S 22° 30 W ½ a mile ...

HYDROG:
OFFICE
23 MY. 42

N° 8.
Campbell I. S. Pa

and smoke in great profusion; at first the smoke appeared like snow drift, but as we drew nearer, its true character became manifest. The discovery of an active volcano inso high a southern latitude cannot but be esteemed a circumstance of high geological importance and interest, and contribute to throw some further light on the physical construction of our globe. I named it "Mount Erebus" and an extinct volcano to the eastward little inferior by height, being by measurement ten thousand nine hundred feet high, was called "Mount Terror"...

'At 4pm Mount Erebus was observed to emit smoke and flame in unusual quantities, producing a most grand spectacle. A volume of dense smoke was projected at each successive jet at great force, in a vertical column, to the height of between fifteen hundred and two thousand feet above the mouth of the crater, when condensing first at its upper part, it descended in mist or snow, and gradually dispersed, to be succeeded by another splendid exhibition of the same kind in about half an hour afterward, although the intervals between the eruptions were by no means regular. The diameter of the columns of smoke was between two and three hundred feet, as near as we could measure it; whenever the smoke cleared away, the bright red flame that filled the mouth of the crater was clearly perceptible, and some of the officers believed they could see streams of lava pouring down its sides until lost beneath the snow which descended from a few hundred feet below the crater, and projected its perpendicular icy cliff several miles into the ocean'

Ross proceeded to sail east by south-east along this icy cliff for around a hundred nautical miles, noting that many small fragments of ice lay in the water at the foot of the ice shelf. Ultimately, they would sail for over 250 nautical miles along this Antarctic feature, which was at the time named the Barrier, or the Great Ice Barrier, by the crew. In time it was renamed the Ross Ice Shelf in the explorer's honour.

As well as observing the geology and coastline of Antarctica, Ross continued to note the various species of wildlife that he encountered, aided by his zoologist, Joseph Hooker. In his entry for 28 January 1841, he noted that he '*saw several white Petrels*', and at the sixth hour in the afternoon he '*saw a dusky Petrel*'. That afternoon, he also '*saw several Penguins*'. At the eighth hour, again, he '*saw a penguin*'. Ross's record-keeping was clearly accurate and meticulous, as would

Franklin Island. S16W 6miles   S36W Jan'y 27th 1841 at 3.20 P.M.

be expected on a scientific expedition. The coastal topography and the outlines of Mounts Erebus and Terror were also captured in a series of beautiful colour sketches which are now held at The National Archives.

On 2 March, he was still navigating the ice shelf, attempting find a route through:

Approaching Franklin Island, drawn by I. E. Davies, on 27 January 1841. **ABOVE**

> *'In passing through the streams of ice, that lay off the pack edge during night, our ship sustained some very heavy blows; and soon after midnight the shackle of the Terror's bobstay was thus broken: as soon as they made the signal we hove to, that they might replace it. This operation, however, was one of great difficulty, owing to the darkness of the night; the ships' bows and rigging being thickly encrusted with ice, and so much swell as to endanger the lives of the brave fellows that were engaged for nearly two hours, slung over the bows, up to their necks in water at every plunge the ship took, before they could accomplish it; and this with the thermometer at 12 degrees below freezing. We made all sail at daylight along the pack edge to the north, with a light breeze form*

METEOROLOGICAL REGISTER.

H	Ther.ᵐ Air	Ther.ᵐ Sea	Barometer	Attached Thermometer	Corrected Barometer	Hygrometer Air	Hygrometer Dew	Hygrometer Diff.	Winds Direction	Force	Weather	Other Phenomenas
1	23.7	29	29.004	61	28.999				S W	3	4 b c	A.M.
2	23	30	28.992	56	999				6 f t w	3	"	Saw several White Petrel
3	23.5	30	900	52	996				"	3	1 b c	
4	24	30.5	970	50	090				"	3	"	
5	25.5	29	940	40.5	071				"	3	"	
6	25.5	31	938	47.5	063				"	3	"	Centre of Island bore one last night
7	27.5	31.5	938	46	067				"	3	"	W p S Small Island J p W extremes of
8	29	31	934	47	061				"	3	"	large Island from J p E to S E ½ E & W p E
9	29	31	934	52	040	30	18	12	"	3	"	N on East of large Island S E ½ p E to S p
10	28	31	940	52	054				"	3	"	Burning Mountain S E ½ p S Centre of
11	29	30	944	52	080				J W W W	3	6 b c v	Smaller Island N S w Ship H d 28 E few
12	29	30	944	51	060	30	22	8	"	3	"	whale popd as here, then
1	27	30	28.932	52	28.046				S W ¼ w	3	6 b c v	P.M. Thos I suppose to be Mt Sabine
2	28	29.5	988	51.5	053				"	3	"	Saw several Penguins
3	32	30	940	51.5	055	33	32	10	"	3	"	
4	33	32	930	53	041				"	3	"	
5	8.5	29.5	950	55	056				"	0	"	5 Saw a dusky Petrel
6	29.5	31.5	950	50	060				"	0	"	
7	29.5	29	956	56	061				S E ½ E	4	6 b c	
8	28	29	956	54	061				"	4	"	9 Saw a Penguin
9	28	28.8	974	58.5	075	29	23	6	"	4		Mount running along Fixed Ice about
10	28	28.5	988	59	080				"	4	4 b c	7 Miles distance extreme of Island
11	27.5	29.5	29.016	55	926				"	4		S E ¼ E extreme of Fixed Ice N ¼ w
12	27.7	29.5	040	52	959				S S E	4		passed several pieces of Loose Ice

the westward; and at noon were in lat. 68 27' S., long. 167 42' E, the dip 85 19', and variation 34 32' E. We had no soundings with 400 fathoms line, the temperature at that depth 36: the surface 28° 2', and the air 27. We met with fewer streams of ice off the pack, and were favoured with very fine weather, the thermometer having risen to a more comfortable temperature.'

Eventually the lateness of the season meant that Ross was unable to advance any further, and the expedition turned back for Tasmania, having weathered gales and conditions which had encrusted the vessels in ice. Yet they had succeeded in discovering the Ross Ice Shelf and the two volcanoes, Mount Erebus and Mount Terror, and returned laden with valuable scientific data.

Ross would make another trip to the Antarctic the following year, when he surveyed the eastern side of what is now known as James Ross Island and gathered ornithological, magnetic and botanical data, returning to England on 4 September 1843. That expedition confirmed the existence of the southern continent, and for this achievement Ross was awarded the Gold Medal of the Société de Géographie in 1843, elected to the Royal Society in 1848 and knighted in 1844.

DOC. 1 Meteorological data taken on the expedition 1 January to 30 June 1841.

Mount Terror S 16.15 W 45 Miles , Mount Erebus S 34 W 50 miles .

N.B. The Bearin

Mount Erebus and Mount Terror, sketched
by I. E. Davies on 28 January 1841. TOP

The Southern Islands, sketched by I. E.
Davies on 28 January 1841. BOTTOM

2

Mutiny & Piracy

Pirate or privateer?

HENRY MORGAN ... 1635–88

Henry Morgan's seafaring life was one of an adventurous buccaneer who plied his trade in the turquoise waters and white sands of the Caribbean. His name has been immortalised in books and films, and even as a popular brand of Jamaican spiced rum.

Morgan was licensed by the Crown as a privateer, to capture and plunder ships of hostile nations and to retain captured booty, in return for the Crown and the Admiralty receiving a share. However, there is still debate as to whether Morgan was a legitimate privateer, or in reality a pirate who frequently overreached his remit from the Crown.

Henry Morgan, 1635–88. **ABOVE**

He was born near Tredegar in South Wales in 1635 and first ventured to the West Indies in 1655 as part of an expedition to conquer the Spanish island of Hispaniola. This failed, and the English force instead conquered Jamaica, where Morgan was granted land and settled.

It was in 1662 that Morgan would experience his first taste of privateering. He served with naval commander Christopher Myng, who raided the Cuban city of Santiago de Cuba, and the following year they attacked the coastal town of San Francisco de Campeche, now in Mexico, using the open-ended instructions of their king, Charles II, to trade with the Spanish colonies by force as justification for their raids.

Following the appointment of the new governor of Jamaica, Thomas Modyford, in 1664, Morgan co-commanded a fleet of privateers along with Englishman John Morris and a Dutchman, David Martien. The privateers trekked through swamp and jungle to raid Villahermosa, a provincial capital in Mexico, and paddled several hundred miles in canoes up the San Juan River to sack Gran Grenada in Nicaragua. Morgan returned to Jamaica in triumph, his pockets lined with looted Spanish gold.

In 1668 he sailed from Port Royal in southeastern Jamaica with ten ships and 500 buccaneers, and orders to capture Spanish prisoners with the aim of verifying rumours of Spanish plans to invade the island. Morgan's successful capture of the Cuban town of Puerto Principe yielded the information he needed. Then, according to the following carefully worded account that the privateers relayed to Modyford, who conveyed it to London, they made for Porto Bello on the Panama coast, where they had learned levies were being raised against Jamaica:

A map of Jamaica from John Sellar's *Atlas Maritimus*, published in 1698. **BELOW**

'... *leaving our ships on June 26 last, about 40 leagues to the leeward of Porto Bello ... we took to our canoes, being twenty three in number, & with them rowing along the*

coast … we landed the boats within two leagues of the westward of the harbour. At 3 of the clock in the morning, and at sunrise, [we] arrived at the castle where finding the Spaniards in arms and firing at us, we thought it reason to answer them in the same language. Presently our first division made their best way into the town … whom following we continued there till about 8 of the clock [in the morning] when seeing we could not refresh ourselves in quiet, we were enforced to assault their castle … which we took and entered by storm about two of the clock the same day, the enemy in the interim telling us that they would not give nor receive quarter. We found the castle provisioned with all sorts of ammunition and provision only undermanned, being in all about 130 men, whereof we found 74 killed, among which the Castiliano was one. In the dungeon 11 Englishmen in chains which had been there two years in misery; and upon further enquiry we were informed that a great man had been carried from thence six months before to a place called Lima of Peru on the south sea, who was formerly brought from Porto Rico, as also the certainty of their intentions against us here and that the Prince of Monte Cerea had been there with orders from the King of Spain to raise 2,200 men (as part of his army) out of the Province of Panama which Porto Bello stands in, the certainty whereof was confirmed us by all the Grandees we had both prisoners and hostages.'

The next day, the privateers recounted, they sent a message to the governor of the second castle demanding that he give their ships free entry into the port:

'… which he refusing and we concluding no other way safe for us, we were forced to attempt the taking of it but after a short time the Governor delivered a treaty which ended in his delivering up the castle and marching according to his desire with arms and colours flying. This done but with one hundred, the third castle was immediately surrendered to five or six of our men and now having possession of the town and three castles, (whereof there were no less than 900 men that bore arms)'

On their fifth day in Panama, Morgan and the other privateers were confronted by *'about 3,000 men'*, whom they fought off, causing more damage to the enemy than to themselves:

Shipps Names	Commanders Names	Tonns	Guns	Men
A List of the Shipps vnder the command of Admirall Morgan				
The Satisfaction Freg	Adll Henry Morgan	120	22	140
The Mary Fregate	Capt Thomas Harris	50	12	70
The Mayflowre	Capt Joseph Bradley	70	14	100
The Pearle	Capt Lawrce Prince	50	12	70
Civillian	Capt Erasmus	80	12	75
Dolphin Fregate	Capt John Morris	60	10	60
Lilly fregate	Capt Rich Norman	50	10	50
Port Royall	Capt James Delliatt	50	12	55
The Gift	Capt Thos Rogers	40	12	60
John of Vaughall	Capt John Pyne	70	6	60
The Thomas	Capt Hump Throston	50	8	45
The Fortune	Capt Rich Ludbury	40	6	40
Constant Thomas	Capt Coone Darbraunce	60	6	40
The Fortune	Capt Rich Dobson	25	6	35
The Prosperous	Capt Henry Wells	16	4	35
Abraham Offerenda	Capt Rich Taylor	60	4	30
Virgin Queene	Capt John Bennet	15	—	30
Recovery	Capt John Sheppard	18	3	30
The Sloope Wm	Capt Tho Woodriffe	12	—	30
The Betty Sloope	Capt Wm Curson	12	—	25
The Fortune Catch	Capt Jem Symons	40	4	40
The Endeavour	Capt John Harmanson	25	4	35
Bonadventure	Capt Roger Taylor	20	—	25
Prosperous	Capt Patrick Dunkarr	10	—	16
Endeavour	Capt Charles Swan	16	2	30
The Lambe Sloope	Capt Rich Powell	30	4	30
Fortune	Capt Jonas Reekes	16	3	30
The Free Guift	Roger Kelly	15	4	40
French Shipps		1120	180	1326
St Katherine	Capt Tributor	100	14	110
Galliardena	Capt Gascoone	80	10	80
St John	Capt Diego	80	10	80
St Peter	Capt Pearse Hantot	80	10	90
Le Deauble Volaut	Capt Demaugla	40	6	50
Le Serfe sloope	Capt Joseph	25	2	40
Le Lyon sloope	Capt Charles	30	3	40
Le St Maria	Capt John Linaux	30	4	30
		155	59	520
English Shipps in all		28	180	1326
French Shipps in all		8	59	520
Totall		36	239	1846

A list of the thirty-six ships under the command of Henry Morgan in 1670. **LEFT**

'...... insomuch that the very next day they sent for a treat, proffering in money for delivery of the town, castles, and 300 negroes which were in our possession ... it being 100,000 pieces of eight ... which being paid, we repaired on board and thence being under sail sent the hostages on shore, leaving both town and castles entirely and in a good condition, as they found them.'

The success of this last raid no doubt provided an impetus for the next. Morgan assembled a fleet, including his flagship, HMS *Oxford*, south-west of Hispaniola in January 1669. Unfortunately, the accidental explosion of the powder magazine on board HMS *Oxford* killed 200 men and sent the ship to the bottom of the sea.

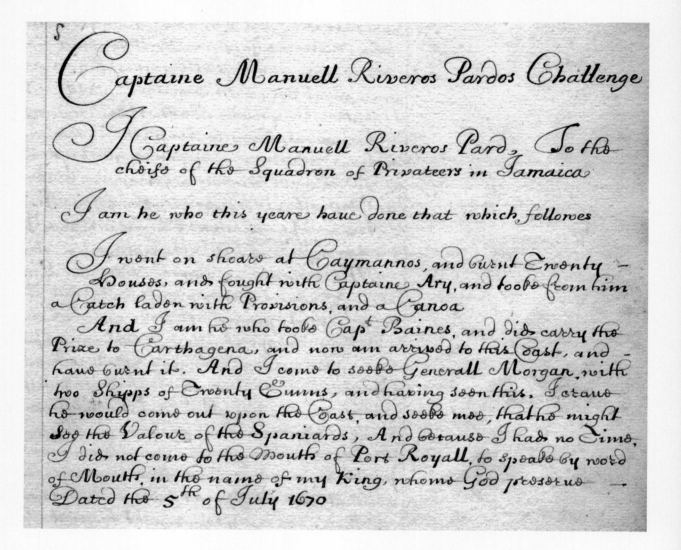

Captaine Manuell Riveros Pardos Challenge

I Captaine Manuell Riveros Pard, To the choife of the Squadron of Privateers in Jamaica

I am he who this yeare haue done that which followes

*I went on shoare at Caymannos, and burnt Twenty — Houses, and fought with Captaine Ary, and tooke from him a Catch laden with Provisions, and a Canoa And I am he who tooke Cap*ᵗ *Baines, and did carry the Prize to Carthagena, and now am arrived to this Coast, and haue burnt it. And I come to seeke Generall Morgan, with two Shipps of Twenty Gunns, and having seen this, I craue he would come out upon the Coast, and seeke mee, that he might See the Valour of the Spaniards, And because I had no Time, I did not come to the Mouth of Port Royall, to speake by word of Mouth, in the name of my King, whome God preserue — Dated the 5*ᵗʰ *of July 1670*

Morgan himself was lucky to escape, but he was forced to modify his plans, successfully sacking the town of Maracaibo in a Venezuelan lagoon instead. Spanish ships blockaded the lagoon entrance and, believing they had well and truly trapped the wily captain, re-manned a fort previously lost to Morgan's buccaneers. However, by attacking and destroying several of the Spanish vessels and then feigning a landing near the Spanish fortress, guarding the entrance to the lagoon, Morgan and his fleet were able to slip out under cover of darkness and escape.

Retribution would come, however, as the Spanish commissioned their own privateers to target English ships and raid Jamaica. The Portuguese privateer Captain Manuel Riveros Pardos issued the following challenge to Morgan: '*with two shipps and twenty guns … I crave he would come out upon the coast and seeke mee that he might see the valour of Spaniards.*'

The challenge made by Captain Pardos to Henry Morgan in July 1670. **ABOVE**

Morgan never answered the challenge, but his superiors in Port Royal were determined to resume hostilities against the Spanish despite the Anglo-Spanish peace agreement. He was appointed admiral of a fleet of ships manned by privateers commissioned to '*doe and performe all matter of exployts which may tend to the preservation and quiet of Jamayca*', an extremely open-ended remit. Morgan interpreted it to mean nothing less than the successful capture and sacking of the wealthiest city in the Americas – Panama City. He set sail from Port Royal on 14 August 1670 with thirty-eight ships and 2,000 men, and, together with sixteen English privateer captains, signed a pledge to safeguard Jamaica from Spanish invasion.

A drawing of a Spanish frigate c. seventeenth century. **BELOW**

'... for the security island of his majesty's island of Jamaica to prevent the invasions of the Spaniards ... we thought [it] might be most feasible and just to take for the good of Jamaica and honour of our nation ... to take Panama the president there of having ranted several commissions against the English.'

The men, having reached central Panama, successfully made their way up the Chagres River and then overland, spying their objective on 17 January 1671. Morgan described what happened as the Spanish assembled to confront them before the gates of Panama City:

'About 4 in the afternoon, after the men having refreshed themselves, we marched and about five [o'clock in the afternoon] we came in sight of the enemy in battalia [divisions] with 2,100 foot and 600 horse... The next morning being the 18th betimes in the morning I gave the order to draw our men in battalia, it was accordingly performed and they were drawn up in the form of a tertia. The vanguard [was] led by Lieutenant-Colonel Lawrence Prince and Major John Morris, they being in number 300 men, the main body containing 600, the right wing was led by myself, the left by Colonel Edward Collyer, and the rearward of 300 commanded by Colonel Bledry Morgan. After having viewed my men and a little encouraged them I commanded the officers [and] every man to repair to his charge the enemy being drawn at such advantage they still kept their station although often provoke[ed] yet would not stir from their ground with their foot. I presently perceived [this] and gave order that the officers should wheel our body to the left and endeavour to gain the hill ... [which] the hill and a dry gutt[er] accordingly gained the enemy then was forced to fight upon their long march having not room enough to wheel his battle ... whereupon one Francesco de Harro gave the charge with his horse upon the vanguard so furiously that he came upon the full speed, I having no pikes gave order that they should double their ranks to the right and close their files to the right and left inward to their close order but his career could not be stopped till he lost his life in the front rank of our vanguard upon which the horse wheeled off to the right and their foot advanced, but met with such a warm welcome and pursued so close that everyone thought it best to retreat but they were so closely plied by our left wing ... that the enemies' retreat came to plain running, though they did work such a stratagem as has been seldom heard of that when the foot engaged

141

Loss Having three men Slightly wounded but y̅ Enemys Loss wee could never Learne January y̅ 15th wee arriued at venta Cruse w̅ is a very fine village y̅ place where they Land and Embarque all y̅ Goods that Comes and goes to Pannama where wee thought wee might bee releaued haueing Marched 3 dayes without victualls but found it as y̅ Rest all afire and the Enemy fleed, y̅ 16 wee began our March y̅ Enemy Constantly gauling vs by Ambuscadaos and small Partys and wee still beating them for a league togeathor, although they had all the advantage y̅ Could bee of vs, y̅ way being soe narrow that wee could March but foure abrest, and such a Deepe hollow one of y̅ Enemy lay over our heads about noone wee got to y̅ Savanas off safe, with y̅ Loss of three men kild out right and six or seauen Wounded and of y̅ Enemy 20 kild and one Capt besides many wounded wee marched 3 miles further and then tooke vp our Quarters to refresh our men and thank them for that dayes seruis, y̅ 17th wee began our March but had noe opposition and about Nyne a Clock in y̅ Morning I arriv'd y̅ desired place y̅ South Seas and Likewise a good spell of Cattle and horses whereupon I Commanded a Generr: halt to bee made, and o̅ men did kill horses and beefe enough to serue them all, about 4 in the after noone, our men haueing Refreshed themselues wee Marched againe and about fiue wee came in sight of the Enemy where hee lay in Battalia with 2100 foote and 600 Horse but finding the day farr spent I thought it not fitt to Engage but tooke vp my Quarters within a Mile of them, where wee lay very quiett not being as much as once alarumed y̅ next morning being y̅ 18th betimes in y̅ morning I gaue order to draw our men in Battalia it was accordingly p̅formed and they were drawne in y̅ forme of A tertia y̅ vantgard was led by Leut. Collo̅ll Lanrence Prince and Majs John Morriss they being in Number 300 men y̅ maine body Conteyning 600, y̅ Right Wing was led by my selfe and y̅ Left Collo̅: Edward Collyer the rearward of 300 was commanded by Collo̅: Bledry Morgan after haueing vewed my men and a Little Encouradged them I Commanded y̅ officers every man should repaire to his Charge y̅ Enemy being drawne at such advantage they still kept theire station although often prouoke, yett would they not stirr from theire Ground with theire foote which I presently perceaued and gaue order that the Officers should wheele our body to y̅ left and Endeavour to gaine a hill y̅ was hard by which if gained wee should force y̅ Enemy to fight to theire disadvantage by reason hee could not bring out of his great body noe more men to fight at A time then I should out of our small body and y̅ likewise I should haue y̅ advantage both of the sun and Wind y̅ Officers putting this Comand in execution and y̅ Hill

51   131 and

759

And a dry gutt accordingly gained y(e) Enemy then was forced to fight
vpon their long march hauing not roome enough to wheele his
battle by reason of a bogg y(t) was drawne behind on purpose as
he thought to entrap us but wee taking another Ground in y(e) end
prooved a snare to himselfe whereupon one Francisco de Starre
gaue the Charge with his Horse vpon the vantgard and soe
furiously that he came vpon y(e) full speed J hauing noe Pikes
gaue order that they should double their Rankes to y(e) right and
Close their files to y(e) Right and Left inward to their close Order,
but his fauoore could not be stoped till hee lost his life in the
front Rank of our vantgard vpon which y(e) horse wheeled of
to y(e) Right And their foot advanced to try their fortunes, butt
it prooved like their followers for wee being ready with the maine
Battle to Receaue them, gaue them such a warme welcome and
pursued soe close that every one thought it best to retreat, but
they were soe closely plyed by our left wing, who could not come
to Engage at y(e) first by reason of y(e) hill that y(e) enemies wheate
came to plaine Runing although they did worke such a stratagem
that hath been seldome or never heare of (that is) when when the
foote Engaged us in y(e) fflank hee attempted to drine two drones
of Cattle of 1500 a peece into y(e) Right and Left angles of y(e) Reare,
but all came to one effect, and helped nothing for they continued
their fligh to y(e) Citty where they had 200 fresh men and two
fortes one with 6 brass guns and the other with Eight And the
Streete Barracaudoes and great guns in Every streets w(ch) in
all amounted to 32 Brass Guns but Instead of flighting hee
Comandoes to bee fired and his Cheife floart to bee blowne
vp y(e) which was done Jn such hast: that hee Blew vp
fforty of his Souldiers in it wee followed into the Towne
where in y(e) Markett place they made some Resistance and
fixed some great guns, Killed us 4 men and wounded fiue,
at 3 of Clock after Noone wee had quitt possession of y(e)
Citty although on fire with noe more Loss on our side in
this dayes worke then fiue Killed and tenn Wounded and
of the Enemyes about 400 where wee were all forced

10

& Lastly

To Endeavour to put ȳ fire out of ȳ Enemyes houses but it was for vaine for by 12 at night it was all Consumed that might bee called the Citty butt of ȳ Subbarbes there was saved two Churches and three hundred Houses,

142

Thus was Consumed ȳ fameous and anciont Citty of Pannama which is ȳ greatest mart for silver and gould in ȳ whole world for it receives all ȳ goods into it ȳ comes from Ould Spaine in ȳe Kings greate fleete and Likewise delivers to ȳ fleete all ȳ silver and gold that comes from ȳ Mines of Pora and Potazi, herein this Citty wee stayed 28 dayes Makeing dayly Incursions vpon the Enemy by land for twenty Leagues Round aboute, without haueing as much as one Gun shott at us in anger, although wee tooke in this time neere 3000 prisoners of all sortes and Kept Likewise Barques in the South Seas a Cruseing and fetching of prisoners that had fledd to ȳ Islands with their goods and familyes February the 14th wee begun our March towardes our Shipps with all our prisoners and ȳ next day came to Venta Cruse aboute two in the after noone which is from Pannama 5 English Leagues where wee stayed refreshin our soldiers till ȳ 24th ȳ 26th wee came to Chaugra where ȳ plunder was Deuided amongst the Souldiers and Seamen wch amounted to aboute 30000: the 6 of March wee fired the Castle Spiked ȳ Guns and begun our voyage for Jamaica where some are arrived and ȳ rest dayly expected ȳ reason that there was noe more wealth was because they had two Months notice of us & it was all Imbarked in to 2 greate Shipps ye one of 350 tun & ye other of 700 tunns as wee had it fro ye Prisoners they wee both Laden with wch money Plate & gould & Jewells all this I auer to be truth Except ye Last wch I haue traditionally as wittnes my hand

Hen Morgan

51   220   132

(3)

*us in the flank he attempted to drive two droves of 1,500 cattle into the right and left
angles of their rear. In the city they had 200 fresh men and two forts one with 6 brass
guns and the other with eight, and the streets [were] barricaded, and great guns in every
street, which in all amounted to 32 brass guns, but instead of fighting he commanded it to
be fired, his chief fort to be blown up, the which was done in such haste that he blew up
40 of his soldiers in it. We followed into the town where in the market place they made
some resistance, but at 3 of [the] clock after noon we had quiet possession of the city,
although on fire, with no more loss on our side in this day's work than five killed and ten
wounded, and of the enemy about 400… Thus was consumed the famous and ancient
city of Panama which is the greatest mart [trading centre] for silver and gold in the
whole world.'*

The plunder gathered in the smoking ruins of Panama City amounted to
750,000 pieces of eight – about £46 million today – over half of which was
Morgan's personal share.

   This was to be Morgan's last venture against the Spanish as England
repaired ties with Spain. Governor Modyford was replaced by a pro-Spanish
governor and the man known as 'Panama Morgan' was arrested and brought
back to England to be tried. Luck was on his side, however, as the fragile state of
peace with Spain broke down, and instead of being punished, Morgan's popular
reputation so impressed Charles II that the king had him knighted in 1674.
Morgan returned to Jamaica a vindicated man, but his privateering days were
well and truly over. With substantial land holdings, he settled down and served
as deputy governor of the island. Ironically his duties involved the prosecution
of pirates, some of whom he had served with. In 1680, he signed the death
warrants for Bartholomew Sharp and John Coxon, who had just successfully
raided Porto Bello.

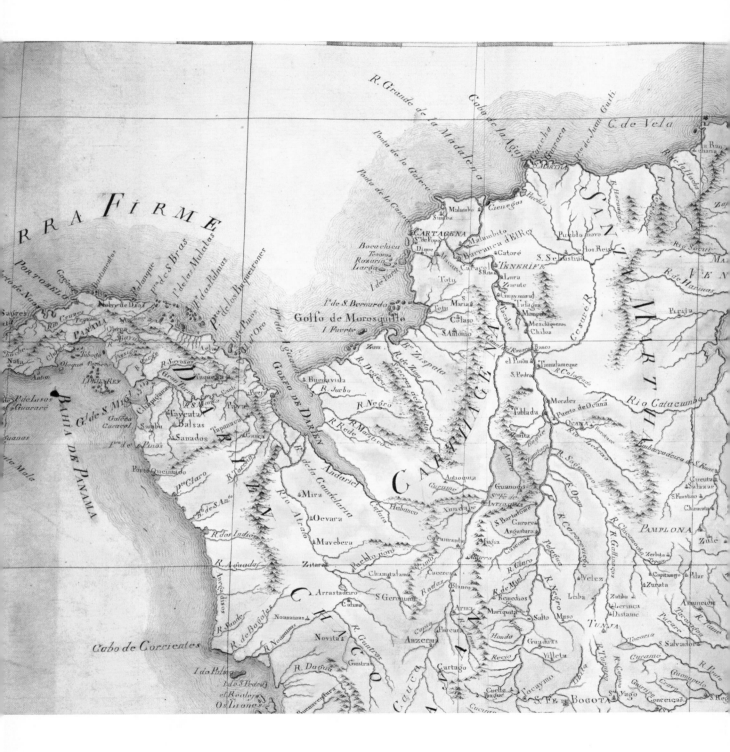

A privateer's commission

CAPTAIN WILLIAM KIDD ... c.1695–1701

Little is known about the early life of the legendary William Kidd, but he was probably born within sight of the sea at Greenock, Scotland, sometime in 1645. He emerged from historical obscurity in 1689 when he became the captain of the *Blessed William*, a privateer vessel licensed to seize enemy ships in the Caribbean during the Nine Years' War against France. Though essentially a privateer, Kidd also played his part in Admiral Codrington's raid on the French colonial island of Marie-Galante.

Kidd's crew objected to full-scale naval action, so they commandeered the *Blessed William*, leaving its captain stranded. But his role at Marie-Galante stood Kidd in good stead in the eyes of the naval authorities, and he was given another ship, the *Antigua*, and permission to hunt down his mutinous crew. He made his way to New York, where he assisted Governor Henry Sloughter in suppressing a rebellion. Once again, he found favour with the authorities so that by 1695 he was a prosperous citizen of New York, married to a wealthy widow, Sarah Oort.

Captain William Kidd c.1645–1701. **ABOVE**

Kidd soon became restless, however, perhaps hankering for the seafaring life and the possibility of making his fortune. New York was a haven for pirates active in the Caribbean and Indian Ocean, as it was a place where they could sell their loot without fear of reprisal. Kidd must have been familiar with this scene and devised a plan for leading a privateering expedition against pirates. He joined up with Robert Livingston, a Scot active in New York business and politics. The pair departed for Britain in the hope of receiving a royal commission as privateers.

With William III on the throne and the Whigs in government, Kidd and Livingston approached Richard Coote, Earl of Bellomont, a prominent Whig politician with financial worries of his own. Bellomont became Kidd's chief patron in a Whig syndicate that would share the profits from Kidd's expedition. They persuaded King William to grant Kidd a commission to apprehend pirates and seize French ships.

'Whereas we are informed ... wicked and ill-disposed persons, and do against the law of nations commit many and great Pyracies, Robberies and Depredations on the seas ... do hereby give and grant to the said William Kidd ... full Power and Authority to apprehend, seize and take into your Custody ... as all such Pyrates, Pyrates, Free Booters and Sea Rovers, being either our Subjects, or of our Nations associated with them, which you shall meet with upon the Seas, or Coasts of America, or upon any other Seas or Coasts, with all their Ships and Vessels; and all such Merchandizes, Money, Goods and Wares as shall be found on board, or with them, in Case they shall willingly yield themselves; but if they will not yield without fighting, then you are by Force to compel them to yield...'

Captain William Kidd's privateering commission 1695. **BELOW**

Kidd chose as his ship the *Adventure Galley*, a hybrid vessel powered by either sail or oars. At close quarters or in calm weather, the latter could give the ship a real advantage. Heavily armed with thirty-four cannon, it seemed ideal for hunting down buccaneers. Early in 1696 Kidd left London in the *Adventure Galley*, first for New York to complete his crew, and then to the Indian Ocean, where pirates preyed on the rich Mughal convoys travelling between India and the Red Sea.

Kidd arrived at the buccaneer town of Tulear in Madagascar early in 1697, soon heading for the Mandab Strait at the entrance to the Red Sea. He intended to intercept wealthy ships crossing the Indian Ocean from Surat to make the pilgrimage to Mecca. But each time he tried to capture a ship he was beaten off, leading to the crew, which by now included many habituated pirates, becoming increasingly frustrated and rebellious. Kidd imposed his authority on them by killing a gunner, William Moore, smashing his skull with a bucket. A sailor, Joseph Palmer, later described the incident in giving evidence at Kidd's trial:

> '... then sailed for Callient upon the same coast of Mallabar and sailing upon that coast there happened some words between Captain Kidd and his gunner whose name was William Moore and Kidd calling him lousy dog and said Moore replied if I am so it is you that have brought me to it, upon which Kid was so enraged that be took up an iron bound bucket by the strap (?) and struck (?) Moore with it over the head as he sat at work grinding his chisel and struck him down ... and Moore ... bid the Company farewell for Kidd had given him his last...'

Kidd found himself in a dangerous situation with nothing to offer his patrons, and with an insubordinate crew on board. Piracy offered a way out of this predicament.

Acts of Piracy

Kidd abandoned the Red Sea and sailed south along the western coast of India looking for prey. His chance came when he spotted the *Rupparell*, a Dutch-owned trading ship. The *Adventure Galley* was flying French colours, which tricked the *Rupparell*'s captain, Michael Dickers, into producing a 'French pass', showing that the *Rupparell* was nominally a French ship and giving Kidd's seizure of it a

Map of the western East Indies, including the Arabian Gulf and the coast east Africa from John Sellar's *Atlas Maritimus*, 1698. RIGHT

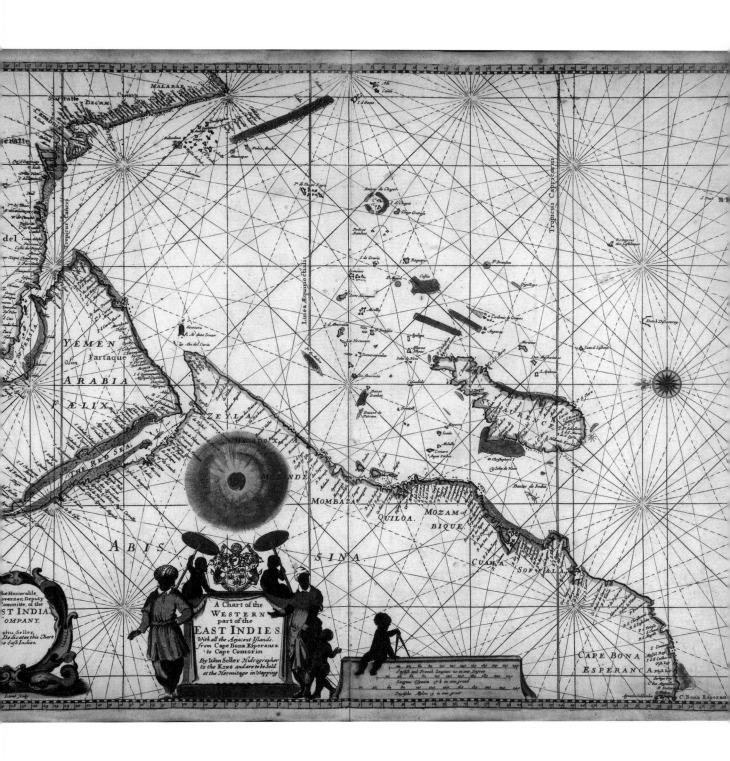

semblance of legality. Kidd duly claimed his prize and then sold off the cargo, distributing the money among the crew, which bought him some time. Soon afterwards, he seized another two small trading vessels; there was no longer any question about it – this was out-and-out piracy.

However, Kidd knew that these relatively meagre prizes would not be enough to satisfy his patrons – he needed something bigger. This came in the shape of the *Quedah Merchant*, a 500-ton ship returning to Surat from Bengal and carrying a rich cargo of fabrics, opium and sugar, much of which was owned by a prominent politician at the Mughal court. The *Quedah* was sailing north along the western coast of India when on 30 January 1698 it met the *Adventure Galley* off Kochin. The ship was unescorted and Kidd saw his chance. Again he used the ploy of flying French colours and again the captain, this time John Wright, made the mistake of producing French documents, as Kidd later described:

> 'And that about the first day of February following upon the same Coast under French colours with a designe to decoy met with a Bengall Merchant man belonging to Suratt of the burthen of 4 or 500 Tons, and he commanded the Master on board and a Frenchman Inhabitant of Suratt and belonging to the French Factory there and gunner of sd ship came on board as master and when he came on board the Narrator caused the English Colours to be hoysted, and he sd Master war surprised and said you are all English, and asking which was the Captain whom when he saw said here is a good prize and delivered him the French pass. And that with the said two prizes sailed for the Port of St Marie in Madagascar. And sailing hither the sd Galley was so leaky that they feared they would have sunk every hour...'

The *Quedah Merchant* was a rich prize, but its links to the Mughal court were to prove instrumental in Kidd's downfall.

The seaworthiness of the *Adventure Galley* was deteriorating as the monsoon season loomed and the crew were working hard at the pumps to keep her afloat. After an abortive pursuit of an East India Company ship, *Sedgewick*, Kidd decided that there was nothing further to be achieved in the Indian Ocean. He headed to the island of Saint Marie, lying to the north of Madagascar and a haven for pirates. Here some of the cargo was sold and the crew were paid off.

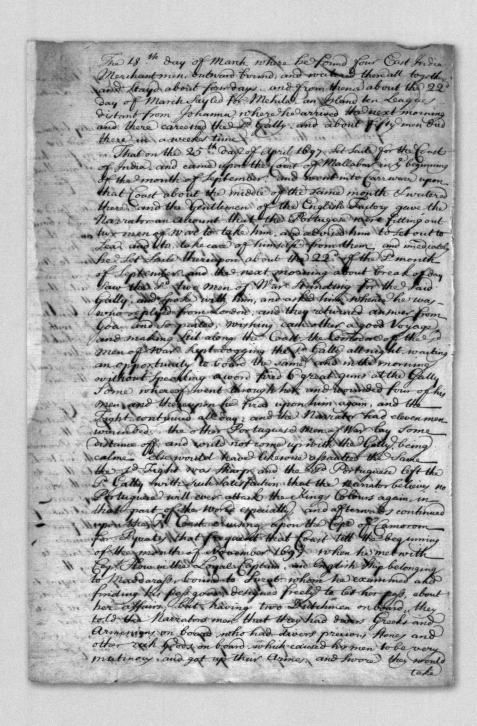

The 18th day of March, where he found four East India
Merchant men, outward bound, and watered there all together,
and stayd about four days, and from thence about the 22d
day of March sayled for Mehila, an Island ten Leagues
distant from Johanna where he arrived the next morning
and there careened the sd Gally, and about fifty men dued
there in a weeks time

That on the 25th day of April 1697, set sail for the Coast
of India, and came upon the Coast of Mallabar in ye beginning
of the month of September, and went into Carrwar upon
that Coast about the middle of the same month & watered
there, and the Gentlemen of the English Factory gave the
Narrator an Account that the Portugais were fitting out
two men of War to take him, and advised him to set out to
Sea and to take care of himself from them, and imediately
he set Saile thereupon about the 22d of the sd month
of September, and the next morning about break of day
Saw the sd two men of War standing for the said
Gally, and spoke with him, and asked him whence he was
who replyed from London, and they returned answer from
Goa, and so parted, wishing each other a good Voyage,
and making Sail along the Coast the Comadore of the sd
men of War kept dogging the sd Gally all night, waiting
an opportunity to board the same, and in the morning
without speaking a word fired 6 great guns at the Gally
Some whereof went through her and wounded four of his
men, and thereupon he fired upon him again, and the
fight continued all day, and the Narrator had eleven men
wounded. the other Portugais Men of War lay some
distance off, and could not come up with the Gally, being
calme, else would have likewise assaulted the same
the sd fight was sharp, and the sd Portuguese left the
sd Gally with such satisfaction that the Narrator believes no
Portuguese will ever attack the Kings Colours again, in
that part of the World especially, and afterwards continued
upon the sd Coast cruising upon the Cape of Camoroon
for Pyrats, that frequent that Coast, till the beginning
of the month of November 1697, when he met with
Cap't Stow in the Loyal Captain an English Ship belonging
to Maddarass, bound to Suret, whom he examined, and
finding his pass good, designed freely to let her pass, about
her affairs, but having two Dutchmen on board, they
told the Narrators men that they had divers Greeks and
Armenians on board, who had divers precious Stones and
other rich goods on board, which caused his men to be very
mutinous, and got up their Armes, and swore they would
take

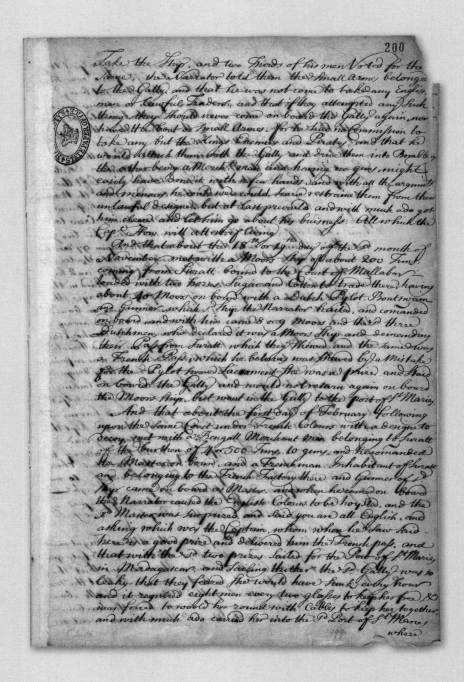

Take the Ship, and two Thirds of his men Voted for the
Same, the Narrator told them the Small Armes belonge
to the Gally, and that he was not come to take any Englis
men or lawful Traders, and that if they attempted any Such
thing, they Should never come on board the Gally again, nor
have it about the Small Armes, for he had no Commission to
take any but the Kings Enemies and Pirates, and that he
would attack them with the Gally and drive them into Bombay
the other being a Merchant man and having no guns, might
easily have done it with a few hands, and with all the arguments
and menaces he could use, would scarce restraine them from their
unlawful designes, but at last prevailed and with much ado got
him cleare and let him go about his buisness. All which the
Capt. Now will attest of being

And that about the 18th or 19th day of the month of
November met with a Moors Ship of about 200 Tuns,
coming from Suratt, bound to the Coast of Mallabar,
loaded with two horses, Sugar and Cotton to trade there, having
about 40 Moors on board with a Dutch Pylot, Boatswain
and Gunner, which Ship the Narrator heired, and comanded
on board, and with him came 8 or 9 Moors and the 3 three
Dutchmen, who declared it was a Moors Ship and demanding
their Pass from Suratt which they Shewed, and the same was
a French Pass, which he believes was Shewed by a Mistake
for the Pylot knew Sacrament she was a prize, and Staid
on board the Gally and would not return again on board
the Moors Ship, but went in the Gally to the port of St Marie,

And that about the first day of February following
upon the same Coast under French Colours with a designe to
decoy, met with a Bengall Merchant man, belonging to Suratt
of the burthen of 4 or 500 Tuns, 10 guns, and he comanded
the Master on board, and a Frenchman Inhabitant of Suratt
and belonging to the French Factory there and Gunner of s'd
Ship came on board as Master, and when he came on board
the Narrator caused the English Colours to be hoysted, and the
s'd Master was surprized and said you are all English, and
asking which was the Captain, whom when he saw said
here is a good prize and delivered him the French pass, and
that with the s'd two prizes Sailed for the Port of St Marie,
in Madagascar, and Sailing thither the s'd Gally was so
Leaky, that they feared she would have Sunk every hour
and it required eight men every two glasses to keep her free &
was forced to woold her round with Cables to keep her together,
and with much ado carried her into the s'd Port of St Marie,

199
where

Kidd sank the *Adventure Galley* before setting sail for New York via the West Indies on the *Quedah*, now renamed *Adventure Prize*, with enough plunder to pay off his backers, but without the ship's logs.

The trial

By the end of 1698, when Kidd left Saint Marie for New York via the West Indies, a lot had changed and news of his activities was circulating. Members of the Mughal court under the Emperor Aurangzeb were outraged by the loss of the *Quedah Merchant*. They believed that the East India Company was complicit in continuing piracy and detained some of its officials until compensation was paid. As a result, senior company officials were after Kidd's blood. In Britain, the Piracy Act of 1698 was an early sign of the government's determination to root out robbery on the seas. When Kidd reached Anguilla in April 1699, he discovered that he was a wanted man. He disposed of the *Quedah Merchant* and acquired a sloop, the *San Antonio*, before making for New York.

Kidd approached New York stealthily, hoping to avoid the authorities. He thought that he could bargain with Bellomont, who had been appointed governor, and use the 'French passes' that he had retained to justify the seizure of the two ships. He sent his lawyer, James Emott, to meet Bellomont in Boston. Emott duly handed over the passes as key evidence in support of Kidd's story. It was a fateful mistake to have relinquished them, however, as the documents disappeared and were not found again until long after Kidd's trial. Meanwhile, Bellomont lured Kidd to Boston with the possibility of obtaining a king's pardon, but in reality he had distanced himself from the matter to protect himself. On Bellomont's orders, Kidd was arrested on arrival and held in Boston's Stone Prison before being transported to London on HMS *Advice*.

Advice arrived in Greenwich in April 1700. After a lengthy interview at the Admiralty, Kidd was taken to Newgate, the notorious and noisome prison near the Old Bailey. Here his health, already damaged by close confinement during the Atlantic voyage, deteriorated further until it seemed that death might cheat his accusers of justice. Only at the last moment did the authorities relent, allowing him medical treatment, exercise and better food. Kidd then set about constructing his defence, requesting access to the evidence, perhaps pinning his hopes on the 'French passes' as they might be taken as proof of legitimate privateering. In all of this, he was well aware that he was taking the blame for others, and as he noted, he knew their motives:

> 'If ye design I was sent upon, be illegal, or of ill consequence to ye trade of ye Nations, My Owners who knew ye Laws, ought to suffer for It, and not I, whom they made ye Tool of their Covetousnesse. Some great men would have me dye for Solving their Honour, and others to pacify ye Mogull for injuryes done by other men, and not my selfe, and to secure their trade; but my Lord! Whatsoever my fate must be, I shall not Contribute to my own destruction by pleading to this Indictment, till my passes are restored to me. It is not my fault if I admit my selfe a pyrate as I must doe I plead without having those passes to produce.'

Kidd was charged with the murder of William Moore and with several counts of piracy. The trial began on 8 May 1701, with Kidd conducting his own defence. The court heard the murder charge first. Kidd argued that he had never intended

to kill Moore, but even the evidence of his own witnesses was dubious. As the indictment for piracy was still being read, the jury returned a verdict of guilty of murder.

Kidd was facing the death sentence even before the jury had considered the piracy charges and the cards were stacked against him. Key evidence was missing, and neither were the 'French passes' to be found. Many interests were ranged against him, the judges were hostile and the witnesses were compromised. The trial lasted only two days and the jury declared Kidd guilty on 9 May. He now faced two death sentences.

Kidd probably hoped for a reprieve, but it never came. The execution was set for 28 May and on that day Kidd was carted eastwards along Holborn towards the execution dock at Wapping, where he had lived before the ill-fated expedition. Noisy crowds gathered along the route and Kidd arrived drunk to deliver a defiant speech. Even Kidd's hanging went wrong, as the rope snapped during the first attempt. The hangman returned Kidd to the gallows and this time the rope held true. The corpse was tarred and gibbeted, to be displayed at Tilbury Point on the Thames — a gruesome warning to passing sailors.

The River Thames at Greenwich, sketched in 1662. **BELOW**

The pirate Blackbeard

EDWARD THATCH ... c.1716–18

The image of the pirate has been embellished by larger-than-life depictions in stories, films and on television over the years, but there are few who conjure up a more terrifying image than Edward Thatch, Teach or Thack, alias Blackbeard.

Edward Thatch operated as a pirate along the North Atlantic coasts of America and the Caribbean for a relatively short period – no more than three years – and yet his reputation and legacy have long outlived both his short career and his lifespan. Like many pirates during the 'golden age of piracy' in the late seventeenth and early eighteenth centuries, Thatch cultivated his reputation to such an extent that the mere mention of his name was enough for many ship's captains to surrender without a fight. His customary practice of wearing lit fuses poking out from under his hat in preparation for a battle, coupled with his large untamed black beard covering his entire face up to his eyes, must have given him a truly terrifying appearance. It is interesting to note, however, that while image was of crucial importance in a successful piratical business, the more astute pirates preferred not to fight if it could be avoided, relying instead on their demonic reputation to stave off most affrays.

Little is known about Edward Thatch's early life; there is an assumption that he hailed originally from Bristol, but he is documented as being in the West Indies in 1716 as part of renowned privateer and pirate Benjamin Hornigold's crew. At this time pirates typically raided shipping and coastal regions of the Caribbean during the winter before sailing up the coast of North America and repeating the trick during the summer months.

The government's approach to privateers during this period was often one of acquiescence. During periods of war governments were happy to issue letters of marque to privateers, in essence licensing them to fit out an armed vessel and then use it to harass and capture enemy merchant shipping. Thatch probably ended up in the West Indies during the early part of the century as a privateer before being recruited by Hornigold.

Edward Thatch, 1680–1718, in a cartoon of 1715. His hair and beard are woven with flaming fuses to increase his fearsome appearance. **ABOVE**

DOC. 1 A proclamation offering a pardon to all pirates, 1698.

By the King,
A PROCLAMATION.
WILLIAM R.

Hereas We being Informed by the frequent Complaints of Our good Subjects Trading to the East Indies, of several wicked Piracies committed on those Seas, as well upon Our own Subjects as those of Our Allies, have therefore thought fit, for the Security of the Trade of those Countries, by an utter Extirpation of the Pirates in all parts Eastward of the Cape of Good Hope, as well beyond Cape Comorin as on this side of it, unless they shall forthwith Surrender themselves as is herein after directed, To send out a Squadron of Men of War under the Command of Captain Thomas Warren; Now We to the Intent that such who have been Guilty of any Acts of Piracy in those Seas, may have Notice of Our most Gracious Intention of extending Our Royal Mercy to such of them as shall Surrender themselves, and to cause the severest Punishment, according to Law, to be inflicted upon those who shall con-

tinue Obstinate, have thought fit, by the Advice of Our Privy Council, to Issue this Proclamation, hereby Requiring and Commanding all Persons who have been guilty of any Act of Piracy, or any ways Aiding or Assisting therein, in any place Eastward of the Cape of Good Hope, to Surrender themselves within the several respective times herein after limited, unto the said Captain Thomas Warren, and the Commander in Chief of the said Squadron for the time being, and to Israel Hayes, Peter Delanoye, and Christopher Pollard, Esquires, Commissioners appointed by Us for the said Expedition, or to any Three of them, or (in case of Death) the Major part of the Survivors of them. And We do hereby Declare, That We have been Graciously Pleased to Impower the said Captain Thomas Warren, and the Commander in Chief of the said Squadron for the time being, and Israel Hayes, Peter Delanoye, and Christopher Pollard, Esquires, Commissioners aforesaid, or any Three of them, or (in case of Death) the Major part of the Survivors of them to give Assurance of Our most Gracious Pardon unto all such Pirates in the East Indies, (viz. all Eastward of the Cape of Good Hope) who shall so Surrender themselves for Piracies or Robberies committed by them upon the Sea or Land; Except nevertheless such as they shall Commit in any place whatsoever, after Notice of Our Grace and Favour hereby Declared; And also Excepting all such Piracies and Robberies as shall be Committed from the Cape of Good Hope, Eastward, to the Longitude or Meridian of Socatora, after the last day of April, One thousand six hundred ninety nine; And in any Place from the Longitude or Meridian of Socatora, Eastward, to the Longitude or Meridian of Cape Comorin, after the last day of June, One thousand six hundred ninety nine; And in any place whatsoever Eastward of Cape Comorin, after the last day of July, One thousand six hundred ninety nine; And also Excepting Henry Every alias Bridgeman and William Kid.

Given at Our Court at *Kensington*, the Eighth Day of *December*, 1698. In the Tenth Year of Our Reign.

God save the King.

London, Printed by *Charles Bill*, and the Executrix of *Thomas Newcomb*, deceas'd; Printers to the Kings most Excellent Majesty. MDCXCVIII.

Hornigold soon delegated responsibility for one of his vessels to Thatch and in tandem they carried out numerous acts of piracy. Hornigold was a canny operator and keen to preserve his privateer status, so he refused to attack British shipping. Such an approach was not overly popular with his crew, who must have felt hugely frustrated to have to watch rich pickings passing them by on their captain's orders. In November 1717 Hornigold lost the support of his crew and was effectively deposed, and once news reached him of a general pardon issued by George I 'For Suppressing Pirates in the West Indies', he retired. Under this royal proclamation, former pirates had the slate wiped clean if they surrendered to the governor of a colony of the British Empire. It also offered financial rewards for the capture of existing pirates.

Edward Thatch had assumed command of most of Hornigold's crew and vessels, and he was not tempted by the lure of a pardon. With his flagship *Queen Anne's Revenge*, a forty-gun former French merchant vessel, he continued to plunder ships in the region.

Thatch was rapidly becoming a serious threat to shipping and trade and was beginning to amass a formidable flotilla. Perhaps his most audacious act was his blockade in May 1718 of Charles Town, modern-day Charleston, in South Carolina. Thatch stopped ships sailing in or out of the harbour, ransacking them, holding their passengers captive and making various demands on the colonial government of South Carolina.

In spite of these actions, in September 1718 Thatch accepted a king's pardon from Charles Read, second governor of the colony of North Carolina, on condition that he would give up piracy. However, such abstinence could not continue for long, and he soon resumed his piratical lifestyle. Thatch's favourite base was Ocracoke Island in North Carolina, where, unseen, he was able to view passing shipping. His presence in the area, along with other notorious pirates, was making the neighbouring colonies very nervous. Successive attempts to apprehend the pirates proved unsuccessful, but the governor of Virginia, Alexander Spotswood, proved more tenacious in his pursuit. Having obtained valuable information from one of Thatch's former crew members, Spotswood enlisted two captains, Gordon and Brand, and Lieutenant Robert Maynard to seek out Thatch and capture or kill him. Captain Gordon's ship's log dating from 17 November 1718 takes up the tale:

'... about noon gave an order to my 1st Lieutenant Mr Robert Maynard to go commander in chief by sea of two sloops the Jane and Ranger, hired by Governor Spotswood, and mann'd and arm'd out of His Majesty's Ships Pearl and Lyme to proceed to North Carolina to attack one Edward Thack, commonly call'd Blackbeard; this day he sail'd from hence, with one month's provisions at whole allowance for 35 men, in the Jane which I mann'd out of the Pearl , and 25 in the Ranger mann'd arm'd and victuall'd by Captain Brand out of the Lyme.'

DOCS. 2 & 3 Captain's log for HMS *Pearl* giving details of the hunt for the pirate Blackbeard in 1718.

It was Maynard who, on 22 November, sailed into Ocracoke Inlet with two sloops and took Thatch and his depleted crew by surprise, apprehending them on board *Adventure*. Nevertheless, the Thatch's vessel had formidable fire power and turned her guns on Maynard's sloops, which almost proved devastating, Maynard losing around twenty-one crew members in the process. Ultimately, the larger of Maynard's two sloops, *Jane*, drew alongside *Adventure* and Thatch saw his chance to board the vessel and claim his prize. A later account by Captain Gordon described the mayhem that ensued when the Adventure broadsided the sloop in order for the pirates to board it:

'After they were so near that the compliment past betwixt them of not giving each other quarters; Thatch observing all his men upon deck gave them a broadside; his guns being sufficiently charged with Swan shot, partridge shot, and others; with this broadside he killed and wounded (most by the swan shot) one and twenty of his men... Thatch observing his decks clear of men presently concluded the vessel his own , and then sheers on board Lieutenant Maynard's sloop enters himself the first man with a rope in his hand to lash or make fast the two sloops:'

What Thatch did not know was that when the *Jane* was broadsided by the *Adventure*, Maynard had ordered most of his crew below decks before his ship was boarded:

'Mr Maynard finding his men thus exposed, and no shelter order his men down into the hold, giving himself into the cabin aloft; ordering the midshipman that was at the helm or Mr Butler, his pilate to acquaint him with anything that should happen...'

mand of Cap.t Geo: Gordon, at Hampton in Virginia

Remarkable Occurrences &c

Moderate gales & fair weather.

The former part moderate & fair, the latter fresh gales & cloudy weather; yesterday in the afternoon came aboard 29 bushells of Callevances & 25 firkins of Butter.

Hard gales & squally rainy weather most part of this 24 hours; yesterday P.M came aboard the Pork that was sent ashore to be cut into mess pieces; at 4 A.M. lower'd yards & Topmasts.

The former part fresh gales & rainy weather, the latter fair. yesterday in the afternoon the longboat brought aboard of 4 Inch One coile new, of 3 Inch twice layd one, of 3 & one of 2½ —

Moderate gales & fair weather; yesterday in the afternoon the longboat brought ab.o Nine hundred weight of bread from hampton & four Barr.els of Farr from the s.d place

The former part moderate & fair, the latter hard gales & much rain; at 2 A.M lower'd yards & Topmasts; gott up the spare cable & an old cast cable, got about 4 Tunns of ballast into the longboat for a sloop taken up to go against the Pyrats in N.o Carolina —.

The former part fresh gales & cloudy weather, the latter moderate & fair; about noon gave an Order to My 1.st L.t Mr. Rob.t Maynard to go comander in chief by sea of two Sloops the Jane & Ranger, hird by Governour Spotswood, & mannd & Armd out of his Ma.ties Ships Pearl & Lyme to proceed to North Carolina to attack one Edward Thach, commonly calld Blackbeard; this day he saild from hence, with one months provisions at whole Allowance for 35 men in the Jane which I mannd out of the Pearl, & 25 in the Ranger mannd Armd & Victuald &c by Cap.t Brand out of the Lyme

Moderate gales & fair weather; dry'd all the sails; unbent M.sail F.sail, stay-sails & put them down —

Wind & Weather D.o yesterday in the afternoon the longboat came aboard with her load of water; this morn sent ashore 10 Sick persons to Sick Quarters in hampton —

Moderate gales & fair weather; the longboat came aboard with water.

Weather for the most part the same; the longboat came aboard with water.

Weather D.o hoisted yards & Topmasts.

Weather D.o; the longboat came aboard with water 556 fresh beef —

Weather D.o; the longboat came aboard with water, D.o sent her ashore to return some cordage;

Moderate gales & fine weather; the longboat brought aboard 48¼ fresh beef

Fresh gales & fair weather Weather; at 5 P.M lower'd yards & Topmasts; this morning Jn.o Dellamote the Cook dyd.

Honor:d S:r

Having aquainted you yesterday for their Lordps: information
that I had reason to finde fault w:th the acount Livet: Maynard
late of his Maj:ties Pearle under my Command made to his Maj:tie
in his petition lately Layed before him in Counsell.

In order to this I shall very briefly lay before their Lordt: all ye:
Steps of that action with Thatch alias Blackbeard

After they were so near, that the Compliment past betwixt them of
not giving each other quarters; Thatch obseving all his men upon
Deck gave them a broade Side; his guns being Sufficiently charged
with Swan Shot, partridge Shot, and others; with this broad Side
he killed and wounded (most by the Swan shott) one & twenty of
his men, Mr: Maynder findeing his men thus exposed, and no
Shelter order his men down into the hold, giving himself into the
Cabin abaft, ordering the midshipman, that was at the helm, or
Mr: Butler his Second to aquaint him with any that should
haappen. Thatch observing his deck clear of men, presently concluded
the vessel his own, and then Steers on board Livet: Maynards
Sloop enters himself the first man, with a rope in his hand to
Lash or make fast the two Sloops: Mr: Butler aquainting Livet:
Maynard with this, turned his men upon deck, and was himself
presently among them: wherein less then Six minnits tyme
Thatch and five or Six of his men were killed; the rest of these
rogues Jumped in the water where they were demolished, one
of them being discovered Some dayes after in the reeds by the fowls
howering over him: the Sloop in w:ch the Lymes people were in, had the
misfortune to have the three officers that commanded them killed, a
head of his Sloop: & another Shot through the body in Thatches Sloop
by one of our men, takeing him by Mistake for one of the pirates
This Sr: is the true, and real Steps of that action, given in upon
oath at his Maj:ties Court of Admr: in Virginia, by himself & people
the truth of which if need be Livet: Governor Spotswood can Justifie
& So Capt: Brand: there being no Such thing given out there
of boarding Thatch Sword in hand; as he is pleased to tell his

When Butler advised Maynard that Thatch and his crew were boarding the vessel, Maynard '*turned his men upon deck, and was himself presently among them…*' Whether by accident or design, the ruse worked a treat, and Thatch could not beat off the crew who surrounded him, eventually losing his head in a face-to-face sword fight with Maynard:

DOC. 4 Captain Gordon's ship's log from HMS *Pearl* on 1 January 1719.

Map of the West Indies and North America from John Sellar's *Atlas Maritimus*, 1698.
BELOW

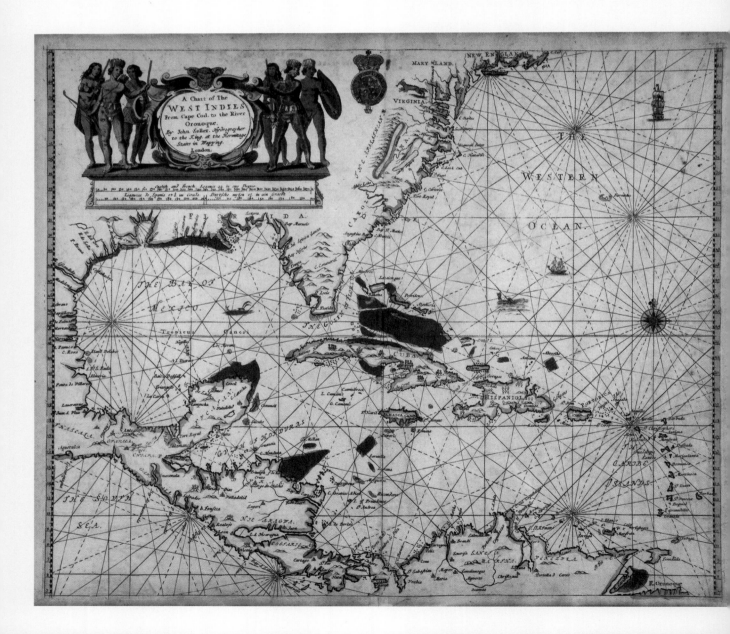

of Capt: Geo: Gordon, at Kiquotan, in Virginia

Remarkable Occurrences &c:

Fresh gales & cloudy weather.

Weather D:º this day Justice Ballard of hampton sent aboard 3 Pyrats & 2 evidences.

Fresh gales, toward the end moderate & fair weather; dry'd all our Sails.

Moderate gales & fair weather; yesterday in the afternoon brought aboard 1000 of bread, some wood, & this morn 570 fresh beef.

Moderate gales & cloudy weather the former part, the latter fresh gales with rain.

The former part moderate gales with rain the latter fair; sent in a Sloop up James river Bт. Cwt. qrs Barr 1 - 7 .. 14 .. 3 with 172 Iron hoops, to be fill'd with beef.

Moderate gales & close cloudy rainy weather.

The former part fresh gales with rain, the middle hard gales with abundance of rain, the latter more moderate; at 5 PM lower'd yards & topmasts; about 4 in the morning my Small bower coming home, let go the Sheat Anchor; at 7 the wind abating hove it up again.

Winds & weather very uncertain with abundance of rain.

Moderate gales & close weather; this morning took in the small bower & new moor'd the Ship; got up yards & Topmasts; cut up 20 fa of 3 inch for a new fore bowline, the old for repairing the service on the Small bower.

Moderate gales & fair weather; dry'd all our Sails.

Weather D:º

Weather D:º

Fresh gales & cloudy, towards the end some snow; sent the longboat for wт.

Moderate gales & fair weather; yesterday in the afternoon the longboat came aboard with water.

Fresh gales & cloudy weather.

Weather D:º

The former part fresh gales & cloudy, the middle & latter very hard gales & cold raw weather.

Moderate gales & fair weather this morn sent the Pyrats & Evidence in my Pinnace to their Tryalls at Williamsburgh; sent the longboat for water.

Winds & weather D:º yesterday PM the longboat came aboard with water & wood.

The former part D:º but terminates with hard gales & thick rainy wт. yesteray PM the longboat came aboard with 12:º Cwt. qrs of beef & 2 barr of suit; at 11 AM lower'd yards & Topmasts.

mand of Cap.t Ge.o Gordon, at Higustan in Virginia

Remarkable Occurrences &c

Moderate gales & fair weather.

The former part moderate & fair, the latter fresh gales & cloudy weather; yesterday in the afternoon came aboard 29 bushells of Callavances & 25 firkins of Butter.

hard gales & squally rainy weather most part of this 24 hours; yesterday PM came aboard the Pork that was sent ashore to be cut into mess pieces; at 4 AM lower'd yards & Topmasts.

The former part fresh gales & rainy weather, the latter fair. yesterday in the after =noon the longboat brought aboard of 4 inch One coile new, of 3 inch twice layd one, of 3 & one of 2½

Moderate gales & fair weather; yesterday in the afternoon the longboat brought ab.d five hundred weight of bread from hampton & four Barr.es of Tarr from the S.o place

The former part moderate & fair, the latter hard gales & much rain; at 2 AM lower'd yards & Topmasts; gott up the spare cable & an old cast cable, got about 4 Tunns of ballast into the longboat for a sloop taken up to go against the Pyrats in N.o Carolina.

The former part fresh gales & cloudy weather the latter moderate & fair. about noon gave an Order to My 1.st L.t Mr Rob.t Maynard to go comander in chief by sea of two Sloops the Jane & Ranger, hird by Governour Spotswood, & mann'd & Arm'd out of his Ma.ties Ships Pearl, & Lyme to proceed to North Carolina to attack one Edward Thach, commonly called Blackbeard; this day he sailed from hence, with one months provisions at whole Allowance for 35 men, in the Jane which I mann'd out of the Pearl, & 25 in the Ranger mann'd Arm'd & Victuald &c by Cap.t Brand out of the Lyme

Moderate gales & fair weather; dry'd all the sails; unbent M. sail, F. sail, stay =sails & put them down

Wind.s & Weather D.o: yesterday in the afternoon the longboat came aboard with her load of water; this morn.g sent ashore 20 Sick persons to Sick Quarters in hampton

Moderate gales & fair weather; the longboat came aboard with water.

Weather for the most part the same; the longboat came aboard with water.

Weather D.o hoisted yards & Topmasts.

Weather D.o; the longboat came aboard with water 556 fresh beef

Weather D.o: the longboat came aboard with water, D.o sent her ashore to return some cordage.

Moderate gales & fine weather; the longboat brought aboard 48¼ fresh beef

Fresh gales & fair weather Weather; at 5 PM lower'd yards & Topmasts; this morning Jn.o Dellamote the Cook dyd.

'... where in less than six minutes tyme Thatch and five or six of his men were killed; the rest of these rogues jumped in the water where they were demolished, one of them being discovered some dayes after in the reeds by the fowls hovering over him.'

DOC. 5 Captain Gordon's ship's log from HMS *Pearl* on 15 December 1718.

Any of the pirate crew who were subsequently captured were put on board Captain Gordon's own ship Pearl before being transported to Williamsburg in Virginia for trial and, ultimately, execution.

On 15 December Captain Gordon wrote in his log: *'Moderate gales and fair weather this morn sent the Pyrats and Evidence in my Pinnace to their Toyalls at Williamsburgh.'*

On 1 January 1719, Captain Gordon's wrote in the ship's log of the conclusion of the Blackbeard episode:

'Moderate gales and fair weather, yesterday in the afternoon the Ranger Sloop that was manned, armed Captain Brand of His Majesty's Ship Lyme, on the expedition against Edward Thack commonly called Blackbeard, a Pyrat, arriv'd here from North Carolina, which acquainted us with the destruction of the aforesaid Thack and most of his men, and the seizure of their effects, by our men.'

The demise of the legendary Blackbeard marked the beginning of the end of the 'golden age of piracy' in the West Indies. The end of the war between France and England left the Royal Navy free to protect merchant shipping in the region, and with the destruction of the lawless capital of the pirate world, the island of New Providence, by government-backed forces in 1718, pirates no longer had a reliable black market for their ill-gotten gains. All that remained was the imagined glamour and romance of this lost but often brutal age in the fertile minds of children and adults alike.

Mutiny on the *Bounty*

CAPTAIN WILLIAM BLIGH ... 28 APRIL 1789

Captain William Bligh, 1754–1817.

The tale of the mutiny on HMS *Bounty* led by master's mate Fletcher Christian against Captain Lieutenant William Bligh has been told and retold in print and on film for over 200 years. To this day there has been heated debate as to whether the mutiny was a justified stand against tyrannical leadership or flagrant disobedience against the righteous rule of authority.

Buried among the log books of the Admiralty is the written account of Captain William Bligh on the fateful voyage of HMS *Bounty*. This account reveals in fascinating detail Bligh's experience of the mutiny and his 4,000-mile voyage in an open boat. His narrative does not, however, fully reveal the motives of the mutineers or the depravations they had suffered at the hands of their captain's venomous temper. Nevertheless, Bligh's narrative, together with other accounts, allows us to begin to piece together why, as well as how, the mutiny on the *Bounty* transpired, and what then befell Bligh and the mutineers.

HMS *Bounty* was dispatched in December 1787 to collect and transport bread fruit trees (named thus because of their use in bread making in the islands of the Pacific) from the island of Tahiti to the West Indies. The intention was to provide a cheap and sustainable source of food for the slave populations in the British colonies of the West Indies.

Assigned to captain this vessel was Lieutenant William Bligh, an experienced sailor, reputed for his skill in navigation and cartography and familiar with the seas and islands of the Pacific from his time spent serving with Captain James Cook in 1776. His crew of forty-six included a botanist, David Nelson, and a gardener, William Brown, to oversee the transfer of the fruit trees to the ship and their care on the voyage.

No one could have predicted at the beginning of the voyage that a mutiny would occur, let alone one led by Fletcher Christian. Christian had previously served under Bligh on voyages to the West Indies and the two had become good friends. Bligh had a deep respect for Christian as a competent and reliable sailor and even promoted him to lieutenant of the third watch on the *Bounty*'s outward voyage.

Bligh was an exceptional officer but he had no tolerance for mistakes, incorrect seamanship or challenges to his authority, and he was prone to dramatic outbursts of temper against members of his crew. For reasons about which we can only speculate, Bligh's temper became more unpredictable and malicious after the *Bounty* left Tahiti on 5 April 1789, and Christian was singled out for unnecessary public humiliation and contemptuous treatment over increasingly tenuous issues.

Bligh seemed to be naïvely unaware of the effect that his outbursts were having on the crew, but he did recognise the negative effect on discipline of spending over five months in the exotic surroundings of Tahiti — especially as

Captain Bligh and his eighteen loyal crew members are cast adrift in a longboat by Fletcher Christian and the *Bounty* mutineers. **BELOW**

Christian and other crew members had acquired mistresses there. He reflects in his journal: '*The mutineers had flattered themselves with the hopes of a more happy life among the Otaheiteans [Tahitians], than they could possibly enjoy in England.*'

Bligh describes in detail what happened on that fateful morning of 28 April 1789:

'I kept near the island Kotoo until 5 o'clock this afternoon on hopes to have had some cannon off but I saw none. I therefore directed my course to the West and went to the southward of Tofoa. Mr Fryer the master had the first watch. Mr Peckover the gunner the middle, and Mr Christian one of the mates the morning watch. This was the tour of duty for the night.

Just before Sun rise Mr Christian, Mate, Charles Churchill, Ship's Corporal, John Mills gunner's mate and Thomas Burkett, seaman, came into my cabbin while I was asleep and seizing me, tyed my hands with a cord behind my back and threatened me with instant death if I spoke out or made the least noise. I however called so loud as to alarm everyone, but the officers found themselves secured by centinels at their doors. There were four men in my cabbin and three outside viz. Alexander Smith Mr Sumner and Matthew Quintal. Mr Christian had a cutlass in his hand, the others had musquets and bayonets. I was forced on deck in my shirt, suffering great pain from the violence with which they had tyed my hands. I demanded the reason for such a violent act, but I received no answer but threats of instant death if I did not hold my tongue. Mr Hayward and Hallett were on Mr Christian's watch, but had no idea that anything was doing until they were all armed. The arms were all secured so that no-one could get them from the centinels. Mr Elphinstone the Mate was secured to his berth. Mr Nelson Botanist, Mr Peckover Gunner, Mr Jedward Surgeon and the Master were confined to their cabins, as also Mr Samuel (clerk) but who from finesse got leave to come upon Deck. The Fore Hatchway was guarded, by centinels, the Boatswain and Carpenter were however allowed to come on Deck where they saw me standing abaft the mizzen mast with my hands tied behind my back, under a guard with Christian at their Head.

The Boatswain was now ordered to hoist the boat out, with a threat that if he did not do it, instantly to take care of himself. Mr Hayward and Hallett, Midshipmen, and Mr Samuel were ordered into the boat upon which I assumed my authority and demanded the cause of such an order, at the same time endeavouring to bring someone to a sense of their duty, but it was to no effect. "Hold your tongue or you are dead this 'instant' was constantly repeated to me." The Master by this time has sent to be allowed on Deck, and was permitted, and as soon was ordered back to his cabin again, where he returned. I continued to endeavour to change the tide of affairs, when Christian changed the cutlass he had in his hand to a bayonet that was brought to him, and holding me with a strong grip by the cord that tied my hands he continued to threaten me with instant death if I could not be quiet. The villains round me had their pieces cocked and bayonets fixed and particular people were now called upon to go into the boat, and were hurried over the side, with these people of course I concluded that I was to be set adrift. I therefore in making another effort to bring about a change expected myself in such a manner as to be saluted with "blow his brains out". The boatswain and seaman who were to go into the boat, collected twine, canvas, lines, sails, cordage and eight and twenty gallon cask of water, and the Carpenter got his tool chest. Mr Samuel got 150 lbs of bread with a small quantity of rum and wine. He also got a Quadrant and compass into the boat but forbid on pain of death from touching any maps whatsoever.'

DOCS. 1, 2, 3 & 4 Extracts from the log book of HMS *Bounty*, kept by Captain William Bligh from 6 August 1787 to 20 August 1789.

The captain and eighteen of the ship's crew were then set adrift amid the turbulent waters of the Pacific. In his journal Bligh lists the names of crew members who were ordered into the open boat with him, and below records the remaining twenty-five crewmen who, in his words, 'remained on board as pirates and under arms'. The latter list, however, includes at least four loyalist crew members who had been ordered to remain on the ship under duress (Michael Byrne, Joseph Coleman, Charles Norman and Thomas McIntosh).

Bligh's voyage across the Pacific in the launch vessel is an epic tale in its own right. Between 28 April and 14 June 1789, Bligh and his crew sailed 4,000 miles in an open boat from the island of Tofua in the Tonga archipelago to the Dutch outpost of Kupang on the Island of Timor. Most days they survived on an ounce of bread and a quarter of a pint of water and fought to keep the ship afloat in the rough seas and turbulent weather of the Pacific. As if this wasn't enough, the crew were attacked by hostile natives on the island of Tofua, as Bligh relates in the journal entry for 3 May 1789:

Remarks Tuesday 28th April 1789 at Sea

Light Winds and Cloudy Wr. Wind NE. E and ESE.

I kept near the Ozodoo untill 5 oClock this afternoon in hopes to have had some Canoes off but I saw none. I therefore directed my Course to the West and went to the Southward of Tofoa — Mr. Fryer the Master had the first Watch. Mr. Peckover the Gunner the Middle, and Mr. Christian one of the Mates the Morning Watch — This was the tour of duty for the Night. —

Just before Sun rise Mr. Christian, Mate, Chas. Churchill, Ships Corporal, John Mills Gunners Mate and Thomas Burkitt, Seaman, came into my Cabbin while I was asleep and seizing me tyed my hands with a Cord behind my back and threatned me with instant death if I spoke or made the least noise. I however called so loud as to alarm every one, but the Officers found themselves secured by Centinels at their Doors — There were four Men in my Cabbin and three outside viz:- Alexr. Smith, Jno. Sumner and Matt. Quintal — Mr. Christian had a Cutlass in his hand, the others had Musquets and Bayonets — I was forced on Deck in my Shirt, suffering great pain from the Violence with which they had tied my hands — I demanded the reason for such a violent act, but received no Answer but threats of instant death if I did not hold my tongue. —

Mr. Hayward & Hallett were in Mr. Christians Watch, but had no Idea that any thing was doing untill they were all armed. — The Arms were all secured so that no one could get near them for Centinels. — Mr. Elphinstone the Mate was secured to his Berth. Mr. Nelson Botanist. Mr. Peckover Gunner. Mr. Ledward Surgeon & the Master were confined to their Cabbins, as also Mr. Jno. Samuel, (Clerk) but who from fences got leave to come upon Deck — The Fore Hatchway was guarded by Centinels, the Boatswain and Carpenter were however allowed to come on Deck where they saw me standing abaft the Mizen Mast with my hands tied behind my back, under a Guard with Christian at their Head. —

The Boatswain was now ordered to hoist the Boat out, with a threat if he did not do it instantly to take care of himself. ——

Mr. Hayward and Hallett, Midshipmen, and Mr. Samuel were now ordered into the Boat, upon which I assumed my Authority and demanded the Cause of such an Order, at the same time endeavouring to bring some one to a sense of his duty, but it was to no effect. "Hold your tongue Sir or you are dead this Instant" was constantly repeated to me. —

The Master by this time had sent to be allowed to come on Deck and was permitted, and as soon was Ordered back to his Cabbin again, when he returned. —

I continued to ...... avor to change the Tide of affairs, when Christian changed the Cutlass he had in his hand for a Bayonet that was brought to him, and holding me with a strong Grip by the cord that tied my hands, he continued to threaten me with instant death if I did not be quiet — The Villains round me had their peices Cocked & Bayonets fixed, and particular People were now Called upon to go in the Boat, and were hurried over the side, with these people I concluded of course I was to be set a drift. I therefore in making another effort to bring about a Change expressed myself in such a Manner as to be saluted with "Blow his Brains out". —

The Boatswain and Seamen who were to go in the Boat, collected twine, canvas, lines sails, Cordage an eight and twenty Gallon Cask of Water, and the Carpenter got his Tool Chest. Mr. Samuel got 150 lbs Bread with a small quantity of Rum and Wine. He also got a Quadrant and Compass into the Boat, but forbid on Pain of death of touching any Map whatever. Ephemeris Book of Astronomical

Observations – Sextants – Time Keeper or any of my Surveys or drawings –

    The Mutineers were now hurrying every one into the Boat, and the most of them being in, Christian directed a Dram to be served to each of his Crew – I was now exceedingly fatigued, and unhappily saw I could do nothing to effect the Recovery of the Ship. every endeavor was threatened with death, and the following People were now in the Boat. —

John Fryer	Master
Tho.s Denm.n Ledward	Surgeon
David Nelson	Botanist
Will.m Peckover	Gunner
Will.m Cole	Boatswain
Will.m Purcell	Carpenter
Will.m Elphinstone	Masters Mate
Tho.s Hayward	Mid.n
John Hallett	Mid.n
John Norton	Q.r Master
Peter Linkletter	Q.r Master
Law.ce Lebogue	Sail Maker
John Smith	Ab
Tho.s Hall	Ab
Geo: Simpson	Q.r Masters Mate
Rob.t Tinkler	Ab
Rob.t Lamb	Ab
John Samuel	Clerk

    There remained on board as Pirates and under Arms

Fletcher Christian	Masters Mate
Peter Heywood	Mid.n
George Stewart	Mid.n
Edw.d Young	Mid.n

351

Charles	Churchill	Ships Corporal
John	Mills	Gunners Mate
James	Morrison	Boatsn Mate
Thos.	Burkett	Ab
Mathew	Quintal	Ab
John	Sumner	Ab
John	Millward	Ab
Willm	Mickoy	Ab
Henÿ	Hilbrant	Ab
Willm	Muspratt	Ab
Alexr.	Smith	Ab
John	Williams	Ab
Thos.	Ellison	Ab
Isaac	Martin	Ab
Richd	Skinner	Ab
Mathew	Thompson	Ab
Willm	Brown	Botanists Assistant
Michl	Byrne	Ab
Joseph	Coleman	Armourer
Chas	Norman	Carpenters Mate
Thos	McIntosh	Dos Crew

—— In all 25 Hands and the most able

Men on board the Ship. ——

This is breifly the Statement of the Case. — The Officers were called
and forced into the Boat. while I was under a Guard abaft the Mizen Mast,
Christian holding me by the Bandage that secured my hands with one hand
and a Bayonet in the other. The Men under Arms round me had their
Pieces cocked which so enraged me against those ungratefull wretches that

'After dinner, we began by little and little to get our things into the boat, which was a troublesome business, on account of the surf and I carefully watched the motions of the natives, who I found still increasing in numbers; and that, instead of their intention being to leave us, fires were made, and places were fixed on for their residence during the night. Consultations were also held among them, and everything assured me we should be attacked. I sent the master orders, to keep the boat well in upon the beach when he saw us coming down, that we might get in.

I had my journal on shore with me, writing the occurrences [in the cave], and in sending it down [to the boat], it was nearly taken away, but for the timely assistance of the gunner.

Every person, who was now on shore with me, boldly took up his proportion of things, and carried them to the boat.

When the chiefs asked me if I would not stay with them all night, I said, "No, I never sleep out of my boat; but in the morning we will again trade with you, and I shall remain untill the weather is moderate, that we may go, as we have agreed, to see Poulahow, at Tongataboo." Macca~ackavow now got up, and said, "You will not sleep on shore? Then Mattee," (which directly implies we will kill you) and he left me. The onset was now preparing; every one, as I have described before, kept knocking stones together, and Eefow likewise quitted me. We had now all but two or three things were in the boat, when I took Nageete by the hand, and we walked down the beach, every one in a silent kind of horror.

When we came down, Nageete wanted me to stay to speak to Eefow; but I found he was encouraging them to the attack, in which if they had then begun, I determined to have killed him and I ordered the carpenter not to quit me untill the other people were in the boat. Nageete, therefore finding I would not listen to him, quitted my hold and went off, and we all except one man got into the boat, who, while I was getting on board, quitted the boat's side, and ran up the beach to cast the stern fast off, notwithstanding I heard the master and others calling to him to return, while they were hauling me out of the water.

I was no sooner in the boat than the attack began by about 200 men; this unfortunate poor man was first knocked down, and the stones flew like a shower of shot. Many men [Indians] got hold of the stern fast, and were near hauling us on shore; and would certainly have done it, if I had I not had a knife in my pocket, with which I cut [the rope]. We then hauled off to our grapnel, every one being more or less hurt. In the course of this I saw five of the natives about the poor man they had killed struggling [with] who should get his treasures, and two of them were beating him about the head with stones in their hands.

We had not time to reflect, before to my surprise, they filled their canoes with stones, and twelve men came off after us to renew the combat, which they did so effectually as nearly to disable all of us. Our grapnel was foul, but Providence here assisted us; as the fluke broke, and we got to our oars, and pulled to sea. They, however, could paddle [a]round us, so that we were obliged to sustain the attack without being able to return it, except with stones as lodged in the boat, and in this I found we were very inferior to them. We could not close, because our boat was lumbered and heavy. I therefore adopted the expedient of throwing overboard some clothes, which beguiled them and they lost time picking them up and by this means and the night coming on they at last quitted [the attack and leaving] us to reflect on our unhappy situation.

The poor man I lost was John Norton: this was his second voyage with me as a quarter-master, and his worthy character made me lament his loss very severely. He has left an aged parent, I am told, who he supported.

I once before sustained an attack of this nature, with a smaller number of men, against a multitude of Indians: (after the death of Captain Cook),on the Morai at Owhyhee, where I was left by Mr- King to act on the defensive as he calls it. Yet, notwithstanding [this experience], I did not conceive that the power of a man's arms could throw stones, from two to eight pounds weight, with such force and exactness as these people did. Here, unhappily, I was without [fire]arms, and the Indians soon discovered it; but it was a fortunate circumstance that they did not begin the attack on us in the cave; in that case nothing could have saved us and we have nothing left but to dye as bravely as we could close together in which I found eveyrong cheerfully to join me. It was from the appearance of such a resolution that awed them, supposing that they could effect their purpose without risk after we were in the boat.

Taking this as a sample of their natural dispositions, there were little hopes to expect much where I was going [visiting Poulaho]; for I considered their good behavior hitherto owing to a dread of our fire-arms, which, now knowing us to have none would not be the case, and, that supposing our lives safe, our boat, compass and quadrant would be taken from us, and thereby I should not be able to return to King and country to give an account of the transaction.'

DOC. 5 & 6 Extracts from the log book of HMS *Bounty*, kept by Captain William Bligh from 6 August 1787 to 20 August 1789.

<u>Rem in the Bountys Launch Sunday 3d. May 1789 at Tofoa.</u>

Fresh Gales at SE and ESE varying to NE in the latter part and a Storm of Wind. — After Dinner we began by little and little to get our things into the Boat which became troublesome on account of the Surf and I carefully watched the Motions of the Natives who I found still encreasing in numbers, and that instead of their intention being to leave us, fires were made and places were fixed on for their residence during the Night. — Consultations were also held among them & every thing assured me we should be attacked. and I sent the Master Orders to keep the Boat well in upon the Beach when he saw us coming down that we might easily get in. —

I had my Log with me in the Cave writing up the occurrences and in sending it down it was nearly taken away but for the timely assistance of the Gunner.

Every Person who was now on Shore with me boldly took up their proportion of things and carried them to the Boat, when the Chiefs asked me if I would not stay with them all Night. I said no. I never sleep out of my Boat, but in the Morning we will again trade with you and I shall remain untill the Weather is Moderate that we may go as we have agreed to see Paulehow at Tonga= =taboo. — Macca-ackavow now got up and said you will not sleep on Shore then Mattie. (which directly implies we will kill you,) and he left me. — The onset was now preparing, every one as I have described before kept knocking their Stones to= =gether, and Eefow likewise quitted me. — We had now all but two or three things in the Boat, when I took Nageetee by the hand and we walked down the Beach every one in a Silent kind of horror. — When we came down Nageetee wanted me to stay to speak to Eefow, but I found he was encouraging them to the attack, in which case if it had then begun, I determined to have killed him. and I ordered the Carpenter not to quit me untill the others were in the

Boat. — Nageetee therefore finding I would not listen to him quitted my
hold and went off, and we all except one Man got into the Boat, who while
I was getting on board quitted the boats side and ran up the Beach to cast
the Stern fast off. notwithstanding. I heard the Master and others calling to
him to return while they were hauling me out of the Water. —

I was no sooner in the Boat then the attack began by about 200 Men,
this unfortunate poor Man was first knocked down. and the Stones flew
like a shower of Shot — Many Men got hold of the Stern fast. and were near
hauling us on Shore, and would certainly have done if I had not had a
Knife in my pocket to cut, we therefore hauled off to our Grapnel with
every one more or less hurt. — In the course of this I saw five of the Natives
about the Poor Man they had killed struggling who should get his Trowsers, and
two of them were beating him about the head with Stones in their hands. —
We had not time to think before; to my surprize they filled their Cannoes
with Stones and twelve Men came off after us to renew the Combat. which
they did so effectually as nearly to disable all of us. — Our Grapnel was foul
but providence here afforded us, as the Fluke broke and we got to our Oars
and pulled to Sea, they however could paddle round us, so that we
were obliged to sustain the Attack without being able to return it but with
such Stones as lodged in the Boat, and in this I found we were much inferior
to them. — We could not close with them because our Boat was lumbered
and heavy. — I therefore adopted the expedient to throw over some Cloaths.
which beguiled them and they lost time in picking up, and by this
means and the Night coming on they at last quitted us to reflect on
our unhappy Situation. — The poor Man I lost was called Mr Norton,
this was the second Voyage with me as Quarter Master, and his worthy

Character made me fell his loss very severly. — He has left an Aged Aunt I am told who he supported. —

I once before sustained an Attack of this Nature with as small a Number of Men against a Multitude of Indians (after the death of Capt⁰ Cook) on their Morai at Owhyee, where I was left by M⁰ King, to act on the defensive as he calls it it. — Yet notwithstanding; I did not conceive that the power of a mans Arm could throw stones from 2 to 8 lbs Wright with such force and exactnep as these People did. — here unhappily I was without Arms and the Indians soon discovered it; but it was a fortunate circumstance that they did not begin the attack on us in the Cave, in that case nothing could have saved us, and we had nothing left but to dye as bravely as we could fighting close together, in which I found every One cheerfully to join me. —

It was from the appearance of such a resolution that awed them, supposing they could effect their purpose without risk after we got into the Boat. —

Taking this as a Sample of their natural dispositions, there were little hopes to expect much where I was going; for I considered their good behaviour behaviour hitherto owing to a dread of our Fire Arms. which now knowing us to have none would not be the case; and that supposing our lives were safe, Our Boat, Compap. and Quadrant would be taken from us, and thereby I should not be able to return to my King and Country to give an account of the transaction. — While my mind was thus anxiously employed to consider what was best to be done as we were sailing along the west side of the Island, I was sollicited by all hands to take them towards home, and when I told them that no hopes of relief for us remained but what I might find at New Holland. untile I came to Timor, a distance of full 1200 leagues, where was a Governor, but that I had no Idea of the part of the Island the settlement was at, they all agreed to live on One ounce of Bread

Bligh and his bedraggled and emaciated crew finally reached the Dutch port of Kupang on 14 June. Despite the miraculous survival of most of the crew on the perilous voyage there, five more would tragically perish before they reached England.

Amid all this adversity, Bligh's journal records new discoveries that were made as the open boat charted its way through the unexplored islands of the Fijian archipelago. He describes an uninhabited island discovered on 29 May which he named in celebration of the welcome discovery of oysters and fresh water there:

> '*This day being the anniversary of the restoration of King Charles the second [29 May 1660], and the name not being inapplicable to my present situation, for it has restored us to fresh life and strength, I named it Restoration Island.*'

Bligh would have a chance to properly chart and document these new discoveries three years later on a second, successful expedition to Tahiti to transfer bread fruit trees to the West Indies.

So what happened to the remaining crew of HMS *Bounty*? After a failed attempt to establish a colony on Tabuai in the Austral Islands, they decided to return to Tahiti, where two-thirds of the crewmen decided to remain. However, Christian, seven other mutineers, six Tahitian men and fourteen Tahitian women made their way in HMS *Bounty* to Pitcairn Island. The community they established on this remote island, whose location had still not been precisely documented, would remain undiscovered for several years.

In November 1790 HMS *Pandora* was dispatched to hunt down the mutineers and bring them back to England for trial. All fourteen crew members on Tahiti were successfully detained, but the ship foundered on the outer Great Barrier Reef and four of the mutineers drowned. A court martial was convened in Portsmouth on 12 September 1792 on board HMS *Duke* for the surviving mutineers and loyalists. Three of the mutineers, Thomas Burkett, Thomas Ellison and John Millward, were convicted and hanged, and a fourth mutineer, William Muspratt, would also have been hanged but won a stay of execution on a legal technicality. Four loyalist crewmen, Coleman, McIntosh, Norman and

DOC. 7 Extract from the log book of HMS *Bounty*, kept by Captain William Bligh from 6 August 1787 to 20 August 1789.

Byrne, were acquitted and two others, Peter Heywood and James Morrison, received a royal pardon.

The community established on Pitcairn Island under Christian's leadership was tragically torn apart in its early years by rivalry and discontent. Christian and several of his fellow mutineers were murdered, along with several of the Tahitian men. Fortunately, however, this notably bloody chapter in the community's history did not last, and under the direction of the last two surviving mutineers, John Adams (who had served on the *Bounty* under the false name of Alexander Smith) and Edward Young, it was transformed into a thriving, God-fearing Christian community. With Young's death in 1800, Adams became the sole surviving mutineer and was later pardoned for his involvement in the mutiny. He would remain as head of the community until his death at the age of sixty-one in 1829. Despite Christian's tragic demise, he would unknowingly achieve celebrity status in the public eye, and left a legacy of fairness and justice on Pitcairn Island, which was the first community in the world to give women the vote.

The final word should, however, go to Bligh, whose career would continue to be dogged by controversy. He became known as 'the Bounty Bastard' among crew members, his controversial conduct overshadowing his exceptional skills and competency as an experienced naval officer. Nevertheless, following his death in 1817, a junior officer serving under him on HMS *Providence* paid the following tribute to Bligh's ability as an officer:

> 'Let our old Captain's frailties be forgotten and [let us] view him as a man of science and [an] excellent practical seaman.'

Captain Bligh's chart of Bligh's Islands, drawn c.1792. He records that the broken line shows the track followed by the *Bounty*'s launch when he first discovered the islands in 1789. The plain line shows the track taken by the *Providence* and *Afistount* in 1792. Those parts tinged in green were seen by the *Bounty*'s launch. RIGHT

A later watercolour of Tahiti, sketched c.1852. BELOW

East end of Tahiti.

A CHART
of
[B]LIGH'S ISLAND'S.

BY *Wm Bligh*

... Line. shews my Track in the Bounty's
... I discovered these Islands in 1789
... Line my Track in the Providence and
... 1792. The Reefs tinged Green
... the Bounty's Launch.

Tahiti.   Eimeo.

1   2   3   4   5 Degrees.

Scale.

A savage mutiny

The most infamous and barbaric case of mutiny in the history of the Royal Navy occurred on HMS *Hermione* on 21 September 1797, resulting in the murder of Captain Hugh Pigot and nine of his officers.

Pigot, born on 5 September 1769 in Patshull, Staffordshire, was the son of Admiral Hugh Pigot. At the age of twelve, he began his naval career on 5 May 1782 by joining his father on HMS *Jupiter* as an admiral's servant, a post his father had secured for him. Admiral Pigot, a Lord Commissioner of the Admiralty, was sailing to Jamaica, having been appointed Commander-in-Chief of the West Indies. His influence would be an important factor in his son's future progress.

Between 1782 and 1789, Pigot gained the six years' sea service that was

The former *Hermione*, now known as *Santa Cecilia*, after it was handed over the Spanish following the mutiny, is cut out at Puerto Cabello by boats from HMS *Surprise* on 25 October 1799. **BELOW**

required before he could take the examination to assess his suitability for the rank of lieutenant, which he passed on 7 October 1789.

The certificate he received for passing the exam includes a record of his service on HMS *Hermione*, a ship which would also feature tragically later in his life. It also records that his father made '*representations*' to authorise the time his son served on HMS *Trusty*, as otherwise, technically, he would not have been able to take the examination.

Pigot had no immediate guarantee of employment as a lieutenant. With the Royal Navy facing personnel cutbacks in peacetime, there were more deserving unemployed candidates than the inexperienced 21-year-old he was at the time. However, on 21 September 1790 his father's standing led him to be commissioned as a fifth lieutenant to HMS *Colossus* under Captain Hugh Cloberry, his father's friend. After HMS *Colossus*, from 1792 to 1794, Pigot served on HMS *Assistance*, HMS *London* and HMS *Latona*. On 10 February 1794, he was given his first command, of HMS *Incendiary*, and eleven days later, he was put in command of HMS *Swan*.

By now aged only twenty-four, Pigot had made rapid progress. However, although he was now in a position of command, he had only limited experience of captaincy and what this entailed. The following three years of his career were marked with some highpoints, but more notably with controversy and a growing reputation for tyranny and brutality.

During his captaincy of HMS *Swan*, on 18 April 1794, sailing from Torbay to Barbados with HMS *Vanguard*, captained by John Stanhope, escorting a trade convoy, Pigot's ship collided with the *Canada*, a merchant ship under their protection.

Pigot's letter to the Admiralty dated 15 July 1794 shows an early tendency towards poor judgement, acting hastily and not considering the consequences of his actions. He blamed the collision wholly on John Sewell, master of the *Canada*, claiming that he had fired a warning shot across the bows of the *Canada*, and that Sewell had disobeyed sailing orders, had not helped in extricating the *Canada* from HMS *Swan*, and had used '*the most insolent provoking and abusive language*' towards him during the incident. He further claimed that he believed Sewell had done this on purpose. The Admiralty, persuaded by Pigot's

DOC. 1 Lieutenants' passing certificates, 1787–89.

DOC. 2 Pigot's letter to the Admiralty 18 July 1794.

IN Purfuance of the Directions of the Right Honble the Lords Commiſſioners of the Admiralty, ſignified to Us by Mr. *Stephens's* —— Letter of the *3ᵈ October 89* We have examined Mr. *Hugh Pigot* —————— who by Certificate appears to be more than *20* —— Years of Age, and find he has gone to Sea more than *6* —— Years in the Ship, and Qualities under-mentioned, Viz.

Ships.	Entry.	Quality.	Diſcharge.	Time			
				Years	M.	W.	D.
Jupiter	10 May 1782	Adᵐˡ Retie	13 July 1782		2		2
Formidable	14 July "	Dᵒ	30 July 83	1	"	2	3
Aſsistance	10 October 83	Dᵒ	21 Decᵣ "		2	2	3
Dᵒ	22 Decemr "	Ordᵈ & Ab	30 Sepᵗ 84		10	"	4
Dᵒ	1 October 84	Mid	16 June 85		9	1	
Hermione	17 June 85	Ab	30 Augᵗ "		2	2	5
Trusty	2 April 86	Capᵗ Serᵗ	11 Decᵣ 86		9		2
Dᵒ	12 Decᵣ "	Mid	22 Janry 89	2	1	2	
Southampton	8 May 89	Ab	8 July "		2	"	6
			case Book				
Mr. Pigot is allowed the time he is rated as Captains Serᵗ in the Trusty, in consequence of a representation from Admᵗ Pigot of his being actually onboard & doing duties of a similar nature of 3 Decᵣ 87 & 30 Decᵣ 88				6	1	1	4

He produceth Journals kept by himſelf in the *Trusty and Southampton* and Certificates from Captains *Bertinck Wolseley & Sᵣ and Aᵈ I. Douglas.*

of his Diligence and Sobriety: He can Splice, Knot, Reef a Sail, work a Ship in Sailing, ſhift his Tides, keep a Reckoning of a Ship's Way by Plain Sailing and Mercator; obſerve by Sun or Star, and find the Variation of the Compaſs, and is qualified to do the Duty of an Able Seaman and Midſhipman. Dated at the Navy-Office, the *7 Octᵣ 89*

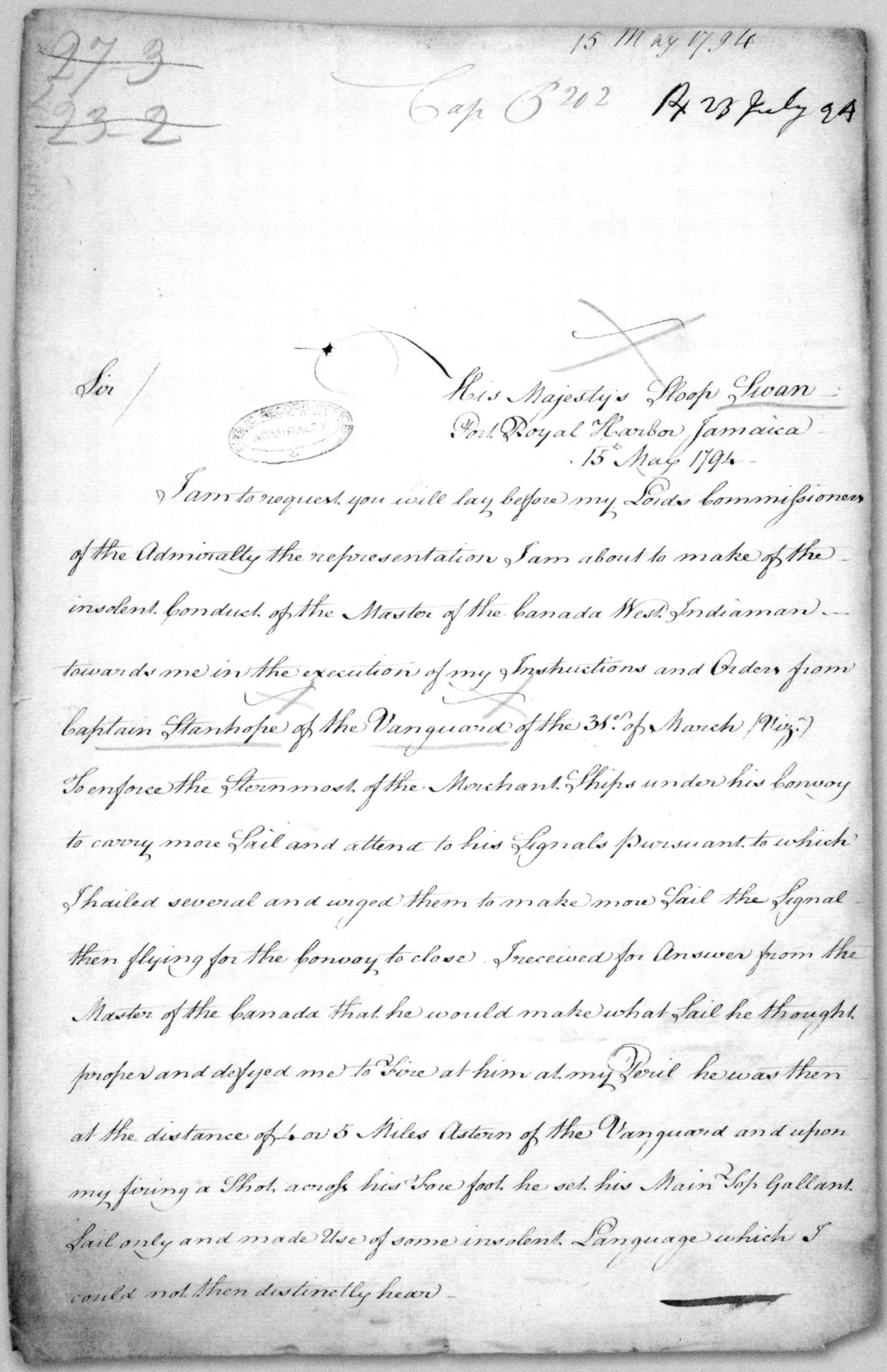

27 9
23 2

15 May 1794

Cap C° 202   R 23 July 94

Sir/

His Majesty's Sloop Swan
Port Royal Harbor Jamaica
15th May 1794.

I am to request you will lay before my Lords Commissioners
of the Admiralty the representation I am about to make of the
insolent Conduct of the Master of the Canada West Indiaman
towards me in the execution of my Instructions and Orders from
Captain Stanhope of the Vanguard of the 31st of March (Viz.)
To enforce the Sternmost of the Merchant Ships under his Convoy
to carry more Sail and attend to his Signals Pursuant to which
I hailed several and urged them to make more Sail the Signal
then flying for the Convoy to close I received for Answer from the
Master of the Canada that he would make what Sail he thought
proper and defyed me to Fire at him at my Peril he was then
at the distance of 4 or 5 Miles Astern of the Vanguard and upon
my firing a Shot across his Fore foot he set his Main Top Gallant
Sail only and made Use of some insolent Language which I
could not then distinctly hear —

Upon the 18 of April at about 5 oClock P.M. ––

His Majesty's Ship under my command then laying too in the
act of Reefing Topsails the above mentioned Ship fell on board of us –
and I am strongly of Opinion purposely . During the whole of –
the time I was in the Execution of my Duty endeavouring to get
the two Ships seperated from each other (to accomplish which I was
under the necessity of cutting the Lanyards of the Swans Mizen –
Shrouds) the Master of the Canada instead of exerting himself on
the occasion stood upon the Bowsprit of his Ship and addressing –
himself to me made use of the most insolent provoking and –
Abusive Language and continued to do so during the whole of the
time the two Ships remained within hail of each other . I think –
it my Duty to represent such conduct from a Master of a Merchant
Ship to his Majesty's Officers appointed to protect the Trade –
                                    of the Admiralty
and trust my Lords Commissioners will not pass it by with

                    I am Sir
                    Your very obed. humble Serv.

                              Hugh Pigot

So Phillip Stephens Esq.

arguments, which were supported by Stanhope, sent a letter to Lloyds, to be communicated to the owners and insurers of the *Canada*, telling them that behaviour like Sewell's would not be tolerated.

In his third command, of HMS *Success*, starting on 4 September 1794, Pigot began to display brutal and sadistic behaviour by flogging his crew far more excessively than other captains. Between 22 October 1794 and 11 September 1795, with varying degrees of severity and characterised by inconsistency, he eighty-five ordered floggings, amounting to half of the crew, and leading to the death of two men from their resulting injuries.

On 1 July 1796 Pigot was involved in another collision, this time with an American merchant brig, the *Mercury*. This was similar to the 1794 *Canada* incident, but had wider repercussions. HMS *Success* had been escorting a merchant navy convoy near Santo Domingo when the *Mercury* collided with Pigot's ship, becoming entangled in her rigging. Pigot blamed the Mercury's master, William Jesup, and had him '*started*' with twenty rope lashes. This caused a major diplomatic incident, with Jesup's representations of 4 July 1794 to RR Wilfred, Commander of HM forces at Port-au-Prince, providing a conflicting version of events. Jesup claimed:

'*Success ran foul of the Mercury [and] the Captain … ordered his people to cut away everything [rigging] they could lay their hands on… [Jesup] begged Captain Pigot for*

DOC. 3 Pigot's letter to the Admiralty 18 July 1794.

Account of a flogging on board HMS *Success*. BELOW

Copy of the Representation, and of the Proofs of the
Conduct of H. Pigot commander of the British Frigate
Success, towards William Jesup an American citizen.

To his honor R. R. Wilford Esqr. Commander of his Majesty's
Forces at Port-au-Prince.

The Petition of William Jesup,
Master of the American ship Mercury
of New York, humbly sets forth;

That your Petitioner, being on his passage from St. Marc's
to this Port, was laying too about one o'clock on the morning of the
5th inst. in company with a number of transports and his Majesty's
Frigate Success commanded by Captain Pigot, when the Success
wore ship and ran foul of the Mercury: the Captain of the
Frigate ordered his people to cut away every thing they could
lay their hands on. The jib-boom, sprit-sail-yard, fore-stay,
top-mast-stays, stopper, shank-painters, and two strands of his
small bower cable, were cut: — he further ordered his men
to cut away and bring on board the Frigate, the Mercury's jib
and fore-top-mast stay-sail, which was done; Captain Pigot
telling his men, at the same time, they would do to make trowsers.
Your Petitioner begged Captain Pigot, for God's sake, not to cut
any more than he could avoid, or words to that effect.

Captain Pigot forthwith commanded his people to
bring the d — d rascal that spoke on board the Frigate. Your
Petitioner was then seized and ordered on board the Frigate,
where he remained for a few minutes till the vessels were
cleared.

God's sake not to cut away more than he could avoid... Pigot commanded his people to bring the damned rascal that spoke on board the frigate ... [and] desired the boatswain's mates to give the rascal... a good flogging.'

DOC. 4 The diplomatic incident about the *Mercury*, July 1794.

Jesup went on to claim that, having established that he was the *Mercury*'s master, Pigot said:

'"flog him well, and let him flog his officers". These orders were instantly obeyed in so severe and cruel a manner that [Jesup] was nearly bereft of his senses. During the time [Jesup] was ... so brutally beaten and ill treated, ... [he] made no use of offensive language whatsoever, or no kind of resistance, but only begged they would have compassion of him. No attention was paid to his cries, but on the contrary he proceeded to beat him with the same violence until Captain Pigot was supposed to be satisfied.'

Pigot's conduct and indiscriminate punishment were taken up by the American consul, L MacNeal. Accounts of his behaviour appeared in American newspapers, and these came to the Admiralty's notice. Lord William Grenville, Secretary of State for Foreign Affairs, received an official complaint from Robert Liston, the British envoy in Philadelphia, and news of the incident had also reached King George III. Although Sir Hyde Parker, Commander-in-Chief in the West Indies, overlooked the matter, the Admiralty was forced by the intervention by the King and Grenville to hold a court of inquiry in January 1797 to determine whether Pigot should face a court martial. Pigot maintained his innocence but apologised for his conduct and was subsequently exonerated.

Parker, corresponding with the Admiralty on 24 January 1797, suggested that Pigot's behaviour had not been as bad as it had been made out to be. He stated:

'Having in obedience to the directions of the Right Honourable, the Lords Commissioners of the Admiralty, signified to me by your letters of the 22nd September and 7th October last, ordered a strict enquiry to be made into the outrageous and cruel conduct and behaviour of Captain Pigot of His Majesty's Ship Success, to Mr. William Jessup Master of the American vessel, Mercury...

... however unjustifiable his conduct may appear to their Lordships, they will be of opinion with me, that it is, proved to be far very far, more favourable than what has been represented either by Mr Liston or the party aggrieved, and most sincerely hope that His Majesty will be graciously pleased, when these papers are laid before him, to see and consider it in the same manner or light as I do.'

Pigot was due to return to England with HMS *Success* but, fearing a bad reception there, was allowed to exchange ships with Captain Philip Wilkinson, who was in command of HMS *Hermione*. Taking command on 10 February 1797, Pigot brought with him twenty-four men from HMS *Success*. This led to complaints by the existing crew of HMS *Hermione* that their new captain gave his former crew preferential treatment by way of prize money and leave when on 22 March 1797 they captured sixteen vessels at Punta Jigeuro, Puerto Rico. Some of the complainants were confined by Pigot and three were threatened with a court martial.

In April 1797, under heavy fire from enemy batteries, HMS *Hermione*, along with HMS *Mermaid*, HMS *Quebec*, HMS *Drake* and HMS *Penelope*, took fourteen ships from French privateers at Juan Rabal near Cape Nicolas Mole, recovering nine prizes in the form of enemy ships. In May 1797, while sailing off the coast of Caracas, as senior officer Pigot was tasked with targeting enemy ships, with HMS *Ceres* also under his command. HMS *Hermione* was prevented from running aground near the Gulf of Trieste mainly through the quick action of Lieutenant John Harris. Unfortunately for Pigot, however, HMS *Ceres* did strike land. Pigot demanded a court martial into the incident, accusing Harris of neglect of duty and of not keeping a proper lookout. In the subsequent trial on 16 July 1797, praise was bestowed on Harris, who was completely absolved, and he left HMS *Hermione*.

Pigot's unpredictable character and irrational behaviour on HMS *Hermione* continued. On 15 September 1797, Midshipman David Casey was accused by Pigot of negligence because a sailor under his supervision had failed to tie a reef knot. Pigot demanded that Casey apologise on his knees in full view of his shipmates, which Casey refused to do. Pigot had Casey flogged and disrated, potentially ruining his career. This outraged some of Casey's shipmates, who felt he had been punished too harshly.

Joseph Montell late Seamen on board
of His Majesty's Ship Hermione about an
hour before his execution Confessed that he
was a principal, and the principal in the
Massacre of the Officers of that Ship. That
about Ten O'Clock at Night, he having pro-
-cured a bucket of Rum, with three others
whose Names are Bell, Draytenham, and
Farrel, and about Four, or Five, or Six more
entered the Gun Room in the dark, and
were the Murderers of those in commande,
having retired forward, and the wounds of
those who' remained alive of the unhappy
sufferers being dressed by the Surgeon, they
burst a second time into the Gun Room
and fully compleated the Murder, He Joseph
Montell says that he met the First Lieuten
-ant coming out of his Cabin, and ordered
him back but the Lieutenant refuseing, and
endeavouring to make his way through the
Sky-light, he Montell knocked him in the
head with an axe, The Captain who' was
grievously wounded, and Crying for Mercy
was answered by Montell "you have shewn
no Mercy yourself, and therefore deserve
none" and immediately ran him through
with a bayonet on a Musquet, Their bodies
were then thrown overboard, and the Surgeon

Mate

Since taking command of HMS *Hermione*, Pigot had instated the irrational practice of flogging the last man down from working on the highest topsails of the ship. On 20 September he threatened the men working aloft with this punishment. In their rush to get down, two men and a boy tragically fell fifty feet to their death. Pigot contemptuously referred to the bodies as 'lubbers', an offensive insult to sailors, and ordered them to be thrown overboard, flogging those men who remonstrated. This proved to be the main catalyst for the ensuing mutiny.

On the evening of 21 September 1797, the rum stores were broken into and inebriated mutineers attacked the marine sentry on watch outside the captain's cabin, intent on retribution. These mutineers viciously hacked Pigot to near death in his cabin, before jettisoning his body overboard.

Joseph Montell, one of the mutineers found guilty at a court martial held on 17 March 1798, sent a confession to Parker one hour before being executed, stating that:

> 'he was a principal, and the principal, in the massacre of the officers … that about ten o'clock at night, he having procured a bucket of rum with … Bell, Draytenham and Farrel, and about Four or five or six more entered the Gunroom in the dark, and were the murderers of those in Command, having retired forward, and the wounds of these that remained alive of the unhappy sufferers being dressed by the Surgeon, they burst a second time into the Gun Room, and fully completed the murder.
>
> '… he met the first Lieutenant coming out of the cabin, and ordered him back, but the Lieutenant refusing, and indeavouring to make his way through the sky light, knocked him in the head with an axe, the Captain who was grievously wounded and crying for mercy was answered by Montell "you have shown no mercy yourself, and therefore deserve none", and immediately ran him through with a bayonet on a musquet, their bodies were then thrown overboard.'

The initial intention of overthrowing their tyrannical Captain developed into a killing frenzy as more mutineers joined in to brutally slaughter three lieutenants, including Lieutenant Henry Foreshaw, as described in John Halford's testimony provided at a mutineer's court martial on 15 January 1799:

DOC. 6 John Halford's testimony given in Courts Martial papers, January 1799.

(15)

Court. Was Turner the Masters Mate considered as one of the Principal Mutineers.

Ansr. The Command of the Ship was offered to him the next day and he accepted of it.

Court. Do you remember at that time seeing in the Cabbin, Robert McCready, Thomas Nash, John Farrell and James Bell Seaman.

Ansr. I frequently saw them there.

Court. Do you know whether those four Men last mentioned were considered as the principal Mutineers.

Ansr. Thomas Nash & John Farrell were considered so. the other two I cannot say much about.

Court. Did you see Captain Pigot or any of the Officers Murdered.

Answer I saw Lieutenant Foreshaw after being wounded on the Quarter Deck and hove over the Quarter, come in at one of the Ports under the half Deck, with Streams of Blood running down his face, Thomas Nash shortly after came under the half Deck, seized Lieutenant Foreshaw by the arm & said Foreshaw you Bugger, are You not overboard yet, overboard you must and overboard you shall go. he then led him to the Larboard Gangway and by the Assistance of some People on the Gangway, forced him up & hove him overboard.

Court. Did you see either of the Prisoners aiding & abetting in wounding Lieut Foreshaw and Asisting in throwing him overboard.

Ansr. No.

Court.

'I saw Lieutenant Foreshaw after being wounded on the quarterdeck and hove over the quarter, came in at one of the ports under the half deck, with streams of blood running down his face, Thomas Nash shortly came under the half deck, seized Foreshaw by the arm saying "Foreshaw you bugger, are you not overboard yet, overboard you must and overboard you shall go" … and by the assistance of some people … forced him up and hove him overboard.'

The surgeon, the purser, the captain's cook, a marine sergeant with yellow fever taken from the sick berth, a sixteen-year-old boy and the boatswain, William Martin, were also thrown overboard, having been singled out by Richard Woodman, one of the ringleaders of the mutiny, who allegedly proceeded to rape Martin's wife (although Admiralty regulations banned women on royal naval ships, captains often ignored this rule, particularly if the women were officers' wives).

The mutineers knew they were condemned men as the Articles of War, the disciplinary code of the Royal Navy that was read to them weekly, stipulated that mutiny was punishable by death. They decided to sail to La Guaira and surrender HMS *Hermione* to the Spanish authorities in exchange for freedom. Instead, on their surrender, they were each given twenty-five dollars and the choice either of joining the Spanish army, doing heavy labour, or refitting their ship, that had been taken into service by the Spanish.

News of the mutiny and Pigot's death reached Parker on 31 October 1797. In a letter to the Admiralty dated 15 November 1797, Parker reveals his disgust and indignation, and states that rewards are being offered for the capture of any of the mutineers, as well as:

'[a] pardon to any (the principals excepted) who shall turn kings evidence for bringing the principal actors to justice… It being of such importance to the Salvation of the Naval Force of Great Britain, that the cruel Perpetrators of this Piracy should be brought to condign punishment and made most exemplary examples of.'

Posters printed by the Admiralty were circulated as a deterrent against mutiny but also as a statement of its intent to punish the fugitive mutineers from the *Hermione*.

Over the next nine years, thirty-three mutineers were caught, charged and tried, twenty-four of these being hanged and gibbeted, one transported and eight acquitted. In October 1797, HMS *Hermione* was recaptured in a daring raid by Captain Edward Hamilton in command of HMS *Surprise* and symbolically renamed HMS *Retaliation* by Parker. Subsequently, on 31 January 1800, the Admiralty renamed the vessel HMS *Retribution*.

Notice of Court Martial for mutiny, 1798.

BELOW

AT A COURT MARTIAL

Assembled and held on Board His Majesty's Ship *York*, Mole Saint Nicholas, on the Seventeenth Day of March 1798.

PRESENT

GEORGE BOWEN, Esquire, Captain of His Majesty's Ship *Carnatic*, and Third in Command.

PRESIDENT.

CAPTAINS.

EDWARD TYRREL SMITH.   JOHN FERRIER.
MAN DOBSON.   JOHN CRAWLEY.

THE Court, in pursuance of an Order of the fif-teenth of March 1798, from Sir *Hyde Parker*, Kn.t Vice Admiral of the Red and Commander in Chief of His Majesty's Ships and Vessels employed and to be em-ployed at and about *Jamaica*, &c. &c. addressed to *George Bowen* Esq. Captain of His Majesty's Ship *Carnatic*, and Third in Command, being first duly sworn, pro-ceeded to try *Anthony Mark*, alias *Antonio Marco*, *John Elliot*, *Joseph Mansell*, and *Peter Delany*, alias, *Pierre d'Orlanie*, upon an information contained in a Letter from Captain *Mends*, of His Majesty's Sloop *Diligence*, of the 27th of October 1797, to the Com-mander in Chief, and one from Captain *Crawley*, of His Majesty's Ship *Valiant*, dated the 8th of March ins-tant, and also the deposition of *John Mason*, late car-penters Mate of His Majesty's Ship *Hermione*, taken in the presence of the said Captain *Crawley*, and Lieu-tenants *Philpot* and *Hancock*, of the *Valiant*, dated the 2nd of the said month of March, representing that the said *Anthony Mark*, alias *Antonio Marco*, *John Elliot*, *Joseph Mansell*, and *Peter Delany*, alias *Pierre d'Orlanie*, were a part of the Crew of the French Pri-vateer *la Magicienne*, captured by the said Ship; and also a part of the Crew of His Majesty's said Ship *Her-mione*, and were actually on board His Majesty's said Ship *Hermione*, at the time the Mutiny, Murders and Piracy were committed on board her; and for being taken in arms against His Majesty.

And having heard the Evidence produced to identify the Persons of the Prisoners, and very maturely and deliberately weighed and considered the several circum-stances in the Letters, and Paper abovementioned, and

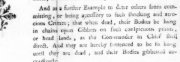

the Prisoners having no Evidence to produce, or any thing to offer in their own defence, THE COURT is of opinion, that the charges of Mutiny, Murder and running away with His Majesty's said Ship *Hermione*, and delivering her up to the Enemy; And being found actually in arms against His Majesty and His Subjects, on board *la Magicienne*, a French Privateer, are fully proved.

THE COURT do therefore adjudge the said *An-thony Mark*, alias *Antonio Marco*, *John Elliot*, *Jo-seph Mansell*, and *Peter Delany*, alias *Pierre d'Orlanie*, to be hung by their Necks until they are dead, at the Yard Arms of such of His Majesty's Ships, and at such times, as shall be directed by the Commander in Chief.

And as a further Example to deter others from com-mitting, or being accessory to such shocking and atro-cious Crimes; that when dead, their Bodies be hung in chains upon Gibbets on such conspicuous points, or head lands, as the Commander in Chief shall direct. And they are hereby sentenced to be so hung until they are dead, and their Bodies gibbeted ac-cordingly.

(Signed) GEO. BOWEN.
EDW.d TYRREL SMITH.
JN.o FERRIER.
MAN DOBSON.
JN.o CRAWLEY.

W.m PAGE, Deputy
Judge Advocate.

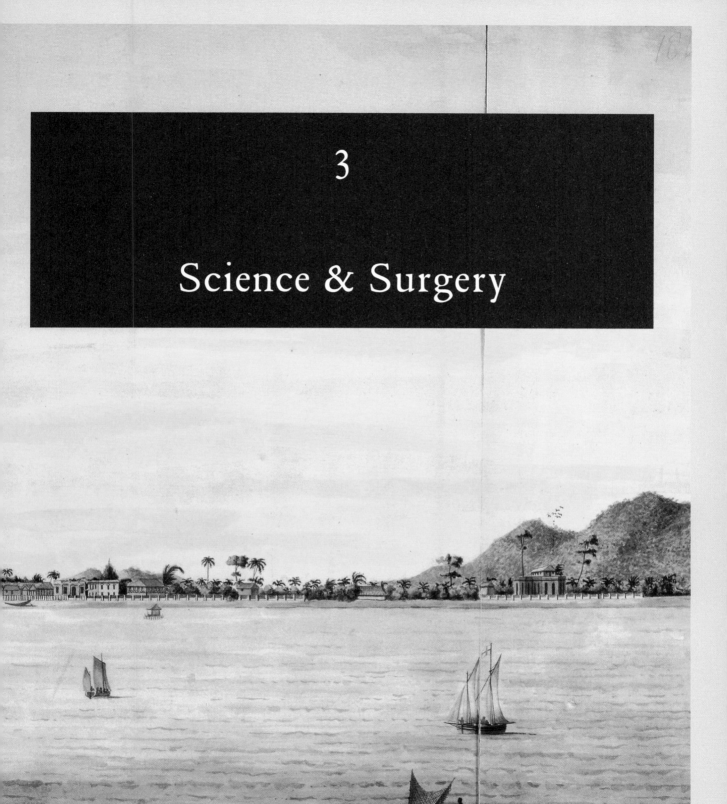

3

Science & Surgery

Measuring the transit of Venus
CAPTAIN JAMES COOK ON HMS *ENDEAVOUR* ... 1768–71

One of the most famous scientific endeavours of the Royal Navy was James Cook's first voyage of discovery from 1768 to 1771. Cook was tasked with observing the 'transit of Venus' under the pretext of scientific discovery, but he was covertly ordered by the Admiralty also to search for *Terra Australis Incognita* – the 'unknown Southern Land' – after expeditions led by John Byron in 1764 and Samuel Wallis in 1766 had failed to find the fabled land:

> *'Whereas the making discoveries of countries hitherto unknown, and the attaining a knowledge of distant parts which though formerly discovered have yet been but imperfectly explored, will rebound greatly to the honor of this nation as a maritime power, as well as to the dignity of the Crown of Great Britain, and may lend greatly to the advancement of the trade and navigation thereof; and whereas there is reason to imagine that a continent, or land of great extent may be found to the southward of the tract lately made by Captain Wallis in His Majesty's Ship the Dolphin... you are therefore in pursuance of His Majesty's pleasure hereby required and directed to put to sea ... so soon as the observation of the Transit of Venus shall be finished, and observe the following instructions...'*

During the eighteenth century 'Age of Enlightenment' there was a growing confidence that 'Science' would resolve such unanswered questions as to whether there truly existed a Southern Continent. In Britain the Royal Society promoted scientific exploration, and Cook's own observations were influenced by the Society's *Philosophical Transactions* of 1665–66, which featured guidelines by Lawrence Rooke entitled 'Directions for Seamen bound for far Voyages'. These 'directions', later adopted by the Admiralty, outlined the type of data, such as meteorological, oceanographic and astrological observations, that voyages of discovery should collect in 'exact diaries'.

One of the oldest mysteries to be resolved concerned the size of the solar

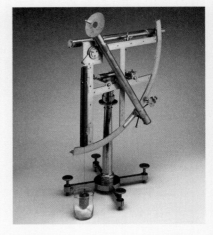

A portable astronomical quadrant made in London by the renowned English instrument maker John Bird (1709–76). It was sent along with one of the Royal Society expeditions to measure the 1769 transit of Venus. **ABOVE**

DOCS. 1 & 2 Additional instructions given to Lieutenant James Cook on board *Endeavour*, 30 July 1768.

64

The Astronomer Royal's Limits for the
Southern Observation of the Transit
of Venus which will happen on the
3ᵈ of June 1769.

Latitude South.	Limits of Longitude West of London.		
5	From 124	to	187
10	126		185
15	128		183
20	130		181
25	133		178
30	136		175
35	139		172.

By &ᶜᵃ

Additional Secret Instructions
for Lieuᵗ James Cook, Com-
-mander of His Majesty's
Bark the Endeavour.

Whereas the making Discoveries of
Countries hitherto unknown, and the
attaining a knowledge of distant Parts
which though formerly discovered have
yet been but imperfectly explored, will
redound greatly to the Honor of this Nation
as a Maritime Power, as well as to the
Dignity of the Crown of Great Britain,
and may tend greatly to the advance-
-ment of the Trade & Navigation thereof;
And whereas there is reason to imagine
that a Continent, or Land of great extent,
may

may be found to the Southward of
the Tract lately made by Capt. Wallis
in His Majesty's Ship the Dolphin
(of which you will herewith receive a
Copy) or of the Tract of any former
Navigators in pursuits of the like kind;
You are therefore in pursuance of His
Majesty's Pleasure hereby required &
directed to put to Sea with the Bark
you command, so soon as the Observation of the Transit of the Planet
Venus shall be finished, & observe the
following Instructions.

You are to proceed to the
Southward in order to make discovery
of the Continent abovementioned until
you arrive in the Latitude of 40, unless
you sooner fall in with it: But not
having discovered it, or any evident
Signs of it, in that Run; you are to
proceed in search of it to the Westward,
between the Latitude beforementioned &
the Latitude of 35 until you discover
it, or fall in with the Eastern Side of
the Land discovered by Tasman and
now called New Zealand.

If you discover the Continent
abovementioned, either in your Run
to the Southward, or to the Westward,
as above directed, you are to employ
yourself diligently in exploring as great
an extent of the Coast as you can;
carefully observing the true situation
thereof both in Latitude & Longitude;
the

system. By the mid-eighteenth century, astronomers knew six planets orbited the sun, as well as their relative range from the Sun and Earth, but exact distances were unknown. The potential answer to this enigma was the 'transit of Venus', which could be viewed by telescope as a small black disk travelling across the Sun. In 1716, Edmund Halley developed an earlier theory proposed by James Gregory in his work *Optica Promota*, that by recording Venus's transit at various times from various locations, astronomers could determine the distance to Venus using the principle of parallax, and thereby accurately deduce the scale of the solar system. However, Halley noted that this phenomenon occurred in a pattern that repeated every 243 years, with pairs of transits eight years apart separated by long intervals of 121 and 105 years.

In 1768 the Royal Society petitioned King George III for a ship to observe the 1769 transit, with added urgency since the next transit would be in 1874. James Cook had previously submitted a paper to the Society's *Philosophical Transactions* about his observations of a solar eclipse from the Burgeo Islands off Newfoundland, and the quality of Cook's work meant he was noticed in influential places. He had surveyed the Bay of Gaspe and the hazardous St Lawrence River in 1758, and his aptitude for surveying and cartography had become apparent quickly. The Admiralty therefore proposed him to lead the voyage, Lord Colville writing the following glowing recommendation to the Admiralty on 30 December 1762:

> *'that from my experience of Mr Cook's Genius and capacity I think him well qualified for the work he has performed, and for greater undertakings of the same kind.'*

The Admiralty provided HMS *Endeavour* for Cook's voyage, while the Royal Society sent Charles Green as the voyage's astronomer and Joseph Banks as the official botanist. Banks privately funded Daniel Solander and Herman Spöring, both naturalists, and two artists, Alexander Buchan and Sydney Parkinson, to join him on the voyage. Cook was tasked with making observations of the transit of Venus in Tahiti. He was limited to a crew of seventy and was anxious to ensure the suitability of every member, as indicated in this letter of 16 June 1768 to the Navy Board:

'I have received your letter ... acquainting me that you have appointed John Thompson, Cook, to the Endeavour ... as this man ... had the misfortune to loose [lose] his right hand; I am of the opinion that he will be of little service and as I am very desirious of having no one on board but what is fully able to do their duty in their respective stations, I hope the Board will not be displeased at my objecting to this man.'

Cook's letters to the Admiralty on 25 and 27 July 1768 show that he was also determined to be equipped with the best scientific instruments:

'Doctor Knight hath got an azimuth compass of an improved construction which may prove to be of more general use than the old ones, please move ... the Admiralty to order the Endeavour ... to be supplied with it.

    'The Navy Board have been pleased to supply ... Endeavour with the reflecting telescope that was on board the Grenville ... for making astronomical observations at Newfoundland, in order to make it of more general use I have got made a micrometer for measuring the apparent magnitudes of the heavenly bodies, which will be of great service in the observation of the transit Venus.'

HMS *Endeavour* sailed from Plymouth on 26 August 1768, reaching Tahiti on 13 April 1769, nearly two months ahead of the transit. This gave ample time for the ship's company to absorb the beauty of Tahiti and make contact with the Tahitians. A portable observatory was set up near Matavai Bay, as Cook noted in his journal on 1 May.

'This afternoon we set up the Observatory and took the Astronomical Quadt. ashore for the first time, together with some other Instruments. The Fort being now finished and made as Tenantable as the Times, Nature & situation of the ground, & materials we had to work upon would admit of – The North and south parts consisted of a Bank of earth 4½ feet high on the inside, & a Ditch without 10 feet broad and 6 feet deep, on the west side facing the Bay a Bank of earth 4 feet high & Palisades upon that, but no ditch, the works being at high water mark: on the East side upon the Bank of the River was placed a double row of casks, &'s this was the weakest side the 2 four pounders were planted there & the whole was defended beside these 2 Guns with 6 Swivels and *generally about 45 Men with small arms including the officers & gentlemen who resided ashore; I now thought myself perfectly secure from anything these people could attempt;——'*

DOCS. 3, 4 & 5 Pages from Captain James Cook's journal on his voyage 27 May 1768 to 10 July 1771.

However, as Cook noted in the next day's entry, the secure fort they also built did not prevent the theft of their astronomical quadrant:

'Tuesday, 2d This morning about 9 o'clock when Mr Green & I went to set up the Quadt.. it was not to be found, it had never been taking out of the Packing case | which was about 18 Inches square | since it came from Mr Bird the Maker; and the whole was pretty heavy, so that it was a matter of astonishment to us all how it could be taken away, as a Centinel stood the whole night within 5 Yards of the door of the Tent where it was put together with several other Instruments, but none of them was missing but this. However it was not long before we got information that one of the Natives had taken it away & carried it to the Eastward.'

In due course, Cook was introduced to Oberea, Queen of the Tahitians. He noted the abundance of old iron on the island, and, as he explained in his journal entry of 9 May, he quickly figured out where it had come from:

'Oberea, the Dolphins Queen, made us a Visit for the first time since the Quadt. was Stolen, she introduce'd herself with a small Pig for which she had a Hatchet, & as soon as she got it she lugg'd out a Broken Axe & several peices of Old Iron, these I believe she must have had from the Dolphin, the Ax she wanted to be mended & Axes made of the Old Iron. I obliged her in the first but excuseed myself from the latter, since the Natives ^ have Seen the Forge at Work, they have frequently brought peices of Iron to be made into one sort of Tool or other, which hath generally been done when ever it did not hinder our own work, being willing to oblige them in every thing in my power; these pieces of Old Iron the natives must have got from the Dolphin, as we know of no other Ship being here and very probably some from us; for there is no species of theft they will not commit to get this Article and I may say the same of the common seamen when in these parts.'

May 1769

Monday 1. This morning Tootaha came onb.d the Ship & was very desirous of seeing into every Chest & Drawer that was in the Cabin I satisfied his Curiosity so far as to open most of those that belong'd to me; he saw several things that he took a fancy to & collected them together, but at last he cast his Eye upon the Adze I had from Mr Stephens that was made in imitation of one of their Stone Adzes or Axes, the moment he lay his hands upon it he of his own accord put away every thing he had got before, & asked me if I would give him that which I very readily did & he went away without asking for any one thing more, which I by experience knew, was a sure sign that he was well pleased with what he had got

This day, one of the Natives who appeared to be a Chief dined with us as he had done some days before; but then there were always some Woman present & one or another of them put the Victuals into his Mouth but this day there happned to be none to perform that Office; when he was helpd to Victuals & desired to eat he sat in the Chair like a Statute without once attempting to put one Morsel to his Mouth, & would certainly have gone without his Dinner if one of the Servants had not fed him; we have often found these Women very officious in feeding of us, from which it should seem that it is a custom upon some Occasions for them to feed the Chiefs, however this is the only Instance of that kind we have seen, or that they could not help themselves as well as us

This afternoon we set up the Observatory & took the Astronomical Quadt. ashore for the first time, together with some other Instruments. The fort being now finished & made as Tenantable, as the Time, Nature & Situation of the ground & Materials we had to work upon would admit of. The N.o & So parts consisted of a Bank of Earth 4½ feet high on the inside, & a ditch without 10 feet broad & 6 feet deep; on the Wt. side facing the Bay a Bank of Earth 4 feet high & Palisades upon that but no ditch, the works being at high water Mark; on the East side upon the Bank of the River was placed a double row of Casks, & this was the weakest side the 2 four pounders were planted there & the whole was defended beside these 2 Guns with 6 Swivels & generally about 45 Men with small Arms including the Officers & Gentlemen who resided ashore, I now thought myself perfectly secure from any thing these People could Attempt

Tuesday 2. This morning about 9 o'clock when Mr Green & I went to set up the Quadt. it was not to be found, it had never been taking out of the packing case (which was about 18 Inches square) since it came from Mr Bird the Maker & the whole was pretty heavy so that it was

a

(74)

Lat: 17½
Long: 149½

Remarkable Occurrences at Georges Island

May 1769   a Matter of Astonishment to us all how it could be taken away, as a sentinel stood the whole night within 5 Yards of the Door of the Tent where it was put together with several other Instruments, but none of them was missing but this, However it was not long before we got information that one of the Natives had taken it away & carried it to the Eastward, immediately a resolution was taken to detain all the large Canoes that were in the bay & to seize upon Tootaha & some others of the Principal People & keep them in Custody until the Quad.t was produced, but this last we did not think proper immediately to put in Execution as we had only Obarea in our power & the detaining her by force would have alarmed all the rest, In the mean time Mr Banks (who is always very alert upon all Occasions wherein the Natives are concern'd) & Mr Green went into the Woods to enquire of Tooboura-tomita which way & where the Quad.t was gone, I very soon was inform'd that these 3 were gone to the Eastward in quest of it & some time after I followed my self with a small Party of Men, but before I went away I gave orders that if Tootaha came either to the Ship or the fort, he was not to be detained for I found that he had no hand in taking away the Quad.t & that there was almost a certainty of geting it again, I met Mr Banks & Mr Green about 4 Miles from the fort returning with the Quad.t this was about Sun set & we all got back to the fort about 8 o'Clock, where I found Tootaha in Custody & a Number of the Natives crowding about the Gate of the fort, My going into the Woods with a Party of Arm'd men so alarm'd the Natives that in the evening they began to move off with their effects & a double Canoe putting off from the bottom of the bay was observed by the Ship, & a boat sent after her, in this Canoe happned to be Tootaha, & as soon as our Boat came up with her, he & all the people were in the Canoe jumped overboard, & he only was taken up & bro.t onboard the Ship together with the Canoe, the rest were permitted to swim ashore, From the Ship Tootaha was sent to the fort, where Mr Hicks thought proper to detain him untill I return'd, The scene between Tooboogatomita & Tootaha when the former came into the fort & found the latter in Custody, was realy moving, they wept over each other for some time, as for Tootaha he was so far prepossess'd with the thoughts that he was to be killd that he could not be made senceable to the Contrary till he was carried out of the fort to the People, many of whom expres'd their joy by embracing him, & after all he would not go away untill some few of the Principal ones were Present, & that appear'd to be owing to our being there, after this was over we were given to understand that we were to go to dinner & were desir'd to follow Tootaha who led us into our own Boat & soon after came a small Pig ready roasted with some Bread Fruit & Cocoa Nutts & here we thought we were to have dinned, but Tootaha after waiting about 10 Minutes made signs to us to put of the Boat & go aboard, which we did bringing him & Tooboweratomita along with us, as soon as we got on board we all dined on the cheer this Chief had provided.——— We soon found the good effect of having made friend with this Man for it was no sooner known to the Natives that he was onboard the Ship, than they bro.ᵗ Bread Fruit, Cocoa Nutts &c. to the Fort.

Saturday 6ᵗʰ & Sunday 7 Nothing remarkable only that the Natives supply us with as much Bread Fruit, & Cocoa Nutts as we can destroy.

Monday 8. Early this morning the Master went to the Eastward in the Pinnace to try if he could not procure some Hogs & Fowls from that quarter but he return'd in the evening without success, he saw but a very few & those the inhabitants pretended belong'd to Tootaha so great is this Mans influence or authority over them that they dare part with nothing without his consent, or otherwise they only make use of his name to excuse themselves from parting with the few they have, for it is very certain these things are in no great plenty with them.———

Tuesday 9, Wednesday 10 & Thursday 11 Nothing remarkable hapned for the 3 days Oberiea the Dolphins Queen, made us a Visit for the first time since the Quad.ᵗ was stoln, she introduced herself with a small Pig for which she had a Hatchet & as soon as she got it she lugged out a broken Axe & several pieces of Old Iron, these I believe she must have had from the Dolphin, the Axe she wanted to be mended & Axes made of the old Iron, I obliged her in the first, but excused myself from the latter since the Natives have seen the Forge at work, they have frequently brought pieces of Iron to be made into one sort of tool or other, which hath generally been done when ever it did not hinder our own Work being willing to oblige them in every thing in my power, these pieces of Old Iron the Natives must have got from the Dolphin as we know of no other ship being here & very probably some from us for there is no species of Theft they will not commit to get this Article & I may say the same of the common Seamen when in these Sloops.

The transit of Venus itself occurred on 3 June 1769. With the astronomer Charles Green, Cook sketched a passage of Venus as it passed across the Sun, which was later published in the *Philosophical Transactions of the Royal Society*. He also recorded the event in his log:

> *'This day proved as favourable to our purpose as we could wish, not a cloud was to be seen the whole day & the air was perfectly clear, so that we had every advantage we could desire in Observing the whole of the passage of the Planet Venus over the Suns disk; we very distinctly saw an Atmosphere or dusky shade round the body of the Planet which very much disturbed the times of the Contact particularly the 2 internal ones. Dr Solander observ'd as well as Mr Green & my self, and we differ'd from one another in observing the times of the Contacts much more than could be expected. Mr Greens Telescope and mine where of the same Mag[n]ifying power but that of the Doctr. was greater than ours, It was nearly calm the whole day & the Thermometer exposed to the Sun about the middle of the Day rose to a degree of heat | 119 | we have not before met with.'*

Following Cook's return to England in 1771, his astronomical observations were quickly overshadowed by his achievement in circumnavigating the globe, charting 5,000 miles of previously unknown coastlines, including New Zealand and the eastern coast of Australia. Banks and Solander returned with prodigious amounts of new species of plants, fish, birds and insects. The transit observations that Cook, Green and Solander each used to calculate the Sun's distance differed significantly from each other and also when compared with the combined results of the other missions owing to a 'black drop effect' which makes it hard to determine the exact timing of the phases of Venus's passage across the Sun. These variations were originally believed to be due to Venus's thick atmosphere, but are in fact caused by turbulence in Earth's atmosphere. Remarkably, Cook's observations have been found to differ from accepted modern values by less than one per cent. In 1771 the British scientist Thomas Hornsby used Cook's observations to calculate that the mean distance of the Earth from the Sun was 93,726,900 English miles. Today, radar has measured the mean distance to be 92,955,000 miles – a testament to the incredible accuracy of Cook's work.

Accident & disease on board

SURGEONS' REPORTS FROM THE GEORGIAN NAVY ... 1730–1830

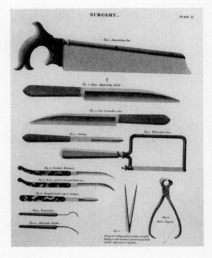

A ship's surgeon in the Georgian navy would have used surgical instruments similar to these. **ABOVE**

At the beginning of the nineteenth century, surgeons at sea were hampered by the limitations of medical knowledge at the time. Major breakthroughs in the field, such as the use of general anaesthesia, and discoveries such as the role of bacteria in disease and the fact that mosquitoes caused yellow fever, were more than half a century away. Many diseases could not be effectively diagnosed, nor could the available medicines – which today would be banned for being too hazardous – treat or cure them.

Disease, not enemy gunfire, was the greatest threat to the Royal Navy throughout the Napoleonic Wars of 1793–1815. Between 1792 and 1815, the Navy employed an average of 109,846 men per year, of whom on average 3,518 (i.e. one man in 31) died as a result of disease or accident; 528 (one man in 208) died through foundering, wreck or fire; and 272 (one man in 403) died in battle. Throughout 1792 to 1815, more than twice as many sailors died of disease in a single typical year than the total number killed (1,483) in the Royal Navy's six major victories during this time (First of June, 1794; Cape of St Vincent, 1797; Camperdown, 1797; Nile, 1798; Copenhagen, 1801; Trafalgar, 1805).

Clearly preserving the health and well-being of its men was in the interests of the Admiralty, from both a fighting efficiency and an economic point of view. Serving men who stayed healthy, and understanding how to keep them healthy and making use of the best medical practices, meant that ships could stay at sea for extended periods, which was particularly important for those on longer voyages – exploration missions, for example – and for those maintaining blockades of enemy ports far from any victualling stations. Healthy crews meant ships could be sailed more efficiently. Health was therefore considered as important as the fighting qualities of the Royal Navy's men and ships – a sentiment summed up by Vice Admiral Nelson, who observed that 'the great thing in all military service is health; and you will agree with me that it is easier for an officer to keep his men healthy, than for a physician to cure them'.

The task of maintaining the health of everybody on board ships of the Royal Navy was the responsibility of the surgeon. Most surgeons received their medical training in Scottish universities, principally those in Edinburgh, Glasgow and Aberdeen. Those who did not attend university served apprenticeships with a practising surgeon ashore, supplementing this with university courses, or by attending lectures by eminent surgeons, or else by observing and assisting in hospitals, familiarising themselves with how patients were treated. What could not be learned in formal education establishments was gleaned from books written by leading surgeons of the Royal Navy – for example, Thomas Trotter's *Medicina nautica* (1799); James Lind's *A Treatise of the Scurvy* (1753); and Gilbert Blane's *Observations on the Diseases of Seamen* (1785). From 1800, those aspiring to become surgeons had to pass a 'viva voce' examination set by the Royal College of Surgeons to test the extent of their medical knowledge in regard to anatomy, surgery and diseases. If a candidate was successful, the college would advise the Royal Navy as to the rate of ship and the capacity in which he should be

Admiral Earl Howe's victory over the French fleet to the west of Ushant, on 1 June 1794 (the Glorious First of June).
BELOW

employed – usually as a surgeon's mate in various classed levels, or in exceptional circumstances as a surgeon before being warranted to a ship by the Navy Board. Admiralty regulations stipulated that surgeons had to provide appropriate medical instruments and medicine chests, which the Royal College of Surgeons checked before each voyage. From 1805, however, medicines were provided free to surgeons.

Surgeons were the only medical officers on board ships, although they were sometimes assisted by a surgeon's mate serving a form of apprenticeship. The surgeon's role combined many of those carried out ashore by surgeons, physicians and apothecaries. They had to treat any medical ailment that presented itself on the ship, including those of a dental and mental nature. As well as carrying out their medical rounds at least twice a day and caring for the sick, from 1806 surgeons were obliged to keep a journal recording the '*general history of the prevailing complaints in the ship; and if any malignant or infectious disease shall have existed to trace their source, and to account for their introduction, stating the means used to destroy the infection and prevent its reappearance*'.

It could be argued that no amount of education or training could have prepared surgeons for some of the unique diseases that were prevalent at sea and that would have stretched to their very limits the medical knowledge and ability of the best surgeons ashore. Diseases such as scurvy, typhus and yellow fever proved fatal in many cases as they incapacitated many and severely reduced the Royal Navy's fighting efficiency; for instance, in 1780, after a six-week cruise, the Channel Fleet had to land 2,400 scurvy sufferers at Haslar Royal Naval Hospital. Aside from scurvy, the deadliest disease that surgeons had to deal with, particularly in tropical climates, was yellow fever.

The journal entries of HMS *Alfred*'s surgeon, W J Warner, reveal that the fever appeared a week after the ship arrived in Jamaica in mid-July 1796, and that of '*more than 200 persons sent from the Alfred*' to Port Royal hospital with the disease, '*not a third survived the third day*'. Warner thought the outbreak had been caused by some crew '*clearing a prize, on … which, were thirty persons, confined to bed, others were at the same time employed to fit out the Malabar, newly arrived from St Nicholas, where she buried most of the officers and crew of a malignant fever*'. Warner graphically describes the disease's symptoms as:

prostration of strength, heavy, sometimes acute pain of the forehead, a severe pain of the loins, joints and extremities, a glazy appearance of with a bloody suffusion of the eye, nausea, or vomiting of bilious, sometimes offensive black matter not unlike coffee grounds, often attended by evacuation by stool of the same kind, the stomach rejecting anything offered, the countenance flushed at other times, pale and dejected with oppressive cold sweating, bleeding at the nostrils, the pulse sometimes for a short period full and quick, but more frequently languid, great thirst, the tongue white and brown at the edge, frequently covered with a white slimy matter, and as the fever advanced, became dry, brown and crusted, a fatal appearance in general ... towards the close of the disorder, a small red rash appeared on the skin, and soon disappeared, leaving livid spots where it had shown itself, and was always a fatal sign'

In these journal entries, Warner then explains the uncertainty among medical officers about the causes of yellow fever, including the opinion of 'Doctor Allenby *... [who] thinks the complaint proceeds from redundancy of bile, or indigested matter, which if not evacuated soon becomes vitiated, and produces the direful symptoms mentioned'*. He also describes the best methods of treatment. Calomel (a derivative of mercury, poisonous in high or multiple doses) was ignored as he was '*not bold enough to give it the trial as recommended*'; strong spruce beer was dismissed as ineffective – '*13 cases on board HMS Dictator treated with this beer, 10 died*'; bloodletting, thought to cure or prevent disease based on the medical theory that blood and other bodily fluids were '*humors*' which needed to be balanced to maintain health, was also not trusted as it was '*an uncertain and perhaps dangerous experiment*', and naval surgeons who used this treatment revealed that '*extreme debility followed, and death soon*' after. Warner extols the merits of Doctor James's Fever products, of camphor (lethal in high doses) along with castile soap and rhubarb, and, having succumbed to yellow fever himself, of '*rhabard pul, calomel, sapon venet in pill form ... followed by Good madeira ... and my common drink ... an infusion of tamarinds with a small glass of brandy to a quart*'.

Surgeons occasionally resorted to unconventional methods to treat medical cases, some of which proved fatal, while others were lifesaving. In his journal, HMS *Atlas*'s surgeon John Duke recounts being called on 20 October 1819 to attend John Baker, a prisoner with pneumonia:

DOCS. 1 & 2 Pages from the journal of WJ Warner, HMS *Alfred*'s surgeon, recounting an episode of yellow fever.

(2)

It is generally allowed to be new in the Country, and is consid=
by most Practitioners a Species of Typhus.

The Symptoms as they appeared on board the Alfred at the
worst period, were prostration of Strength, heavy, some=
=times acute pain of the Forehead, a severe pain of the
Loins, joints, and extremities, a glary appearance of,
with a Bloody suffusion of the Eye, Nausea, or vomiting
of Bilious, sometimes offensive Black Matter, not unlike
Coffee Grounds, often attended with evacuations by Stool
of the same kind; the Stomach rejecting every thing
offered, the Countenance flushed, at other Times Pale
and dejected with oppressive cold sweating, Bleeding
at the Nostrils; the Pulse sometimes for a short period
full and quick, but more frequently languid, great
Thirst, the Tongue white and brown at the edge, frequent=
=ly covered with a white slimy Matter, and as the Fever
advanced, became dry, brown, and crusted; a fatal

(3)

3

appearance in general; but particularly so, when attended with frequent puking and loose Stools; sometimes towards the close of the Disorder, a small red Rash appeared on the Skin, and soon disappeared, leaving livid Spots where it had shewn itself, and was always a fatal Sign.

Of the treatment of this Disorder various modes were tried, all of which I am sorry to say proved ineffectual in very many instances. In speaking of them will first mention Calomel, giving it in frequent doses to a considerable extent with a view to produce Salivation; with respect to its use, I was not bold enough to give it the trial as recommended.

My orders from Captain Drury, were to send every Person the moment of complaining on shore, and in consequence many were sent daily to the Naval Hospital at Port Royal, where the use of Calomel was

'of a most severe and aggravated form ... I was surprised to find him in such a state ...
I found him restless and impatient, sometimes violent and raving, respiration difficult
and labourious ... I immediately abstracted 50 ounces of blood which brought a syncope
(loss of consciousness), and seemed to have relieved him.'

Duke recounts being called again to Baker at 10.30pm to find him:

'in a dangerous state, ... insensible... His respiration was hurried and sterterous, his
features astonishingly shrunk, and his face and neck covered with a cold and clammy
perspiration ... 20 ounces of blood was immediately abstracted ... which again brought
on syncope.'

Having extracted the equivalent of three-and-a-half pints of blood from Baker in
several hours, Duke records that the man died at around 2.15am.

Thomas Tappen, HMS *Arab*'s surgeon, records in his journal how he
medicated James Stevens, who had been bitten twice by a tarantula in the space
of three days. Stevens *'did not complain till the virus had made its way into the system'.*
Tappen described the patients' symptoms *'as sedate melancholy accompanied with*
nausea and a sense of pain in the breast' and observed that *'it is wonderful what a curious*
affect, this poison has on the human frame though not so virulent as that of the scorpion or
centipede, but the melancholy stage is extremely obdurate'. Tappen remedied the situation
by applying *'rum and oil to the affected part'.*

The surgeon on board HMS *Elizabeth* sailing to Quebec recorded journal
entries on 15 June 1825 about Ellen McCarthy, a twelve-year-old girl, after her
mother had brought him a *'lumbricus'* (a tapeworm), eight-and-a-half inches
long, which the patient had vomited. One of these entries reads:

'Complained yesterday evening of pain in the bottom of her belly increased on pressure.
abdomen hard and swollen, picks her nose, starts in her sleep, bowels constipated,
pyrexia, tongue foul, pulse quick, skin hot, great thirst.'

Three days later he observed the child had one motion:

13

Men's Names, Ages, Qualities, Time when and where taken Ill.	The History, Symptoms, Treatment, and daily Progress of the Disease or Hurt.	When discharged to Duty, Died, or sent to the Hospital.
Ellen McCarthys Case Continued	20th a pleasing and evident improvement this morning passed a quiet night takes her drink and recognizes her attendants support the strength continue brandy punch — 21st improves in intellects eyes more lively calls for the bed pan bowells free consistence of ejesta as before makes a large quantity of water repeated Enema without the Turpentine pulse 89 Skin Cool tongue cleaning takes her drink with some difficulty 22nd ut Hora 23rd a shade better this morning passed a quiet night bowells secrete a vast quantity of offensive slimey matter pulse 91 skin cool a great disposition to sleep refuses with much entreaty her drink gets very cross and stubborn 24th a very distressing dry cough	

Men's Names, Ages, Qualities, Time when and where taken Ill.	The History, Symptoms, Treatment, and daily Progress of the Disease or Hurt.	When discharged to Duty, Died, or sent to the Hospital.
	in other respects recovering ℞ Mucil Acacic ℥fs aqua Cinnamoni ℥v ℞ Scillæ ℨi Syr Simpl ℥i ℞ Capus Sit dosis Cochleare Medium urgent tusse — 25th bibere Cont. Medicamenta 26th improving 27th Stools less frequent and approaching to a natural consistence 28th improves rapidly 29th Convalescent —	

*The efficacy of the Ol. Terebinth in worms is pretty clearly to be seen in the foregoing case it will be observed that altho the first dose of Calomel & Jalap dislodged a worm the second had no effect and that persevering in it may bring on incurable debility without the Ol. Tereb. I am confident this little patient would have been lost I have no hesitation in adding my testimony to that of others in favour of the Medicine as the surest and most certain Anthelmintic

'in which two worms were discovered one 13½ inches the other 7. She is very weak and constantly moaning but the heat and fever is decreased and I entertain hopes if she is not too weak of an ultimate recovery support the system with sago and give brandy punch . . . every two hours having no wine on board.'

With the patient fully convalescent by 29 June, the Surgeon reflected that although calomel and jalop dislodged a worm its continued use would have brought about an '*incurable debility*', and he was of the opinion that '*this little patient would have been lost*' without the use of '*ol. Terebenth*' (turpentine oil), adding without hesitation his '*testimony to that of others in favour of the medicine as the surest and most certain anthelmintic*'.

Ben Lara, the surgeon of HMS *Princess Royal*, includes in his journal an amazing lifesaving account of James Callaway, seaman, aged 40, through the ingenious use of tobacco smoke. On 19 January 1802, an apparent corpse was brought on board. It was Callaway, who:

had fallen over the bows of the launch which passed over him . . . another boat endeavouring to assist also drove him under water. He emerged and was again sinking when dragged into the boat. He was about 12 minutes in the water and 20 more elapsed before he was brought on board. He was stripped, laid on a warm bed . . . and rubbed dry with coarse cloths warmed. He was rubbed with dry salt and some heated was applied in a cloth to the scrob cord. He proceeded in this mode for a quarter of an hour without effect . . . Being compelled to relinquish the advantage of the galley . . . he was removed into the bay — here on a warm bed, bottles with hot water, were put under his hams, armpits and to the feet, pewter plates heated and defended with flannel were placed along the spine. Tobacco smoke was conveyed to the lungs through the tube of a common pipe. In three quarters of an hour from his removal into the bay, I observed an obscure palpitation of the heart — the tobacco smoke was urged — In ten minutes from this he sighed faintly and closed his mouth. The smoke was continued — he coughed pulse at the wrist was evident — we desisted from using the smoke he coughed repeatedly — in an hour and 20 minutes from his being brought on board — he spoke — and then swallowed about two tea spoonfuls of brandy and water. In four hours from our first applications he was perfectly collected.'

January 19th. Brought on board an apparent corse — he had fallen over the bows of the launch, which passed over him with a smart breeze — another boat endeavouring to assist, also drove him under water — He emerged, & was again sinking, when dragged into the boat. He was about 12 minutes in the water, & 20 more elapsed before he was brought aboard — He was then stripped, laid on a warm bed, at the side of the galley — & rubbed dry with coarse cloths warmed — He was rubbed with dry salt, & some heated was applied in a cloth to the Scrob. Cord — We proceeded in this mode for a quarter of an hour without effect — Being compelled to relinquish the advantage of the galley fire — he was re=moved into the bay — & here on a warm bed — bottles with hot water, were put under his hams, arm pits & to the feet — Pewter plates heated, & defended with flannel were placed along the Spine. Tobacco smoke was conveyed to the lungs through the tube of a common pipe — In three quarters of an hour from his removal into the bay, I observed an obscure palpitation of the heart — the tobacco smoke was urged — In ten minutes from this he sighed faintly, & closed his mouth — The smoke was continued — he coughed — pulse at the wrist was evident — We desisted from using the smoke — he coughed repeatedly — In an hour & 20 minutes from his being brought onboard — He spoke — & then swallowed about two tea Spoonsfull of brandy & water — In four hours from our first applications, he was perfectly collected.

A naturalist's voyage of discovery

CHARLES DARWIN ON HMS *BEAGLE* ... 1831–36

Charles Robert Darwin was born in 1809 in Shrewsbury. The son of the local doctor, Darwin attended university at Edinburgh and Cambridge, where he initially studied medicine before deciding on a clerical career in the Church of England. At Cambridge, Darwin became fascinated with botany and took part in many field trips. On completion of his studies, he began planning an expedition to Tenerife to study the local flora and fauna of the region.

In 1831, Darwin received a letter from his tutor at Cambridge, the Reverend John Henslow, asking whether he would be interested in serving as a naturalist on a two-year trip to Terra del Fuego, returning home via the East Indies. The letter changed Darwin's life. He accepted, and in December set sail on HMS *Beagle*, a converted ten-gun brig sloop, ninety feet in length, with a crew of seventy-four. Commanded by Captain Robert FitzRoy, a nephew of the Duke of Grafton, the *Beagle* was commissioned by the Admiralty to undertake a hydrographic survey of South America. Intended to last two years, the expedition ended up taking five years to complete, returning to England in October 1836.

The naturalist Charles Darwin, 1809–82, painted in 1840 by George Richmond.
ABOVE

DOCS. 1 & 2 Charles Darwin's letter accepting a place on board HMS *Beagle*, 1831.

The voyage of the *Beagle* was a key event in Darwin's life and one of the most important scientific expeditions in history. It provided an unparalleled opportunity to collect a wide range of plants and animals and to make scientific observations on the geology and topography of the region explored. The *Beagle* was equipped with scientific instruments, including the latest marine chronometers used to calculate longitude and clinometers for measuring angles and elevations.

In the course of the expedition, the *Beagle* visited Brazil (April to July 1832), Tierra del Fuego (December 1832 to January 1833), Patagonia (April 1833 to January 1834), the Galapagos Islands (September to October 1835) and Cape Town (May to June 1836). As Darwin was not a regular member of the crew, he was not involved in the day-to-day duties of running the ship and often

September the 1st Rec'd
Shrewsbury

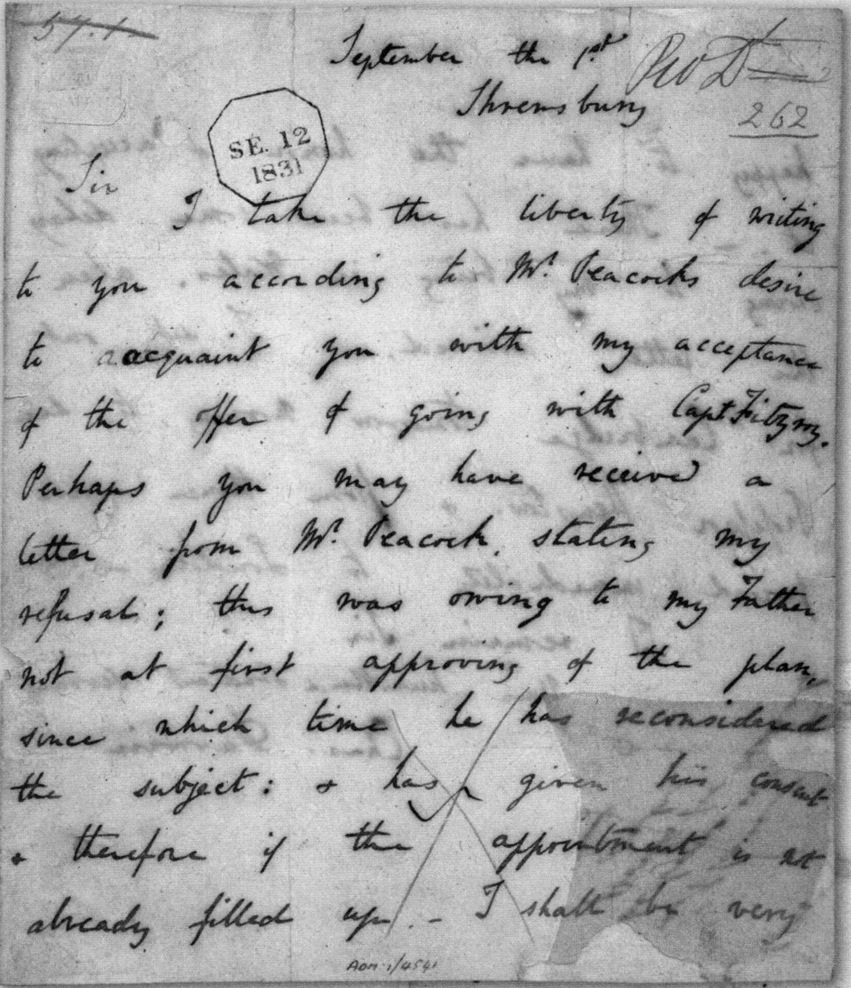

262

SE. 12
1831

Sir
         I take the liberty of writing
to you according to M.r Peacocks desire
to acquaint you with my acceptance
of the offer of going with Capt Fitzroy.—
Perhaps you may have received a
letter from M.r Peacock, stating my
refusal; this was owing to my Father
not at first approving of the plan,
since which time he has reconsidered
the subject: & has given his consent
& therefore if the appointment is not
already filled up.— I shall be very

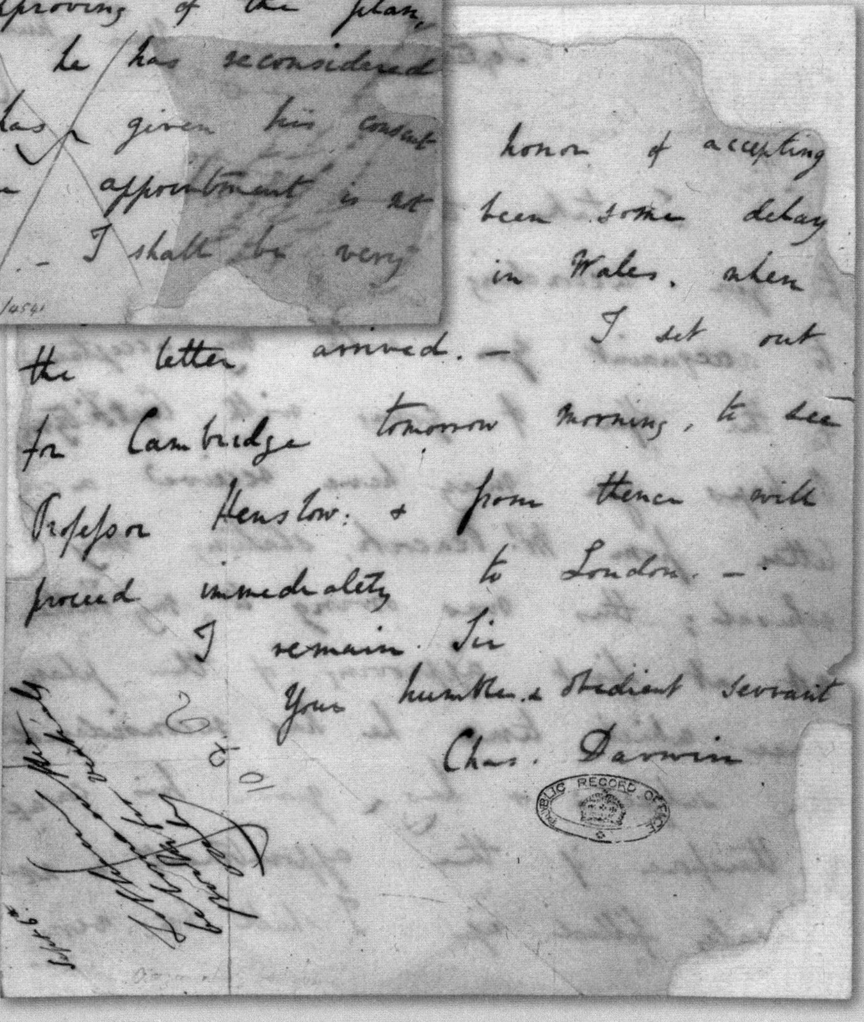

honor of accepting
been some delay
in Wales, when
the letter arrived.— I set out
for Cambridge tomorrow morning, to see
Professor Henslow: & from thence will
proceed immediately to London.—
            I remain Sir
                 Your humble & obedient servant
                          Chas. Darwin

PUBLIC RECORD OFFICE

seized the opportunity to travel overland. These excursions were not without danger. In November 1834, he witnessed the eruption of the Osorno volcano in southern Chile, and in February 1835 he experienced a large earthquake that destroyed the Chilean town of Concepción. On another occasion, he was taken seriously ill with fever and needed five weeks to recover, staying in the house of an old school friend in the port city of Valparaíso, also in Chile. Darwin used his time on the mainland collecting a wide range of fossils, plants and insects that he then carefully catalogued and classified on his return to London.

In September 1835, the *Beagle* sailed to the Galápagos Islands for a five-week study of the island's flora and fauna. According to Darwin, the Galápagos were a paradise for reptiles, boasting three types of turtles, a

A map of Table Bay and Cape Town from 1833 showing wine merchants' stores and warehouses. **BELOW**

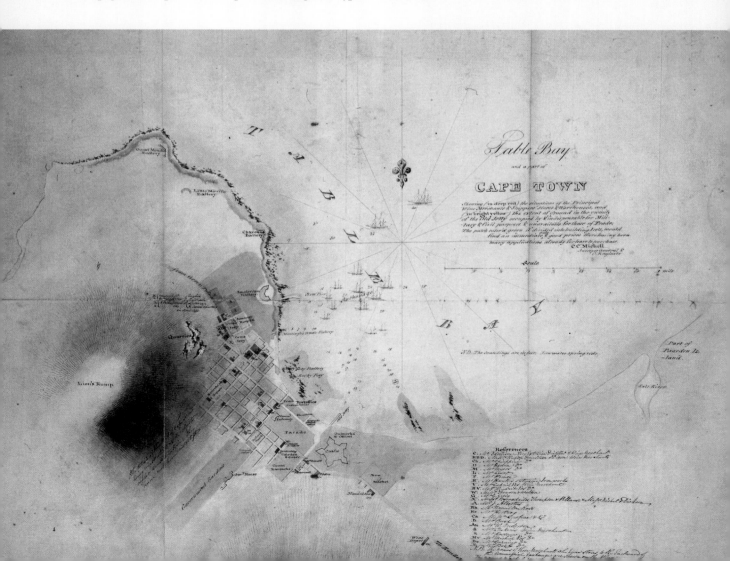

1. Geospiza magnirostris.
3. Geospiza parvula.

2. Geospiza fortis.
4. Certhidea olivasea.

Sketches of four species of finches by Charles Darwin showing the differences in the size of their beaks. **LEFT**

giant tortoise and a variety of black iguanas which were christened 'the imps of darkness'. Darwin was also fascinated by the bird life, particularly taken by the finches and mockingbirds that appeared to be peculiar to the island. The geology of the region was a further puzzle. As a result of the 1835 earthquake, Darwin found the shoreline had been elevated by a few feet, leaving mussel beds high and dry. These observations confirmed his belief that the Earth was not static but had gradually been shaped over millennia, which provided sufficient time for evolution by natural selection to have occurred.

During the *Beagle*'s five-year voyage, its captain, Robert FitzRoy, kept in regular touch with the Admiralty in London via a series of letters that can now be found at The National Archives. In November 1832, he informed London that '*the Beagle had sailed from Monte Video on the 19th of August and from that day to the 8th of September was employed surveying the coast between the River Plate and Bahia Blanca.*' In September 1834, FitzRoy notified the Admiralty that the *Beagle* had arrived safely in the port of Valparaíso and was being refitted for a further voyage. The journey there is described by him in the following terms:

'The Beagle sailed from the Falkland Islands on the 7th of April — employed a month on the western coast of Patagonia and two months in and near the straits of Magellan. She arrived at San Carlos in the Island of Chiloe on the 28th June and sailed hence for Valparaiso.'

On 5 September 1835, FitzRoy informed the Admiralty that:

'on the 29th of June, the Beagle sailed from Valparaiso with eight months stores and provisions on board — she visited Capiapo, and Iquique; and anchored in Callao Bay [Peru] on the 21st of July. I rejoined her, on the 10th of August — since that time the small vessel mentioned in my letter (No.21) has been fitted and in every way prepared for continuing the coast survey of Peru — and many very valuable manuscript documents relating to the hydrography of South America have been obtained.

Views of Chatham Island in the Galapagos, sketched from HMS *Beagle* in 1835. **BELOW**

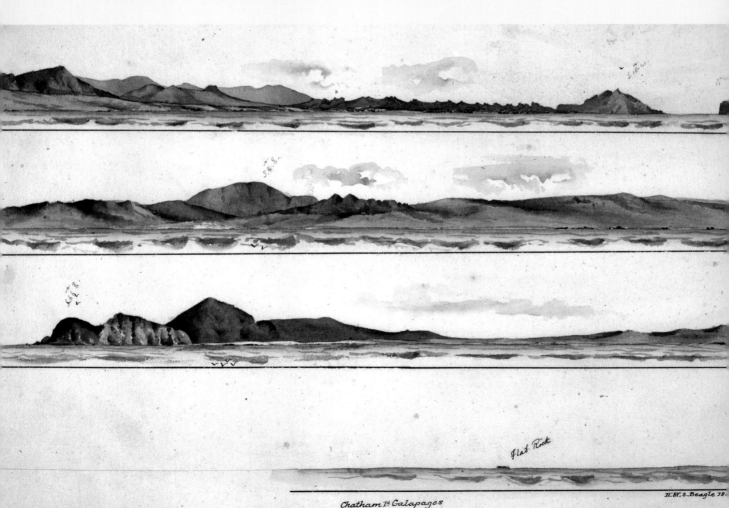

Flat Rock

Chatham I.ᵈ Galapagos

H.M.S.Beagle 18.

Tomorrow (6th September) the Beagle will sail hence – direct for the Galapagos Islands – thence she will go to the Marquesas [French Polynesia] – the Society and Friendly Islands [Tonga] – New Zealand and to Port Jackson in New Holland [Australia].'

DOCS. 3, 4 & 5 Letter from Captain FitzRoy on 5 September 1835 informing the Admiralty of the *Beagle*'s route from Valparaiso.

Evidently this route was altered, as in a letter to the Admiralty dated February 1836, FitzRoy describes the voyage as follows:

'As my letter (No.24 – Sydney – 29th January 1836) may not have arrived I now mention that after the Beagle had completed the survey of the Galapagos Islands; – (in October) – she went to Tahiti – passing through the dangerous archipelago and adding two – if not three, new islands to the list of those known. From Tahiti we sailed on the 26th of November – and on the 21st of December arrived at the Bay of Islands, in New Zealand. Thence the Beagle sailed on the 30th of December – anchored in Port Jackson on the 12th and left that port on the 30th ultimo. From King George's Sound, the Beagle will probably go to Swan River, – and perhaps to the Keeling Islands, – in her way to the Mauritius. She will probably arrive at the Cape of Good Hope about the end of June, and in England during the month of September. A report of the condition of Her Majesty's sloop is enclosed. I have the honour of being, Sir, Your very obedient humble servant. Robt. Fitzroy Captain.'

Darwin was not a natural sailor: he was often seasick, and longed to return home. In October 1836, FitzRoy informed the Admiralty that the *Beagle* had returned to Falmouth and was waiting 'to perform such further service as their Lordships may decide proper'. Darwin did not wait for a reply, disembarking immediately. Two days later he was back with his family in Shrewsbury.

In 1839, Darwin published his daily journal that he had written aboard the *Beagle* of his experiences and observations gained during the voyage. Over the next twenty years, he sought to make sense of how animal species he had seen on the voyage had diversified and adapted to their habitats. His findings were made known to the public in his famous book *On the Origin of Species by Means of Natural Selection*, published in 1859. The book introduced the idea that animal populations evolve over generations via a process of natural selection and

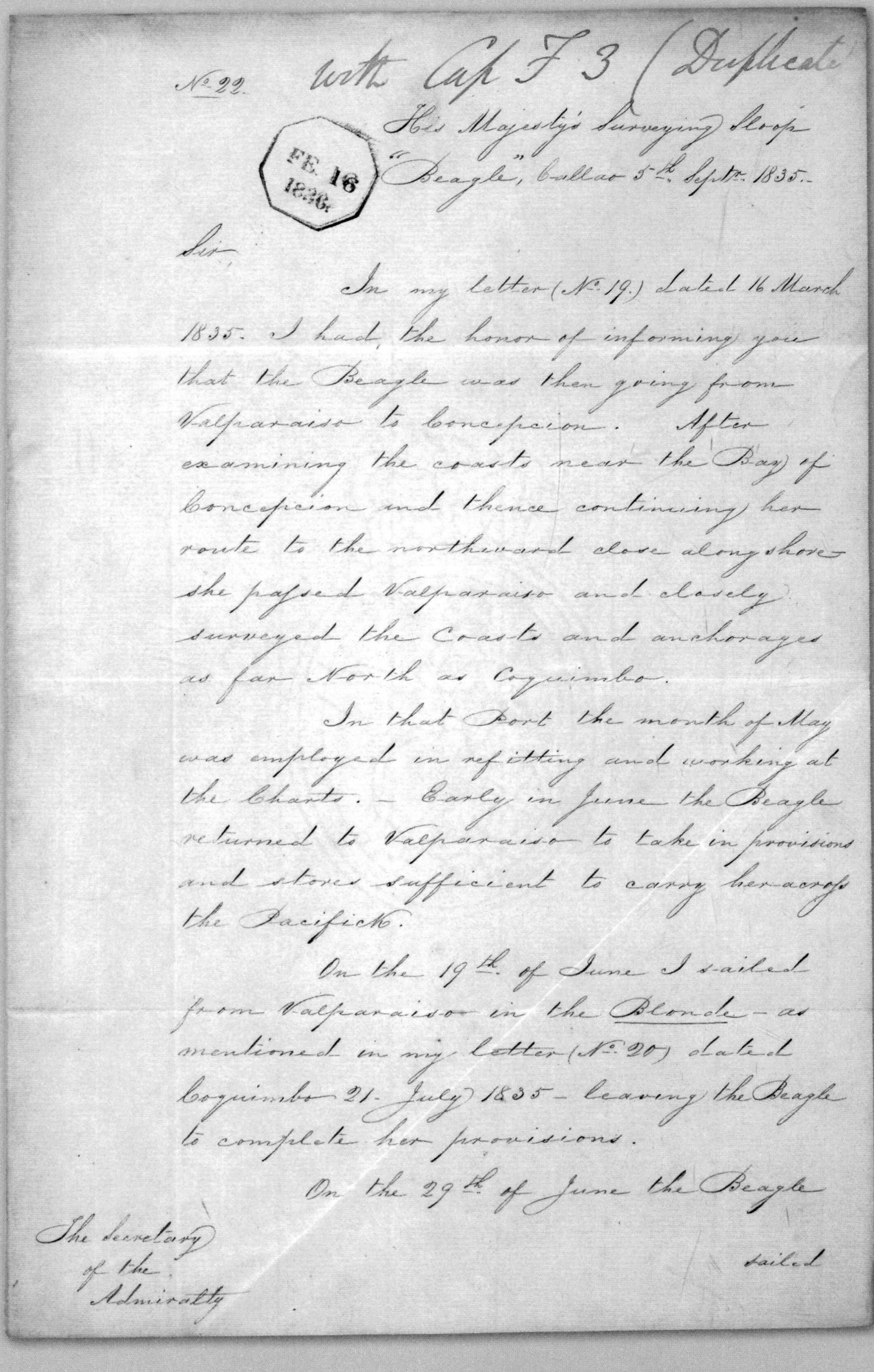

No 22.   with Cap F 3 (Duplicate)

His Majesty's Surveying Sloop
"Beagle", Callao 5th Septr. 1835.—

FE. 16
1836.

Sir,

In my letter (No. 19.) dated 16 March
1835. I had the honor of informing you
that the Beagle was then going from
Valparaiso to Concepcion. After
examining the coasts near the Bay of
Concepcion and thence continuing her
route to the northward close alongshore
she passed Valparaiso and closely
surveyed the coasts and anchorages
as far North as Coquimbo.

In that Port the month of May
was employed in refitting and working at
the Charts.— Early in June the Beagle
returned to Valparaiso to take in provisions
and stores sufficient to carry her across
the Pacifick.

On the 19th of June I sailed
from Valparaiso in the Blonde—as
mentioned in my letter (No. 20) dated
Coquimbo 21. July 1835 — leaving the Beagle
to complete her provisions.

On the 29th of June the Beagle

The Secretary
of the
Admiralty

sailed

sailed from Valparaiso with eight months stores and provisions on board — she visited Copiapo, & Iquique; and anchored in Callao Bay on the 21st of July).

I rejoined her, on the 10th of August — since that time the small vessel mentioned in my letter (No 21) has been fitted and in every way prepared for continuing the coast Survey of Peru — and many very valuable Manuscript documents relating to the Hydrography of South America have been obtained.

To morrow (6th September) the Beagle will sail hence — direct for the Galapagos Islands. — Thence she will go to the Marquesas — the Society and Friendly Islands — New Zealand and to Port Jackson in New Holland.

At that Port I hope to arrive in March.

Passing through Torres Straits — the Beagle will go to the Mauritius — and ought to arrive at the Cape of Good Hope in July). From the Cape she will continue her voyage towards England.

A Report of the condition of

His Majesty's Sloop – Documents for the
Hydrographer – and Periodical Returns
accompany this letter.

I have the honor of being
Sir
Your very obedient
humble Servant.

Robt FitzRoy Captain

suggested that the diversity seen in the natural world arose by common descent through evolution. Darwin based his theory on the evidence that he had gathered during his voyage on the Beagle and on his subsequent experimentation.

Darwin's book proved controversial as it contradicted biblical teaching that all creatures were created by God and unchanging, and he spent the remainder of his life defending his theory of evolution against attacks from the Church and the religious establishment. However, it has been described as one of the most influential books in human history. Darwin died in 1882 and is buried in Westminster Abbey.

Sketch of the 'Beagle Channel' drawn in 1834. **ABOVE**

Scurvy on a convict ship

HENRY W MAHON ON HMAS *BARROSA* ... 1841

While scurvy has been around for a long time, the cure has been lost and found many times through the centuries. The Egyptians recorded cases of scurvy over three and a half thousand years ago, and it was documented by Hippocrates hundreds of years later. It is therefore surprising that by the mid-nineteenth century scurvy was still deadly. It killed those with little access to fresh fruit and a poor diet, and as such, was the scourge of those at sea.

The convict ship *Barrosa* left Sheerness on the north coast of Kent on 30 August 1841 with a 'cargo' of 348 male convicts bound for Van Diemen's Land (now Tasmania) to serve out their transportation sentences. For the first few months of the voyage, the ship surgeon, Henry W Mahon spent his time treating the various diseases that seemed to turn up wherever seamen went, whether on land or at sea. According to his daily sick book, he had encountered gonorrhoea, syphilis, ulcers, hernia, herpes, bronchitis and rheumatism, all within the early stages of the five-month voyage to Australia. But two months into the journey, on 5 November 1841, he treated Abraham Baker for the first symptoms of 'Scorbutus' – scurvy. Entries for Baker for 5, 7, 10 12, 14 and 17 November chart the frightening speed with which the disease took over Baker's body, until an entry made on 21 November simply states: '*Discharged Cured, lime juice was continued to the end of the month when there did not appear any further symptoms of scurvy*'. Unfortunately, however, Baker succumbed again in December.

The 106 cases that Mahon recorded compelled him to emphasise in his log the excellence of the conditions under which the prisoners were kept. His sense of confusion is clear as he writes about the enforced bathing, about the men being shaved twice a week and having to wear clean clothes on a Sunday and about cooks not being allowed to serve 'slush' on pain of punishment. Interestingly, he concludes that the fact that more prisoners continued to succumb to the disease despite these precautions may have been a result of 'their previous habits', and he admits that lime juice was administered primarily to treat diarrhoea.

Citrus Limonum

Lemons and other citrus fruits were known to alleviate the symptoms of scurvy although doctors in the nineteenth century did not know why this should be.
ABOVE

DOC. 1 Page from the journal of Henry Mahon from his time on *Barrosa*.

11

Nature of Disease.	No. of Case	Men's Names, Ages, Qualities, Time when and where taken ill, and how disposed of.	The History, Symptoms, Treatment, and Daily Progress of the Disease or Hurt.
Scorbutus.	7	Abraham Baker Ætat 19. Prisoner put on the Sick list the 5th of November and discharged cured on the 21st November. Readmitted on the 20th of Decr and discharged into the Colonial Hospital at Hobart Town on the 14th of Jany 1842.	This Prisoner is of a fair complexion and plethoric habit of body. States that he observed a spot this morning for the first time a little above the ankle of the left leg. Its size is about that of a half crown piece; colour dark red and on the surface, with slight suffusion; small Papillæ of both legs; appetite bad; skin cool and rough; pulse regular; tongue clean; Bowels costive; no tenderness of Gums, swelling of face or enlargement of tongue. A purgative draught immediately. 1½ Lime juice iced with sugar three times a day. Cold evaporating lotion and bandage to Leg. 7th The livid redness now similar to Petechiæ occupies half the leg and is beginning to appear on the other; not severe. 10th Ecchymosis on both legs of equal extent rather more livid. Papillæ stationary, Legs and feet Ødematous, no pain complained of. Ut Antea 12th Livid colour fading, Petechiæ remain; no uneasiness anywhere complained of. Repeat 14th The appearance on the legs is that of an Ecchymosis when absorption begins, namely yellowness taking place of redness. The Papillæ are also much lighter. Ut supra. 17th Yellowness of the legs only; Ødema much less. Health good, appetite improved. 21st Discharged cured. Lime juice was continued to the end of the month when there did not appear any further symptoms of scurvy.
		December 20th Readmitted with sponginess of Gums, Epigastric pain, purple ecchymosis and livid papillæ on both legs which are somewhat tumefied. Ordered 3oz Lime juice & 2dr (?) twice in the day, which he took till the 31st without much benefit. Jany 1st 3oz L juice daily Salt provisions discontinued 5th Bled to 10oz Coagamentum thick & firm without Serum. 14th Finding no improvement he was sent ashore for Hospital treatment. The Lime juice	which are somewhat tumefied. Ordered 3oz Lime juice & 2dr twice in the day, which he took till the 31st without much benefit. Jany 1st 3oz L juice daily 5th Bled to 10oz Coagamentum thick & firm without Serum. 14th Finding was sent ashore for Hospital treatment. The Lime juice taking place, a Combination of L. juice with Nitre, which he took for ten days, failed. The same may be said of the Lime juice prescribed afterwards. Ten days

(left margin, vertically) Bleeding effected a cure at first, but on the relapse for ten days, failed. The same may be said of the Lime juice prescribed afterwards. Ten days

(left margin) Blee Ecchymosis indeed lumps staying at

(right margin, vertically) to another Regimen and fresh Air. — In number his surgery sent to his surgeon into the hospital, he was discharged cured.

This delay in the appearance of scurvy on the voyage is explained by how the disease actually runs its course. As a by-product of malnutrition, due specifically to a lack of vitamin C, scurvy manifests itself where access to fresh food is limited. A month of little or no vitamin C will cause lethargy and fatigue. Later, patients become short of breath, bruise easily, their wounds do not heal and they may start to lose teeth. Jaundice, fever and convulsions can follow, and, if left untreated, this results in death. The isolation of seafarers, confined to the vessel on which they were travelling, made them scurvy's most notorious victims. Indeed, an estimated 2,000,000 sailors died of the disease between 1500 and 1800, and it wasn't just the sailors who were affected – scurvy posed significant problems too for the most revered of voyagers.

Vasco da Gama had lost half of his crew to scurvy in 1499, the outbreak only being halted as a result of trading with the locals along the east coast of Africa for oranges. As da Gama's crew started to recover, he noted in his journal: '*It pleased God in his mercy that all our sick recovered their health for the air of the place is very good.*'

Ferdinand Magellan, a Portuguese explorer, lost all but twenty-two of his crew of 230 to scurvy, and in 1507, Pedro Álvares Cabral, also from Portugal, had found that citrus fruit was a cure for the disease among his crew. The link between citrus fruits and scurvy was therefore known during this so-called Age of Discovery, and had been the subject of experiments and treatises, including those by the physicians Johan Backstrom and James Lind, the latter of whom published *A Treatise of the Scurvy*, in which the first clinical links were made. As early as 1593, Admiral Sir Richard Hawkins recommended drinking orange and lemon juice to prevent scurvy, and this was backed up in 1614 by the surgeon general of the East India Company, John Woodall, who published *The Surgeon's Mate*, a handbook for apprentice surgeons aboard the company's ships. He could not, however, actually explain why eating citrus fruits prevented and cured scurvy, so his work on the subject was largely ignored by the medical establishment.

Poor communication between sailors and those responsible for their well-being, coupled with lack of facility to store fresh food on board ships, ensured that scurvy continued to ravage crews. Indeed, the British Admiralty

Graphic sketches by Henry Mahon showing the effects of scurvy on various parts of the body. **ABOVE**

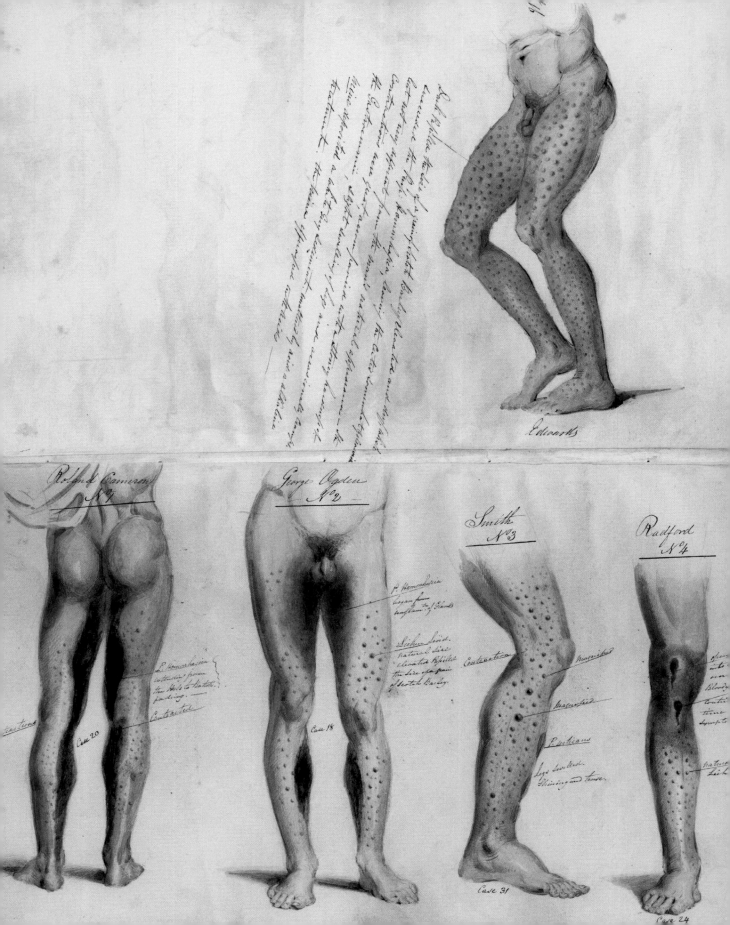

Edwards

Roland Cameron
Nº 1

George Ogden
Nº 2

Smith
Nº 3

Radford
Nº 4

Case 20

Case 18

Case 31

Case 24

was sufficiently concerned to issue citrus juice as standard on its ships from 1795 onwards. However, it was not until 1927, when 'hexuronic acid' (vitamin C) was isolated by Hungarian biochemist Albert Szent-Györgyi, that science could provide a reliable cure. The acid's efficacy in treating scurvy was proved five years later by Charles Glen King and, staying true to the Latin roots of the disease's name, it was renamed ascorbic acid.

Writing in the middle of the nineteenth century, Mahon, like Woodall, knew that there was a link between fresh fruit and scurvy, even if he could not explain it. All of the patients featured in his illustrations were prescribed upwards of two ounces of lime juice to be taken daily, although the results were mixed. Underlining his words to show his frustration, Mahon explains that '*Case 19*', 39-year-old Daniel Keep, whose leg is the middle one of the three to the right in the illustration, was given lime juice for '*twenty days without benefit*'. Similarly, Joseph Shaw, whose leg is illustrated below Keep's, made slow progress in his recovery, although Mahon concedes that the juice '*may probably have retarded its progress towards a fatal issue*'. Ultimately, however, the death count supported Mahon's use of lime juice: of the 106 cases of scurvy on the *Barrosa*, only a handful proved fatal, with most of the deaths occurring in the Colonial Hospital after the ship's arrival on 14 January 1842 in the harbour at Hobart.

Series of graphic sketches by Henry Mahon showing the effects of scurvy on various parts of the body. LEFT

Exotic flora & fauna

ZOOLOGICAL & BOTANICAL RESEARCH, HMS *SAMARANG* ... 1843–46

'The survey of the various coasts and islands of the Eastern Seas made by Sir Edward Belcher in HMS Samarang afforded many valuable opportunities for adding to our knowledge of the Zoology of those parts of the world.'

Expeditions like Belcher's led to exotic discoveries like these previously unknown snakes, thus helping to advance the zoology of that part of the world. In 1849, the Belcher's sea snake, *belcheri* was named in his honour. **RIGHT**

Thus began the zoological report on Edward Belcher's four-year voyage of exploration on its publication in 1850.

HMS *Samarang*, first launched by the East India Company in Cochin in 1822, had seen action in the First Opium War (1839–42) before being placed under Belcher's command for this survey and for extensive zoological studies of the East Indian Archipelago, the East Indies, the Philippines and Borneo. The expedition aimed to use every facility at its disposal in the pursuit of science, making observations, collecting specimens and making sketches and drawings of rare forms to help advance zoological knowledge of that part of the world.

Belcher brought home many drawings of the different animals and plants he had observed, as well many specimens. Many of the drawings had been sketched by Arthur Adams, a Linnean Society fellow, malacologist (expert in molluscs), naturalist and editor of HMS *Samarang*'s zoological report. As the assistant surgeon, Adams was one of two medical officers on board HMS *Samarang*, the other being Henry Walsh Mahon, the surgeon.

It is through the medical officer's journal that Mahon kept that the quality of the zoological research findings and the fine drawing skills of Arthur Adams can be seen and appreciated. Take, for example, Mahon's vivid description of the *hydrophis fasciatus* (striped sea snake):

'head small and triangular, nostrils neither vertical nor acuminated, nose or muzzle dirty yellow, and a streak of the same colour extends backwards above the eye, and another below, along the upper jaw, iris grey, and eyes sunk and piercing, tongue fleshy,

a broad yellow line reaches from the chin along the gular region, bounded on either side by masses of black. Body cylindrical, of a bright grey blue colour, banded with distinct black rings, the grey insensibly blending in the whitish yellow of side and abdomen. Scales of back are regular and uniform, and there is one row of abdominal scuta which on the under surface of the tail subdivides into two series; tail compressed; two edged and flattened like the blade of an oar. Upper jaw furnished on either side by a poison fang – the species from which the figure was taken measured only eighteen inches in length, 1½ in circumference had 50 black bands ⅛ of inch broad, which united on the abdomen. Common in Manila Bay, Sooloo, China and Indian Seas, and coast of Borneo. Varieties of the last described, measuring upwards of six feet in length are frequently seen at sea, and occasionally found in nests coiled together among rocks, above high water mark, where they have glided and secreted themselves for the purpose of casting off the old skin, the colour however is far different being of a faded grey and dirty yellowish white, instead of the bright greyish blue of the smaller species, they are likewise unprovided with poison fangs, notwithstanding which, an officer belonging to HMS Wolf was bitten in 1837, by one of this description and died in the course of a few hours afterwards. The sea snakes swim gracefully on the surface of the water in calm weather, and are not very timid.'

Mahon then describes the medicinal properties and appearance of the *Cassia alata* (or Acapulco of Manila) plant which Philippine natives extolled for its healing qualities '*in curing ring worm and herpes*':

'*… this plant or shrub grows to the height of about nine feet and attains the size of a man's leg; the natives call it by different proverbial names but that by which it is commonly known is Gamot Sa Luni. The natives rub the ringworm or eruption firmly, and for some time with the fresh bruised leaves, until the vessels burst or bleed, they are then cleaned by a napkin, and covered with some simple cerate. This operation is resorted to every fifth day.*'

Mahon's journal also contains a drawing of a *Semnopithecus nasalis* (long-nosed monkey) of Borneo. Tellingly. an annotation on the sketch makes it clear that this specimen did not survive, its skin sent to the Haslar Medical Museum in Gosport.

Observations

on the Sea Snakes of the Southern Ocean

Class Reptilia;   Order Ophidia;   Family Anguis;

Genus Hydrus;   Subgenus Hydrophus

Example of Species. Pelamis Bicolor. This species is common in the China, Sooloo, and Mindoro seas; the head is triangular, distended at the cheeks; muzzle somewhat acute, mouth large, and the eyes projecting a little, are of a dusky color, with a light yellow Iris; dorsal band very black, well defined. and not blending with the yellow of the sides and belly which are of a bright yellow color. Row of abdominal scuta large and scabrous; lozenge shaped marks on the caudal moiety, extending to the vent; tail compressed, flattened and two edged, but rounded at the extremity like the blade of an oar. Teeth maxillary and pallatine without the true prison fang, or venom gland, but there are small apertures at the base of the two terminal pallatine teeth, which are visible under a magnifying power, and may probably serve the same purpose. There were four varieties of this genus observed, differing chiefly in the depth or lightness of the dorsal line in the yellowish white of sides and belly; in the shape of head; turmid throat; likewise spotted tail.

No 2. Hydrophis Circumcinctus _ Chloris? Head small, acuminated and of a greenish brown, plaited with hexagonal scales, nostril vertical and acuminated; body compressed; abdominal Scuta hexagonal, and larger than the other scales; tail flattened and two edged; Color yellow with dark brown rings extending the entire length of the body at equidistant spaces, and broader on the back than belly _ Tail brownish black, with straw colored bands on the upper part _ Has two prison fangs in the upper jaw. Common in the China Sea and in Manila bay. Length from 15 to 20 inches.

No 3. Hydrophis fasciatus vel platurus fasciatus. Head small and triangular; nostrils neither vertical nor acuminated, nose or muzzle dirty yellow, and a streak of the same color extends backwards above the eye, and another below, along the upper jaw.

iris grey; and eye sunk and piercing, tongue fleshy, a broad yellow line reaches from the chin along the gular region, bounded on either side by masses of black. Body cylindrical, of a bright grey blue color, banded with distinct black rings, the grey insensibly blending in the whitish yellow of side and abdomen. Scales of back are regular and uniform; and there is one row of abdominal scuta, which on the under surface of the tail subdivides into two series; tail compressed, two edged, and flattened like the blade of an oar. Upper jaw furnished on either side by a poison fang. The species from which the figure was taken measured only 18 inches in length. 1½ in circumference - had 80 black bands 1/8 of an inch broad, which united on the abdomen. Common in Manila Bay, Sooloo, China, and Indian Seas, and coast of Borneo. Varieties of the last described, measuring upwards of six feet in length, are frequently seen at sea, and occasionally found in nests coiled together among rocks, above high water mark, where they have glided and secreted themselves for the purpose of casting off the old skin, the color however is far different, being of a faded grey and dirty yellowish white, instead of the bright greyish blue of the smaller species, they are likewise unprovided with poison fangs, notwithstanding which, an officer belonging to H.M.S Wolf, was bitten in 1837. by one of this description, and died in the course of a few hours afterward. The sea snakes swim gracefully on the surface of the water in calm weather, and are not very timid. When about to descend, the head is first raised out of the water, it then plunges downward striking with its oar like tail to give impetuosity to its progress. From the contents of the stomach I infer that small fishes, Medusæ and crustacea constitute their principal food. The lungs resemble the air bladders of fishes, being simple sacs, without cell, and having vessels ramifying over its parieties. The species are very numerous, of beautiful exterior and the most poisonous of all the Ophidian race found in the southern seas or its divisions, and are easily distinguished by their peculiar oar shaped tails, and bright yellow

or

The Cassia Alata or
Acapulco of Manila
Leguminosæ. Tribe Mimiosæ

Arthur Adams delt.

A sketch of *Cassia alata* a diuretic shrub from the medical journal of HMS *Samarang*. **LEFT**

Described by Adams as a member of the Semnopithecus family, this monkey is known more commonly as a grey langur. Unfortunately, the sketch makes it clear that this individual didn't survive the voyage; his skin was sent to the Haslar Museum in Gosport. **BELOW**

This report and the success of the zoological aspect of Belcher's expedition mask the trials, tribulations and adventures faced by his crew on board HMS *Samarang* during this voyage. At the outset, Belcher was given carte blanche by the Admiralty to carry '*this great survey into effect*' with the reassurance that it would give implicit directions to the commander-in-chief to prohibit '*his interfering with your proceedings, or permitting any casual Senior officer, with whom you may fall in, to control or meddle with you in an way, unless in cases of extreme exigency, and we shall direct him to keep up your supplies, so as to enable you to carry out this important service with uninterrupted energy, and to continue on it till you receive further orders from us*'.

On leaving Falmouth at the start of the voyage, Belcher received an Admiralty order to visit Sarawak in Borneo to communicate with James Brooke (who had been made Rajah of Sarawak in 1841, having assisted the Sultan of Brunei in crushing a rebellion), and then to proceed to Borneo proper to examine and report on the coal measures of that district and obtain a sufficient amount to trial on board Admiralty steamers.

When HMS *Samarang* reached Sarawak, Mahon described an incident which took place that could have jeopardised the whole expedition:

> '*in the act of dropping down the river [Sarawak] on the 17 July 1843 accidentally got upon a reef of rocks at high water about a mile from the town of Kuchin [Kuching]… The tide falling … [HMS Samarang] … fell over on her beam ends on the starboard side filling the starboard cabins (including that appropriated for me) with water that soon got putrid and of a dark colour. In this condition notwithstanding every exertion used she remained during a period of 11 days, which caused extraordinary deposits of mud in the cabins of the starboard side. The glue used in making chest of draws and desks, became dissolved and thus their contents were scattered about, floating in water, which was up to the hatchways of the ship. In attempting to save my accounts, I sustained some severe contusions and slight but painful wounds of both legs.*'

In claiming compensation for the accident, a dejected Belcher stated: '*I feel perfectly unable to attach any particular value to papers, books and stationery, and other apparatus, chemicals and delicate instruments prepared for this voyage, which have been swept away*', and he went on to bemoan the loss of '*5 years supply of perishable cabin necessaries*'.

DOC. 3 Henry Mahon's report of the expedition reaching Sarawak on 17 July 1843.

original

H. M. S. Samarang Sarawak River Borneo
Aug 11. 1843

Return of Articles of Clothing &c. lost on Service belonging to Dr. Henry W. Mahon Surgeon of H. M. S. Samarang on the 17th July 1843

Articles	£	s	d	Remarks
15 Shirts white	4	15	0	H. M. S. Samarang Commanded
4 do Blue	1	0	0	by Captain Sir Edward Belcher in the
15 Socks cotton	-	15	0	act of dropping down the river on the
2 Waistcoats Elastic under	-	7	6	17th of July 1843 accidentally got
4 do White uniform Kersey	3	0	0	upon a reef of rocks at high water
1 do Blue do	-	17	6	about a mile from the town of
1 Full dress Belt /new	2	15	0	Kuchin: the tide falling she fell over
1 Undress do do	-	18	0	on her beam ends on the Starboard
1 Uniform Undress coat /new	4	10	0	side filling the starboard cabins
1 Do Jacket Blue	1	17	5	(including that appropriated for
2 Uniform Caps	1	1	0	my use) with water that soon
1 Gold Lace for caps	-	11	6	got putrid and of a dark color.
1 Super blue Trowsers /new	2	0	0	In this condition notwithstanding
1 do Black do do	2	0	0	every exertion used she re-
3 White drill Trowsers	3	0	0	-mained during a period of
4 do duck do	1	16	0	11 days, which caused extra-
1 White Jacket /grass cloth	-	15	0	-ordinary deposit of mud in the
12 do Silk pocket handke	2	2	0	Cabin of the Starboard side. The
8 Red do do	2	0	0	Glue used in making Chest of
2 White Cambric	-	6	0	draws and desks &c. became
2 Black Silk do	-	12	0	dissolved and thus their contents
Black do ribbon	-	6	6	were scattered about, floating
6 Gloves white	-	15	0	in water which was up to
Stationary for five Years	5	0	0	the Hatchways of the Ship.
Bedding	7	0	0	In attempting to save my ac-
Books & other necessaries	8	0	0	-counts I sustained some severe
Mess articles	5	0	0	Contusions and slight but painful
£	63	2	6	wounds of both legs, which have

not yet recovered. In justice to myself I beg to state that £ 200. would not defray the expenses of fitting out for a five years servitude in the station and unfortunately purchases must be made on very dis-ad-vantageous terms.

Through the exertions of her crew, however, HMS *Samarang* was recovered and, her provisions having been replenished, completed the object of her mission to Borneo. Once the survey of the off-lying islands of the Eastern Archipelago had been completed, and after an encounter with some Illanon pirates off Gilolo, HMS *Samarang* returned to Singapore, where she joined HMS *Dido* in her Sakarran expedition to suppress piracy. With the aid of an East India Company ship, *Phlegethon*, placed at his disposal by the governor of Singapore, Belcher was involved in searching for an Englishwoman who was thought to be captive in Borneo. He then transported Rajah Muda Hassim and his family to Borneo proper, leaving Brooke in undisputed possession of his territory. During this visit, the original document in which the Sultan offered to cede the Island of Labuan to the British was received by Belcher and transmitted to the government. The search for the Englishwoman proving unsuccessful, HMS *Samarang* then proceeded to Manila, where news was received of the captivity and distress of the crew of the British ship *Premier* crew on the coast of Borneo. She returned to Sooloo to seek help from the Sultan there, who sent his ambassador to negotiate the liberation of all who remained captive and complete treaties of friendship with the Sultans of Gunung Taboor and Bulungan.

In his proceedings of 17 March 1845 mentioning the treaty negotiations, Belcher complained about the charts he had been issued with, he claimed were '*very erroneous*' and had nearly led to the loss of his ship. He went on to describe

E by North.

the difficult conditions that had also hampered the rescue operations, saying that he had experienced:

> 'very great difficulty, by reason of the strong currents, in effecting anything of importance, without the assistance of steam such operations cannot be affected without danger ... I saved the Samarang from a very dangerous position ... had the ship grounded her wreck was inevitable, and having ... but five tons of water on board, many deaths would have resulted.'

Belcher then mentioned that he would be sailing to Hong Kong via the Bashees to refit and resupply the ship and to continue surveying the Meia-co-Shima Islands, and ominously reflected that 'with the exception of a lad who died (from worms) on the passage hither, the crew have been free from any important disease, but unless we remove to a Northern climate shortly officers as well as crew will fall.' Mahon had noted that remittent and intermittent fevers, as a result of malaria and the oppressive heat, had already affected some of the crew, whilst surveying amongst the Philippine group of Islands and North West coast of Borneo.

Mahon's journal also reveals that the dangers had not passed for Belcher, who, on returning to Borneo for more surveying excursions on 22 April 1846, was involved in a shooting incident. Having landed ashore, he was collecting

A sketch of the coast of Luzon in the Philippines, 1844. BELOW

specimens of seashells with Theodoro Miguel, a native of Manila who was a
cting as his interpreter. Miguel had been captured by Bornean pirates three years
earlier and made a slave but had been subsequently rescued by HMS *Samarang*.
On that day in April, while collecting shells with Belcher, Miguel was wounded
by musket fire. Fortunately, however, Belcher was not hit and Miguel's gunshot
wound was slight, and after returning to HMS *Samarang*, Miguel made a
full recovery.

Even the homeward part of the voyage was not without incident, as
Mahon's journal entries reveal that near Java an epidemic of febrile catarrh '*run
through a great portion of the crew, 60 were attacked of whom 48 had it in a slight degree, 12
required remission from duty*'. The journal also shows that Mahon and Adams were
kept very busy as medical officers caring for HMS *Samarang*'s 200 crew: '*during the*

4 years and two months of the voyage, they dealt with 1669 medical cases of which 1615 were discharged cured, 32 were sent to hospital, 12 were invalided and 10 died'.

On completion of the voyage and having returned home, Mahon received some good news: he was awarded the Gilbert Blane Medal in 1847. Instituted by Blane, one of the most acclaimed Royal Navy Surgeons of his time, this was the highest honour bestowed upon any surgeon in the Royal Navy who had demonstrated through his journals the most distinguished proof of skill, diligence and humanity in the exercise of his duties, with consideration given to achievement in research, articles and reports. Having missed out on this award with his previous journal covering his observations of scurvy in 1842 on HMS *Barossa*, receiving it this time was just reward, and in no small part due to Adams' striking drawings.

Colour sketches of Manila presented to Belcher by Captain Frazer of the ship – on 10 October 1833. BELOW

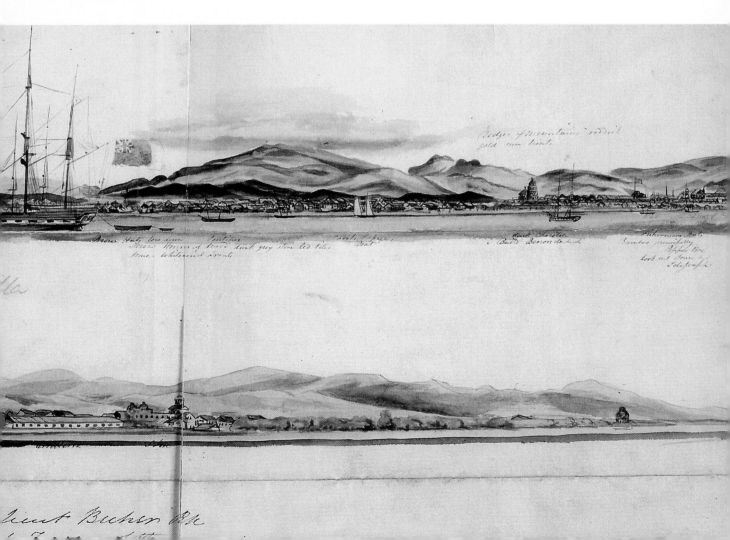

Cholera on a convict ship

COLIN ARROTT BROWNING ON *HASHEMY* ... 1848

William Farr compared the outbreak in cholera in England in 1848 and
1849 to the invasion of a foreign army. It was as if this force, he said, '*had
landed on the coast of England, seized all the seaports, sent detachments over the surrounding
districts, ravaged the population, and, in the year it held possession of the country, slain
fifty-three thousand two hundred and ninety-three men, women and children*'.

Cholera was a 'shock disease': it could live suspended in water, and once it
was ingested by the sufferer, its symptoms started suddenly – within a few days,
sometimes within only hours – profuse vomiting and diarrhoea, lethargy, sunken
eyes and cold, bluish skin. Unchecked and untreated cholera kills half of its
victims. With no understanding of germ theory at the time, and with poor
sanitation, cholera spread rapidly through England in 1848, and its consequences
were terrible.

For us in the twenty-first century it is difficult to fully appreciate how fearful
people in England must have been during the cholera epidemic. How much worse
it must have been, though, for the 237 prisoners aboard the convict ship *Hashemy*,
overwhelmed by the disease during the vessel's long journey to the penal colonies
of New South Wales, Australia.

At the beginning of this journey, as the *Hashemy* made her way around
England's southern coast from Woolwich to Mother Bank, an anchorage in the
Solent off the Isle of Wight, cholera struck. Within the cramped confines of this
packed, insanitary ship it ravaged the condemned men imprisoned in her. The
journal of the *Hashemy*'s surgeon, Dr Colin Arrott Browning, records the progress
of cholera on the vessel.

Anchored at Woolwich, the *Hashemy* had received her first prisoners bound
for Australia on 24 November 1848 – twenty-five boys from Parkhurst Prison on
the Isle of Wight (whether the irony of their circular journey occurred to them we
cannot know). Arrott Brown inspected their physical condition and found that
although they were '*of delicate form and constitution*', they '*manifested no symptoms of
positive disease*'.

Jail cells on a convict ship, 1846. **ABOVE**

Further prisoners embarked on the *Hashemy* over the next few days. On 28 November, one man was received from Millbank Prison, London, and 111 also arrived from Wakefield. On 29 November, 100 men came from London's Pentonville Prison, completing the *Hashemy*'s complement on 237 convicts.

While the London prisoners had been medically certified as fit for living on a crowded ship during its long voyage to the other side of the world, the Wakefield men had not, and were a cause of concern for Arrott Browning. He rejected two of their number immediately and had them removed to prison hulks (old ships that were anchored and that had been converted into fetid, floating prisons). The next day he removed another from the *Hashemy* on account of his '*mania*'.

From the first entry to the last, Arrott Browning's sick book is a testament to the horrors that the prisoners aboard the *Hashemy* endured as they rounded the south coast. Thomas Francis, aged fifty-seven, a prisoner from Wakefield, was Arrott Browning's first patient and perhaps the source of the cholera on board the ship. Francis initially came to Arrott Browning with a severe cold and cough. He had, he explained, been forced at Wakefield to climb into a cesspool to cleanse it, becoming covered in human filth in the process. The prison warders then commanded Francis to 'cleanse' himself by submersion in a bath of cold water while still clothed, and then gave him no means to warm his sodden clothes. He developed a chill on 1 December 1848, just a day after embarking on the *Hashemy*. By his second day in Arrott Browning's care, though, Francis's symptoms had developed. He now had a '*fever, attended with moderate thirst, tongue inclined to dryness, and had some obscure abdominal uneasiness*'. Francis's symptoms persisted and at Arrott Browning's request he was soon admitted to the hospital ship *Senate*, where he recovered.

Francis may have been the source of the scourge that soon ripped through the *Hashemy*, and Arrott Browning later added to his entry in the sick book, under '*nature of disease*', the note '*reported cholera*'. But whether Francis had brought the disease onto the *Hashemy* or not (prolonged exposure to possibly infected faeces in a cesspool makes him a good candidate), cholera was soon rampant among Arrott Browning's charges, quickly claiming its first victim – thirty-year-old Joseph Taylor.

DOC. 1 The first page of Dr Colin Arrott Brown's 'General Remarks' on the *Hashemy*'s voyage, 1848–49.

An Admiralty chart showing 'Spithead and Approaches from the Eastward', 1848.
BELOW

31

GENERAL REMARKS.

The total number of souls embarked in the Hashemy was 344
of which the Ship's Company, consisting of the Master, three mates and
men before the mast, furnished . . . .   41.
The guard, consisting of 2 Officers, Mr Ramsbottom Ensign, 53 rank &
file, 5 Soldiers wives, & 4 Soldier children, supplied . . . .   63.
The Prisoners in number amounted to . . . .   237.
The Religious Instructor . . . .   1.
The Surgeon Superintendent . . . . —————
                                                                        343
also before we sailed, an acting apistant Surgeon, Royal Navy,
came on board and had a passage to Sydney 1. 344

Of the Prisoners, 25 boys were received from Parkhurst, on the 24 Nov
1846, at Woolwich: on the 28 - 1 man was received from Millbank, and 111
from Wakefield. From Pentonville on the 29 were embarked 100. Total 237.

In my Nosological Synopsis, transmitted from Sydney, it was stated
that I had no opportunity of Inspecting the Parkhurst boys until they appeared on board the Hashemy, when three of them were found to be of
delicate form and Constitution but manifested no symptoms of positive
disease.

Respecting the men from Wakefield they brought with them no
Medical Certificate of health and fitness for the voyage, and, from what
I could ascertain from themselves, it did not appear that they had been
before they left their Prison, subjected to any close and scrutinizing In-
spection with reference to their embarking in a crowded Ship, and
entering on a long voyage to the penal Colonies. Two of these men I
rejected at once, on the day immediately following that of their embarkation; I sent a third away, on account of mania; and further observation
and experience, revealed the total unfitness of several of them to proceed
in the voyage, and absolute incapacity to render themselves useful to
the community either at home or in the Colonies. The men from Pentonville
I had, before they were removed from their Prison, an opportunity of Inspecting
in conformity with my "Instructions"

Before I proceed with my remarks on the state of the Prisoners
health during the voyage, I would beg leave to observe that, before we
sailed from the Mother Bank, I had the honor to transmit to the
Director General of the Medical Department of the Navy a Paper on
"The appearance and prevalence of cholera in the Hashemy," and which
considered more or less fully, the following Heads:

First. The protracted Confinement of the Prisoners in the Solitary Cells
            of their respective Prisons.
Second, The Prisoners preparation or Seasoning for Embarkation in
            consideration of the tendency of their prolonged Solitary Confinement.
Third, The Prisoners diet in their several Prisons.
Fourth, The Prisoners clothing and shoes which were wretched, and
            will go far to account for the number of Cases of Catarrh
            and other ailments referrible to the influence of Cold & Wetfeet
Fifth, The Season of the year during which the embarkation took
            place; namely, Midwinter.
Sixth, The place of Embarkation; namely Woolwich, where cholera was
            known to prevail.
Seventh The inclemency of the Weather, and working of the ship from the
                                                                            River

Taylor had arrived on the *Hashemy* from Pentonville Prison on 29 November. He reported to Arrott Browning's clinic on the ship at 8pm on 9 December. By this point, cholera had seriously struck two men on the ship, nineteen-year-old Richard Martin and twenty-one-year-old Henry East, who both eventually recovered. Arrott Browning had in accordance issued orders that any prisoners '*experiencing the slightest deviation from perfect health*' should report to the hospital.

Taylor – or his keepers in the prison – had not obeyed this instruction, as he only arrived there after having '*purged*' six times since that morning, and having experienced sickness for some time already. Arrott Browning prescribed him a menthol stomach compression and tinctures of both cardamom and opium to settle his digestion and told him to remain in bed. However, half an hour later Taylor was carried back into the hospital by a petty officer and some other prisoners. He was experiencing severe cramps. The severity of his condition was apparent on looking at his face, Arrott Browning said, which, though '*full before, seemed to have almost vanished, eyes hollow and surrounded with a dark hue; complexion leaden, countenance ghastly, and exhibiting an expression of the deepest misery*'.

Arrott Browning attempted to treat Taylor's symptoms with a variety of remedies: opium mixed with brandy, a warm bath of water and mustard oil, continual rubbing with blankets, and the application of dry heat with cloth-wrapped hot-water bottles to try and stave off Taylor's cramps. This was to no avail; Taylor's abdominal cramps only increased and he soon became certain of his own fate. Arrott Browning describes how this young man spoke '*very calmly and intelligibly of his spiritual and eternal interests*'. Through the chaplains at Pentonville Taylor had discovered his Christian faith and remained reassured in his last moments that his sins would be forgiven by Jesus and that he would be received into eternal life. Despite Arrott Browning's best efforts, Taylor slipped into unintelligible speech; as '*the vital powers gradually sank*' from Taylor, Arrott Browning remarked that '*the surface became cold and clammy and the tongue and breath … was sensibly cold*'. Taylor died on board the *Hashemy* at 2.30am on 10 December 1848, only eleven days after boarding the ship at the Downs, an anchorage only a few miles off the coast of east Kent.

Taylor's was just the first death from the outbreak of cholera that harried the *Hashemy* as it rounded England's south coast in the bitter cold of December 1848. Twenty-seven-year-old John Collins, the second man to die from the disease, was admitted to Arrott Browning's hospital on 12 December. Arrott Browning's notes, clearly hastily scribbled, give an insight into the degradation of his symptoms, and into his course of treatment, before his death on 19 December 1848 with the ship still anchored at the Downs:

John Collins
Aged 27
Prisoner from Pentonville
Dec 12 1848
Downs
Died – Dec 19 1848

Rather tall of a spare habit of body and very pale. Complaint: states that his bowels were quite natural yesterday, but has had this morning three loose stools attended with abdominal pain which vanished with the dejections. Pulse and tongue and skin natural ... Dose – tincture of opium 3 drops; menthol oil; barley or rice water for drink.

5pm. Two relaxed stools since morning passed with some pain. No apparent constitutional disturbance. Countenance pale ever since he embarked and experienced five successive fits. Repeat his morning dose– Watch, and if necessary repeat the draught.

Dec 13 a.m. Purged twice during the night, feels some pain which extends across the abdomen and is increased while at stool; complains of his belly being internally somewhat cold. Dose Tincture of Opium; Tincture of Zingib [ginger]; Tincture of Cardamom. Hospital watch.

Afternoon: no ailment. Watch, repeat if necessary the morning draught.

Dec 14. Morning visit: Asleep, seems to go on favourably. Continue to watch. Make immediate report at hospital should any change take place.

Dec 15, 9 a.m. Purged once since seven o'clock this morning, no further manifested constitutional disturbances. Pulse and tongue natural, urine said to be in natural quantity. Tincture of opium administered.

Evening. Again some purging with slight pain, expression of countenance natural – Tincture of opium, Tincture of cardamom.

Dec 16 a.m. No purging, some abdominal pain, apply to Belly hot fomentation. Drink and diet as before.

5 p.m. Symptoms less favourable. Repeat the draught, apply to belly turpentine epithem and renew hot stomach bottle. Drink as before. Closely watch.

Dec 17. 1.30 a.m. Abdominal pain increased but no increased purging. Tincture of cardamom; Tincture opium; Spirit aether sulphuricus; Spirit Gallici [brandy]; *Menthol oil.*

7 a.m. No purging since the draught. Abdominal pain increased. Tincture of cardamom; Tincture opium. Apply turpentine epithem and renew stomach bottle. Rice for food and for drink weak brandy and water. Watch.

. . .

Dec 19. 5 a.m. Purged five times since last night and during the fearful prevalence of cholera throughout through the whole person; great abdominal pain, some nausea, pulse rather weak and soft.

. . .

7 a.m. Some abdominal uneasiness but no cramps anywhere, some flatulency.

12 noon. Having been incessantly occupied the whole night with the cholera patients, who had rapidly multiplied, and observing quietness and an apparent cessation pervade the prison, I retired for the purposes of being fomented for relief of the symptoms of the malady by which I was assailed the night that Taylor died and was absent from the prison about two hours. When I returned Collins I found in the grip of the pestilence in its spasmodic stage, no additional precursory indication of the change having appeared. The countenance suddenly exhibited the characteristic and appalling expression. The stools now quite watery and like rice water now flowed involuntarily. Skin clammy and cold, tongue and breath cold. Pulse very feeble, scarcely meeting the finger. Opiates, with other antispasmodics and aromatics, with friction and dry heat were most zealously used., but his skin became more cold and clammy, the watery purging increased, the powers of life seemed suddenly to flow out and forsake him and about half past six o'clock left him under the power and dominion of death!

'Until the morning of resurrection, when he shall be called for by His voice who is able to destroy him that had the power of death.' Hebrews II:14–15.'

There were another twelve deaths from cholera among the passengers of the *Hashemy*, mostly drawn from the ranks of the young prisoners from Parkhurst and Pentonville. William Browning, a forty-six-year-old prisoner from Wakefield, was the last to die, on Christmas Eve 1848, as the *Hashemy* lay anchored off the Isle of Wight on what is known as 'Mother Bank'.

Henry Chilton, a private in the 99th regiment and one of the soldiers tasked with guarding the convicts, was the last man to be stricken by cholera on board the *Hashemy*. He was admitted to the ward on New Year's Eve 1848 and was discharged, having recovered, on 18 January 1849.

On 11 February 1849, some two months after Joseph Taylor's death, the *Hashemy* weighed anchor and left English waters. Arrott Browning's medical journal records his treatment of scurvy and other diseases at sea. In total, during the *Hashemy*'s seven-month voyage to New South Wales, Arrott Browning treated 1,018 sick cases, an average of around three cases for every member of the ship's company. Included in this total were 193 cases of cholera in the short period between December 1848 and January 1849. Far fewer than that number are recorded in Arrott Browning's journal, the *'fearful rapidity'* with which the disease spread preventing him from keeping a full record.

That only fourteen of these 193 men died is a testament to Arrott Browning's meticulous care of his charges, and it is even more surprising given that the physician had never previously encountered the disease. In his journal he remarks on this: '*I never in my life before had seen the disease or witnessed its treatment. The plan I pursued I was led to adopt in consideration of that I had learned from books, and from conversations with professional brethren.*'

Arrott Browning's ability to think on his feet and his commitment to his patients were remarkable. He later wrote a paper on the *Hashemy*'s cholera outbreak and sent this to Admiralty; it is full of criticisms of the horrifying practices that left convicts as such risk of contracting disease – from their poor diets to the thin clothes they were given to endure a winter crossing to the other side of the world, including shoes that were, shockingly, made of nothing more substantial than brown paper.

However, while his heart was certainly in the right place, to modern eyes some of Arrott Brown's medical practices are a little off-putting, including the recommendations he makes in his journal for a physician faced with a cholera outbreak. This '*terrific scourge*', he says, should be properly met by the liberal application of such cure-alls as calomel (mercury chloride, which is highly poisonous) and tartarised antimony (an emetic which induces severe vomiting). Both these, of course, should be complemented by '*the judicious use of laudanum to encounter the appalling assault of the pestilence, in its more fierce and deadly form*'.

DOC. 2 The closing remarks of Dr Colin Arrott Browning's 'General Remarks' on the *Hashemy*'s voyage, 1848–49.

Cholera warning poster from 1853. BELOW

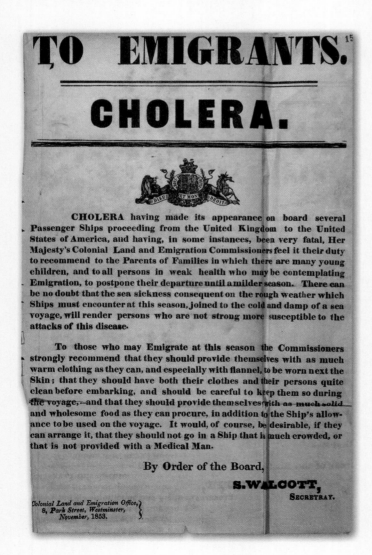

TO EMIGRANTS. 15

CHOLERA.

CHOLERA having made its appearance on board several Passenger Ships proceeding from the United Kingdom to the United States of America, and having, in some instances, been very fatal, Her Majesty's Colonial Land and Emigration Commissioners feel it their duty to recommend to the Parents of Families in which there are many young children, and to all persons in weak health who may be contemplating Emigration, to postpone their departure until a milder season. There can be no doubt that the sea sickness consequent on the rough weather which Ships must encounter at this season, joined to the cold and damp of a sea voyage, will render persons who are not strong more susceptible to the attacks of this disease.

To those who may Emigrate at this season the Commissioners strongly recommend that they should provide themselves with as much warm clothing as they can, and especially with flannel, to be worn next the Skin; that they should have both their clothes and their persons quite clean before embarking, and should be careful to keep them so during the voyage,—and that they should provide themselves with as much solid and wholesome food as they can procure, in addition to the Ship's allowance to be used on the voyage. It would, of course, be desirable, if they can arrange it, that they should not go in a Ship that is much crowded, or that is not provided with a Medical Man.

By Order of the Board,

S. WALCOTT,
SECRETARY.

Colonial Land and Emigration Office,
8, Park Street, Westminster,
November, 1853.

severe; and the same thing can be affirmed of those prisoners who were, during the prevalence of the disease, most actively and humanely engaged in voluntarily attending on their sick mess-mates, or other sufferers. But we require a <u>collection</u> of facts to settle the point at issue.

The *Hashemy* finally sailed from Spithead on the 11th day of February 1849. The organization of the people, in the appointment of Petty Officers and Schoolmasters, was speedily completed, and our whole machinery was at once in active and efficient operation. The health of the Prisoners continued to improve more & more, until we began to approach the Cape of Good Hope, when the appearance of elevated and spongy gums, both in the prisoners and guard, and other marks of failing health, rendered it expedient to put into Simon's Bay for fresh meat and vegetables. From the Cape we sailed on the sixth day after our arrival, carrying with us a sea stock of fresh meat and live sheep. The people soon evinced that they had laid in a stock of health, and they continued to retain their healthy appearance, until we reached Port Jackson.

Two deaths occurred during the passage from England to Sydney. <u>Adam Germain</u> (Case N° 74) died on or close to the Equator, quite <u>Insane</u> and seemed to suffer exceedingly from the heat of an almost vertical Sun.

<u>Frederick Jones</u>, (Case N° 75) was near St Pauls, carried off by <u>~~Hectic~~ Fever</u>, symptomatic of old organic disease of the digestive, and apparently also of the respiratory organs, under which he was reported to have suffered a long while in Prison. Both these prisoners seemed, while they lived, to be reformed men, and to live in accordance with the precepts and hopes of Christianity. The mind of Jones was clear and strong to the last, and his hope vigorous and purifying. Altho' Germain was Imbecile when he embarked his moral principles were good, his disposition amiable, and his conduct gentle and harmless. Both these prisoners and indeed all who were <u>debarked</u> at Portsmouth were from the prison of Wakefield.

Every case of ailment was entered in the Sick Book, with the exception of trifling deviations from usual health, and although the number increased during the voyage; from the day we sailed to our arrival in Sydney, until it reached 359, yet there <u>appeared</u> amongst the people very little of positive disease, — and our practice, wore, to a considerable extent, more of a <u>preventive</u>, than of a <u>curative</u>, aspect.

The issue of biscuit to the prisoners, was very carefully regulated agreeably to the letter of Instructions; never exceeded <u>the pound</u>, and was, for a short time, as low as <u>eight ounces</u>, in accordance with the prisoners' appetite and desire.

Preserved Potatoes being on board, the consideration of the terrible shaking the prisoners had received from their prolonged confinements and our visit from Cholera, induced me to order them to be issued for some time

4

The Navy

Life in the Navy
THE EIGHTEENTH AND NINETEENTH CENTURIES

During the Age of Sail, life at sea on board Royal Navy ships typically involved undertaking laborious routine duties to ensure ships were kept afloat, day in, day out, often without the crew setting foot on land for several years. Ships usually were deployed in gruelling activities such as blockading enemy ports or escorting merchant ship convoys.

Whether it was a first-rate ship like HMS *Victory* with more than 800 crew or a sixth-rate ship such as HMS *Hermione* with only 160 crew, the men on board were usually a cosmopolitan mix from different strands of society. And whether they were experienced seamen, pressed men, quotamen or landsmen, once on board, irrespective of their backgrounds, they had to mould into an efficient and organised unit ready to deal with any emergency at a moment's notice, in all types of weather and in varying sea conditions.

This could only be achieved with tight organisation and discipline and with each man fully understanding his role. The person responsible for a ship's organisation, and for the safety, fighting efficiency and discipline of its crew, was the captain. Under his command, a well-trained crew on a sailing ship – which at that time was the most technically advanced instrument of war, and which, with its masses of rigging and sails, used as its method of propulsion the natural elements – could be the difference between victory and defeat and between life and death.

Life on board was governed by the Articles of War, the Royal Navy's own disciplinary code. Introduced in 1652, this code laid down what was not permissible as well as the likely punishment awaiting someone who transgressed any article at a resulting court martial. Offences ranged from swearing and drunkenness to failure to obey orders, quarrelling, fighting and negligence of duty. Seven articles carried an automatic death sentence, whereas twelve carried a possible death sentence. It was the captain who decided whether a misdemeanour necessitated a court martial.

Although the Articles of War were wide ranging they did not cover every possible disciplinary offence. They were supplemented by *Regulations and Instructions Relating to HM Service at Sea*, and by each captain's own code of conduct, which led to inconsistencies in discipline and punishment. However, the captain's opinion was final in this regard. Under a benevolent captain this was not an issue, but one with more draconian tendencies could make life unbearable for the men.

Admiralty regulations stipulated that captains could authorise floggings of twelve lashes without resorting to a court martial. However, this rule was often overlooked and some captains authorised punishments of up to forty-eight lashes. Minor transgressions could be punished without recourse to an inquiry by

Sailors in hammocks being woken for a night time watch duty. **BELOW**

'starting' with a rope's end. Punishments such as death, imprisonment or floggings of more than forty-eight lashes could only be imposed at a court martial. Death sentences for seamen were carried out by hanging, whereas officers were shot. Apart from the death sentence, the most severe form of punishment was flogging around the fleet. An offender receiving this sentence would have parts of his punishment meted out on every ship in port (as many as 1,000 lashes could be given). In 1778, Thomas Young, a deserter, received such a sentence, which stipulated that he was '*to receive 300 lashes on his bare back with a cat of nine tails alongside such of His Majesties ships and vessels at this port, at such times and in such proportions as shall be directed by the commanding officer of the said ships and vessels for the time being*'.

However, it was how they performed in battle that was the definitive test of the discipline and efficiency of a Royal Navy crew and the sternest test of seamen's character. Although infrequent, battles were the most immediate and horrifying peril a seaman would face, as revealed by Robert Young, surgeon of HMS *Ardent*, which was involved in the Battle of Camperdown (1797). A total of 203 men were killed from the twenty-four British ships present, and of these, HMS *Ardent* had the most fatalities – forty-one, and 107 wounded. Young described the mayhem on board the *Ardent*:

> *Ninety wounded were brought down … the whole cockpit deck, cabins wing berths, and part of the cable tier, together with my platform, and my preparations for dressing were covered with them. So that for a time, they were laid on each other at the foot of the ladder where they were brought down… Numbers, about sixteen, mortally wounded, died after they were brought down, amongst whom was the brave and worthy Captain Burgess, whose corpse could with difficulty be got conveyed to the starboard wing berth. Joseph Bonheur had his right thigh taken off by a cannon shot close to the Pelvis, so that it was impossible to apply a tourniquet, his right arm was also shot to pieces, the stump of the thigh, which was fleshy presented a dreadful and large surface of mangled flesh, in this state he lived near two hours, perfectly sensible and incessantly calling out in a strong voice to me to assist him. The bleeding from the femoral artery although so high up, must have been very inconsiderable, and I observed it did not bleed as he lay. All the service I could tender the unfortunate man was to put dressings over the part and give*

*him drink… Melancholy cries for assistance were addressed to me from every side, by
wounds and dying and piteous moans and bewailings from pain and despair.*

*In the midst of these agonising scenes … the man whose leg I first amputated,
Richard Traverse had not uttered a groan or complaint from the time he was brought
down, and several, exulting in the news of the victory, declared they regretted not the
loss of their limbs. An explosion of a salt box with several cartridges, abreast of the
cockpit hatchway, filled the hatchway with flame and in a moment fourteen or fifteen
wretches tumbled down upon each other their faces black or a cinder, their clothes blown
to shatters and the rags on fire. A corporal of marines lived two hours after the action
with all the Glutei muscles shot away so as to excavate the pelvis. Captain Burgess's
wound was of this nature but he fortunately died almost instantly. After the action
ceased, fifteen or sixteen dead bodies were removed before it was possible to get a
platform cleared, and come at the materials for operating and dressing, those I had
prepared being covered over with bodies and blood.'*

DOC. 1 A graphic account of the surgeon's cockpit in action from the logbook of HMS *Ardent*, 1797–99.

DOC. 2 The log of HMS *Victory* from October 1805.

Casualties were more prevalent in long-range sea battles than they were in
fighting at close quarters. Fatalities and severe injuries were more likely to result as
a cannonball fired from a distance impacted on and hit through wooden hulls,
decks and masts, sending lethal large wooden splinters hurtling across the deck
space, as evidenced by the wounded list for HMS *Victory* at the Battle of
Trafalgar compiled by the ship's surgeon.

The most frequent surgical treatment for injuries sustained in battle was
amputation. Such operations usually were undertaken by surgeons while the
patient was still awake but sedated with laudanum (an opium derivative) or grog,
as no general anaesthetic was available. Following amputation of the limb, the
stump was sealed by either a hot iron or pitch tar. Some surgeons used ligatures to
stem blood loss and covered the stump with the remaining skin. Although they
were often accused of incompetence, most surgeons were in fact skilled in this
procedure and able to amputate a limb in under two minutes.

In 1797 Admiral Nelson led an unsuccessful assault on Tenerife during
which his right arm was hit by enemy fire. Bleeding heavily, he returned to his
ship, HMS *Theseus*, for swift remedial action by the ship's surgeon, Thomas
Eshelby, as noted in the latter's journal: '*Compound fracture of the right arm by a*

Mens Names, Ages and Qualities	When and where put on the Sick List	Statement of the Case when put on the List	Symptoms and Treatment while under Cure.	When discharged to Duty, Died, or sent to the Hospital	REMARKS
John Jennings	—	greatly burnt face & hands			
~~Dav Clff~~ John Downie	—	both heels much torn			
Peter Meloney	—	~~Scalp~~ Cheek cut open from the mouth almost to the ear			
Wm Treek	—	Langridge shot in thigh			
Jas Kid	—	Splinter in mouth and foot			
Wm Robinson		left arm broke in pieces, above the elbow			
John Moriarty	—	bruised back and hands			
John Griffin	—				

and give him drink. In many other instances, to day, I had occasion to observe, that Vessels collapse and bleed little after gun shot or splinter wounds. The Vessel, probably, stretched longitudinally, has its sides brought nearly together and its cavity diminished, when at length transversely seperated by violence the jagged ends retract inward, which with the spasmodic contraction of the circular fibres of the Artery occasioned by the tension, compleatly closes the passage and resists the impetus of the blood from above. Whether ~~or not~~ this attempt to explain be just or not, the fact is deserving of notice, at the same time I am aware that it does not hold universally true. Melancholy cries for assistance were addressed to me from every side, by wounded and dying and piteous moans and bewailings from pain and despair. In the midst of these agonising Scenes I was enabled to preserve myself firm and collected, and embracing in my mind the whole of the Situation to direct my attentions where the greatest and most essential Services could be performed. Some with wounds bad indeed and painful but slight in comparison with the dreadful condition of others were most vociferous for my assistance, these I was obliged to reprimand with severity as their noise disturbed the ~~last dying~~ moments of the dying. I cheered and commended the patient for fortitude of others, and sometimes extorted a smile of satisfaction, from the mangled Sufferers and succeeded to throw momentary gleams of cheerfulness amidst so many horrors. The man whose leg I first amputated, Richd Traverse had not uttered a groan or complaint from the time he was brought down, and several, exulting in the news of the Victory, ~~brought down~~ declared they regretted not the loss of their limbs. An explosion of a salt box with several cartridges, abreast of the Cockpit hatchway, filled the hatchway with flame and in a moment fourteen or fifteen wretches tumbled down upon each other their faces black as a cinder, their clothes blown to shatters and the bags on fire. A Corporal of Marines lived two hours after the action with all the Glutei muscles shot away so as to excavate the pelvis. Captain Burgess's wound was of this nature but he fortunately died almost instantly. After the action ceased, fifteen or sixteen dead bodies were removed before it was possible to get a platform cleared, and come at the materials for operating and dressing, those I had prepared being covered over with bodies and blood, and the store room door block'd up. I have the satisfaction to say that of those who survived to undergoe amputation or be dressed, all were found next morning in the Gun room where they were placed, in as comfortable a state as possible, and on the third day were conveyed on shore in a Steel in good spirits cheering the Ship at

Mens Names	Quality	Nature of Wound	When cured on board, sent to Hospital or Died	
				37
Charles Chappel	Marine	Wounded head on fracture of the finger	15 November	
Samuel Green	Marine	Flesh Wound of the Arm	3d November	
Joseph Gordon	Ordy	Amputated Thigh	27 October	Died of Sudden Spasm
Robert Philips	AB	Flesh Wound of the Leg	13 November	
Thos. Green	AB	Exposed Tibia by a splinter	19 November	
David Connor	AB	Wound on the Head and Arm	10 November	
William Browne	AB	Grape shot through the inferior part of the left cavity of the Thorax	23d October	Died of internal Hæmorrhage
George Graves	Marine	Contused Wound of the fore arm	4 November	
James Tragan	Marine	Contused Wound on the side	5 November	
John Sutton	Marine	Contused Arm by a Splinter	2d November	
Nicholas Lecontre	AB	Several severe flesh Wounds	10 November	
John Smith 2d	AB	Lacerated Wound of the Leg, the Gastrocnemius Muscle torn half way down the Leg	10 January	Sent to the Sussex Hospital ship
James Rogers	Marine	Wounded head	1st November	
George Colstone	Marine	Wounded face by Splinters	10 November	
Thos. Smith 2d	AB	Amputated Thigh, high up		
Richd Jewell	AB	Amputation of the Thigh above the Trochanter major, he had lost a great deal of blood before he was brought to the cockpit	22d October	this man died shortly after the operation, from the great violence done the habit sustained, the removal of so large a portion of the body
Thos. Graham	Boy	Contused Shoulder by a Piece of wood	1st Novr	
Jas Hines	Mar	Compound fracture of the Humerus by a Musquet Ball		
Isaac Harris	Mar	Contused leg by a Splinter	1st November	
Cullen Tamp	Boy	Shot through the abdomen	29 October	Died of Mortification shortly after the action
Wm Smith 2d	AB	Amputated Thigh	2d Novr	died of a Tetanus

Page 16th Mens Names, Ages and Qualities.	When and where put on the Sick List.	Statement of the Case when put on the List.	August 1st Symptoms and Treatment while under Cure.	When discharged to Duty, Died, or sent to the Hospital.	REMARKS.
Geo. McCrohy	Page 15	Contused Wound	The Same. Cont Medic ut heri		
Thos. Ramsey	Page 2d	Amputated Arm	Getting better. Repd Medic ut antea		
John Hoskins	Page 9th	Gunshot Wound Ancl	Repd. Mixt Cinchona et Pil Opii		
Florce Mahony (M)	Page 10th	Fracture of the Cranium	The left side Paralyzed. a large black fungous growing out from the dura mater. Pulse small & quick. sleeps constantly. Repd Medic ut heri		
Admiral Nelson	Page 7th	Amputated Arm.	Continued getting well very fast Stump look'd well no bad symptom whatever occured he continued the use of the Cortex. and a gentle opening Draught occasionally.	Discharged on board the Isabore 20th August	The sore reduced to the size of a Shilling in perfect good health one of the Ligatures not come away
Jas. Holding	Page 7th	Amputated Arm	Getting well. Continued the Cortex &c.	Gibralter Hospl 17th August	
Wm Harrison	Page 7th	Comp fractur Arm	All the muscle sloughed off. large discharge. Repd Medic ut heri		
Sal Harrison (M)	Page 8th	Wounded Hip.	The Same. Rep Mixt Saline et Opii Cont Cataplasm Emoll.		

musket ball passing thro' a little above the elbow, an artery divided; the arm was immediately amputated.' Later Eshelby wrote that Nelson *'continued getting well, very fast. Stump looked well; no bad symptoms...the sore reduced to the size of a shilling in perfect good health'*. Eshelby also noted that, unfortunately and painfully for Nelson, *'one of the ligatures [had] not come away'*.

Apart from battle, other major risks to ships were fire and being shipwrecked. A more unusual hazard was lightning, as reported in 1799 by Thomas Tappen, surgeon of HMS *Arab*:

'John Leggett and two marines were killed by lighting at sea, at the same time our main top mast was splintered to pieces, every man on deck knocked down, many of whom cried out their leg or arm were broke from the violence of the shock; the bolt broke, as it left the main mast, which acted as it's conductor, and issued a most sulphureous stench accompanied with three sharp cracks, the most astonishing of all, was that a man who was up at the main top gallant mast head, remained untouched there was a violent squall of rain and wind, previous and in an instant not a breath of air out of the heavens the mark of violence were most conspicuous in... Leggett, whose side had the appearance of being burnt, the skin all peeled off, tho the shirt remained entire, the two others, had no other appearance than of contusion under the ear and about the forehead, we kept them till evening, to satisfy the credulity and superstition of sailors, when their bodies were committed to the deep.'

Other common hazards on board ships were posed by insanity and sexually transmitted diseases. In Britain, lunacy was more widespread in the Royal Navy than it was ashore. In 1815, Gilbert Blane stated that one serving seaman in every thousand suffered from insanity. James Farquhar, surgeon of HMS *Captain*, had to discharge Walter Bryan, an able seaman, to Plymouth hospital in 1798 because he had *'for some time past been quite deranged... he sits for whole hours together without moving or taking his eyes from one ... object'*. Others tried to play on the surgeon's uncertainty as to their insanity, as revealed by Thomas T Crew, assistant surgeon on HMS *Contest*:

DOC. 3 Report on the amputation of the arm of Admiral Nelson in 1797.

15th W.W. Mistura.
15th W.W. Mist. 14th W.W. Mist.
15th W.J. Sal. Clouds.

on sea, & above, generally counteracted, &c

Thos Leggett.
James Dumble. (M)

Thos Gray.. (M)

These Men were killed by Lightning at Sea on the eleventh of October, at the same time our Main Top Mast was splinter'd to pieces, every Man on Deck knock'd down (many of whom cried out their Legs or Arms were broke) from the Violence of the Shock; the Brass Bolt, broke, as it left the Main mast, which acted as its conductor, and issued a most Sulphureous stench accompanied with three sharp cracks, the most astonishing of all, was that a man who was up at the main top & Mast head, remaind untouch'd there was a violent Squall of Rain & Wind, previous & in an instant not a breath of air out of the heavens the marks of violence, were most inconspicuous in Mr Leggett, whose side had the appearance of being burnt, the Skin all peel'd off, tho the Shirt remaind entire; the Two others, had no other appearance than of Contusion just under the Ear & about the Forehead satisfy the Credulity & superstition of Sailors, when their bodies were committed to the deep

This happend off Cape Canaveral on the Coast of Florida, which place is pretty well known for a number of instances of the same kind, previous to being struck, we saw the Walls, playing around us & descending on the water, which immediately issued out a quantity of Smoke

I had recourse to those means used, for the recovering life, in case of suffocation, but alto as the Patients were bonafide dead,

We kept till Evening, to then

'John Smith an old marine ... shamed a contraction of the knee on examination I saw what he was about and immediately told him he deserved to be flogged but he persisted in his understanding until he had received 8 or 10 dozen. He then shamed mad and sung night and day but I put him on a diet of ½ bisket and half pint of water ... at the end of sometime confessed his villany and returned to duty. He confessed he intended to deceive me as he said he had done 4 other surgeons previously.'

DOC. 4 Reports on three men fatally struck by lightning in the West Indies in 1799 from HMS *Arab*.

Venereal disease was a common affliction among seamen. The Admiralty believed such diseases were self inflicted, and prior to 1795 men paid for their own medical care. This practice was ceased by Thomas Trotter, a famous naval surgeon who believed it deterred men presenting themselves for treatment. This certainly was so in the case of John Squires, as recorded by Samuel Allen, surgeon of HMS *Albion*. Allen noted that Squire's inclusion on his sick list in 1802 was due to swollen testicles following Squire's failed attempt to self-medicate with a strong injection of chemicals to stop the effects of gonorrhoea.

Eating and drinking were generally the highlights of a seaman's day. A weekly ration for a seaman typically comprised 7lbs of biscuits, 4lbs of beef, 2lbs of pork, 2 pints of pease, 1½ pints of oatmeal, 6 ounces of sugar and butter, 12 ounces of cheese and half a pint of vinegar. The lack of fresh vegetables and fruit in this diet, a major contributory factor in the prevalence of scurvy, was often addressed by the captain in the form of a request to the Navy Board for more foods of this kind. This was sometimes met with annoyance by the Navy Board, as evidenced by its response to Captain James Cook in 1768 following such a request:

'The Commissioners of the Navy having been pleased to order a supply of necessaries for the use of the sick on board the Endeavour bark under your command for two years, during which time the currants, an article in the said supply, will inevitably spoil; and almonds being an article hardly at all conducive to the purposes intended; I beg you would be pleased to apply to the Commissioners of His Majesty's Navy for an order to omit the latter and lessen the quantity of the former article, thereby to increase the quantity of sago, and spices, articles highly more useful to the sick.'

Not surprisingly, men often supplemented their diet with fish, but on the occasion recounted here on board HMS *Barrossa* in 1841, it was of an unusual type:

> '*Cape De Verds was passed and observing a shark "squalus glancus" preceded by a pretty pilot fish "scomber doctor" striped brown and white vertically, a baited hook was passed over the side and immediately seized by this voracious monster turning belly upwards; after drawing him in board, he was cut up; fried and eaten by the seamen.*'

DOC. 5 Letter from surgeon WB Munkhouse about HMS *Endeavour*, 14 July 1768.

Sometimes the tasting of local delicacies resulted in unwanted medical conditions, as highlighted in this journal entry by HMS *Arab*'s surgeon in 1799:

> '*a number of men poisoned by a "mangereen apple" … occasioning severe vomiting and violent convulsions … the stomach being corroded by the virulence of this fruit … but the effects of this poison is never properly iradicated.*'

Starting in 1740, in their weekly rations seamen were also given seven gallons of beer, and more if required, from a communal barrel, along with twice-daily grog rations (half a pint of rum with a quart of water). Drunkenness was a severe problem, leading to many accidents and disobedience. In 1813, William Warner, HMS *Ville De Paris*'s surgeon, opined that John McLean had died not from pneumonic inflammation, but because he had been drunk constantly for ten days. Warner lamented that '*drunkenness nowadays in the Navy kills more men than the sword*' and that '*most diseases and accidents can be attributed to grog*'.

Perhaps drinking provided an escape from the drudgery of duty, or was simply a means of entertainment. In 1805, Thomas Simpson, surgeon of HMS *Arethusa*, highlighted the case of John Downie, a man with a:

> '*ghastly wretched appearance [who could] imitate with the greatest possible exactness the howling of a pack of hounds, the crowing of a cock, the bellowing of a bull, cow or calf and a number of other animals. On account of these curious qualifications he is often solicited by his shipmates to give a specimen of talents and a glass of grog is of course his reward.*'

206

125.

Endeavour July 14th 1768

Sir

The Commissioners of the Navy having
been pleased to order a supply of Necessaries for
the use of the Sick on board the Endeavour Bark
under your Command for two years: during which
time the Currants, an article in the said supply, will
inevitably spoil: and Almonds being an article hardly
at all conducive to the purposes intended; I beg you
would be pleased to apply to the Commissioners of
His Majesty's Navy for an order to omit the latter
and lessen the quantity of the former article, thereby
to increase the quantity of the Sago, and Spices;
articles highly more usefull to the sick.

I am

Sir Your obedient servant,

W B Munkhouse

Other party tricks often ended in mishap or complete embarrassment. Surgeon Robert Dickson of HMS *Dryad* recounted in 1829 the case of James Connor who, playing a trick on one of his messmates, slit his genitals with a knife. In 1805, Ben Lara, surgeon of HMS *Isis*, must have been completely flabbergasted when he went to treat John Cummings, who was complaining of '*excessive pain in the stomach and intestines, incapacity of retaining anything in the stomach, smart pain in walking or standing erect*', and concluded that the pain was caused by Cummings having swallowed previously '*19 or 20 clasp pen knives and one penknife*'.

Various species of exotic fish drawn
in 1688.

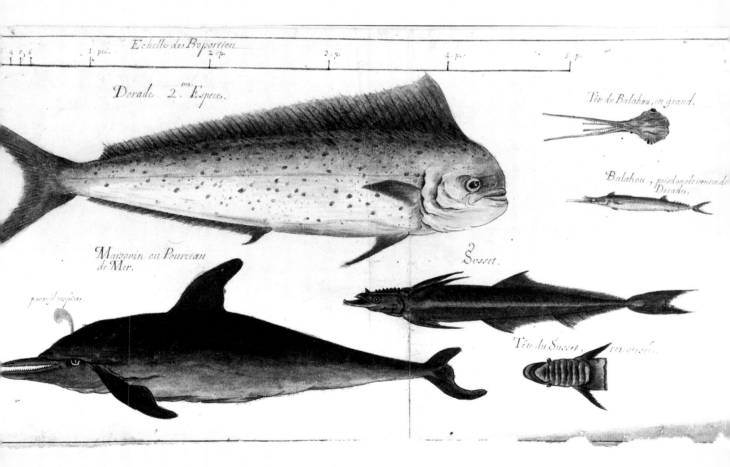

The Battle of Quiberon Bay

20 NOVEMBER 1759

Despite its relative obscurity, the Battle of Quiberon Bay ranks alongside Trafalgar as one of the most significant and crucial naval battles in British history. On a stormy day late in November 1759, a squadron of the Royal Navy under the command of Sir Edward Hawke won a resounding victory over a French fleet as it was entering Quiberon Bay in north-western France. In defeating the French at sea, Hawke effectively prevented an invasion attempt of Britain by the French through Ireland. We have the privilege of understanding what unfolded on that tempestuous winter's day through the accounts written in the log books by the captains of the ships of the British fleet. These log books provide a unique understanding of the battle because they reveal events from the different perspectives and varied experiences of individual ships involved in the fighting.

The French plan had been to dispatch a fleet from Brest to link up with transport vessels gathering in the enclosed Morbihan Sea near Quiberon Bay and escort those ships that were laden with French troops to Ireland. To prevent this from happening, the Royal Navy's western squadron under the command of Admiral Hawke blockaded the French fleet in Brest from May 1759. A smaller

Print of the Battle of Quiberon Bay c. 1765.
BELOW

The location of Quiberon Bay from a map of Brittany in the *Carte Géométrique de la Province de Bretagne*, 1771. **ABOVE**

squadron of ships under the command of Robert Duff was assigned to watch the transports in Quiberon Bay.

It was not until mid-November that a spate of bad weather and a favourable wind gave the admiral of the French fleet, the Comte de Conflans, a chance to escape. Hawke's fleet had been blown back towards Torbay in Devon by severe gales and was confined there for several days. On Wednesday 14 November, the French fleet, consisting of twenty-one ships of the line and six frigates sailed out of Brest for the open sea, unchallenged. Two days later Hawke received news of the whereabouts of the French fleet from a British victualling ship and charted a course towards Quiberon Bay.

Amid gales and rough seas, the French fleet was sighted by the frigate *Maidstone* on the morning of 20 November: '*at 8am we saw a large fleet of ships ahead which we took to be the French fleet; made signal which the Magnanime [formerly a ship of the French Navy, but now part of the British fleet] repeated*'. Between 9am and 10am Hawke made the signal for a general chase, which released the British fleet (with twenty-three ships of the line and two frigates) from a line-of-battle formation to pursue the retreating French fleet at speed. During the course of the battle, ships from Duff's squadron joined the British fleet.

Sketch of Quiberon Bay showing the location of the islands of Houat, Hedic and Dumet, 1800. RIGHT

The captain's log entries for several ships, such as the *Burford*, confirm that at 10:30am Hawke made the signal for the seven headmost ships, which included the *Torbay*, the *Magnanime*, the *Warspite* and the *Resolution*, to form a line of battle ahead of the main fleet. They were to attack the French rear and then overtake them, aiming for the vanguard of the enemy fleet until the rest of the squadron had caught up.

By 2:30pm the leading ships of the British fleet had finally caught up with the rearward French ships. The *Maidstone* was in a good position to observe the battle as it began to unfold, as this entry from the captain's log shows:

> '¾ past 2 the headmost of our ships begun to engage the stern-most of the enemy's at 2 cables length at 46 minutes. After 3[pm] the French rear admiral's fore topmast was shot away [and] when he bore out of the line the Magnanime and another followed him and engaged him.'

The actions of the British fleet must have astonished the French commander as he would have assumed that the British fleet would abandon their pursuit through the unknown waters around Quiberon Bay. Nevertheless, it might still have been possible for the French admiral to have successfully reached the Morbihan Sea with the majority of his fleet intact, had not the weather and wind direction changed. French ships were thrown off course and into confusion.

By this stage the French rear admiral's ship, the *Formidable*, had been battered by several British ships, including the *Torbay*, as they sailed abreast and overtook her. The captain's log from the *Torbay* reads: '*at 4[pm] we got alongside the Formidable ... who had before received the fire of some of our ships and [we] gave her two broadsides which seemed to silence her...*' Shortly afterwards, the Formidable surrendered to Henry Speke of the Resolution.

The Torbay was then locked in a duel with the 74-gun French ship the *Thésée*, which '*seemed determined to engage us. We soon got alongside of her and after exchanging some broadsides the French ship sunk.*' What the log does not say is that due to the gales and rough seas, both ships were heeling and in danger of being

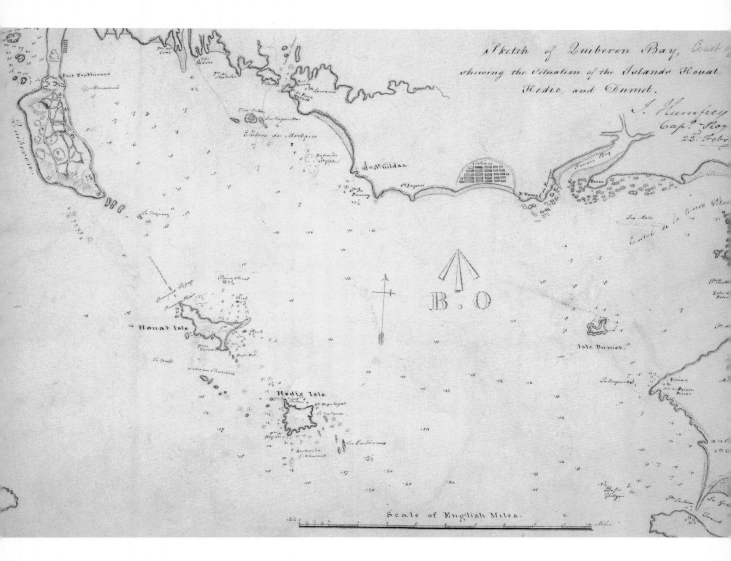

Sketch of Quiberon Bay, Coast of France, Shewing the Situation of the Islands Houat, Hedic and Dumet.

Scale of English Miles.

flooded through their lower-deck gun ports. Unfortunately the *Thésée* did not close her lower gun ports in time and sank with all hands, apart from twenty-two men who were rescued.

Hawke's flagship the *Royal George* succeeded in sinking another French ship, the *Superbe*, after an exchange of broadsides at 4:41pm, according to the captain's log. This was a rare sight indeed as ships of this period were seldom sunk through broadside fire alone. Meanwhile, the badly damaged French vessel *Héros* had surrendered to Viscount Howe, commander of the *Magnanime*. Unfortunately Howe was prevented from taking possession of her due to the proximity of retreating French ships and the worsening weather.

The captain's log entries for the *Royal George* describe vividly the battle that then ensued amid treacherous weather conditions:

Month day and year	Course	Winds	Dist.	Latde.	Longde.	Bearings & Distce. at Noon	Remarks On Board His Majesty's Ship Maidstone 1759.
Novr. 1758 Mondy 19		NEbE to NbE					Mod. & Cloudy Wear. the Whole fleet 7 or 8 Miles a Stern of us a 7 pm Wore Ship & Stod to the Fleet a 9 Wore again a 10 Shortned Sail for the Fleet a 7 am Saw 2 Sails in the NE a 11 the Admiral made our Lieut Signal sent the Boat on Bd of him. Read the Articles of War & New act.
Tuesdy 20		SbW NNW WbN W				Belle Isle N26E 3 or 4 Leag	Hard Gales & Cloudy Wear. a 1 pm Admiral made Signal to call in all Cruizers Dc. Torbay Signal to Chace to the SW Exercised great Guns & small arms. a 11 Shortned Sail for the fleet a 1 1&2 Reff Topsails ½ past 3 made Sail a 5 in 3 Reff Topsails a 8 am Saw a Large fleet of Ships ahead which we took to be the French Fleet made Signal which the Magnanime repeated Admiral made Sail & gave Chace also made Signal to form a Line of Battle a head lost our yaul with the Crew &c
Wednesdy 21		NW NWbN NW NbW				Belle Isle NW½W 5 or 6 Leagues.	Do. Wea. & Squally the Torbay, Resolution & Warspite Magnanime came up with us & gave us 3 Cheers, which we rett 3/4 past 2 the Headmost of our Ships begun to Engage the Sternmost of the Ennemy's at 2 Cables Length at 40 min. after 3 the french W. Admiral fore topmast was Shott away when he bore out of the Line the Magnanime & another followed him & Engaged him more Ships coming up made the Action more General, a 4 a Large french Ship wt a Rear Admiral Flag Struck, saw several of our Ships Disabled ½ past 4 one of the french Ships sunk wth. flying Colours a 5 the french was Obliged to Ware & Come to a general Engagem. the Wind coming more Northerly a ½ past 5 another of them sunk alongside Admr Hawke a 6 pm Anchd. in 10 fm Waydick WbS, several Ships Continued firing Guns of Distress, at day Light saw the Resolution & Essex aground on the Fours, & 2 french Ships on Creisig where they Lost their Masts. a 7 Adm Hawke made Signal to Weigh but in Weighing was Obliged to Cutt the Cable to prevt being foul of the Magnanime a 9 our Mn Mast went by the Bd being Obliged to Carry Sail to prevent being aground on the Fours Sand lost three Sail

'Strong gales and squally; made the signal for all cruisers of the Revenges signal to chase to windward.., at 2 am made the signal to alter course got down topgallant yards close reef the topsails sounded 70 fathom[s], fine grey sand; at 7[am] made the signal and bore away out reef top sails and got up topgallant yard; made Magnanime signal to come within hail, who was ordered to go ahead; at 8[am] made the signal for the line of battle a breast 2 cables length asunder apart; the Magnanime made the signal for a fleet; made the general signal to chase; at ¾ the Magnanime made the signal for the fleet being an enemy; at 10[am] discovered the enemy 18 sail of the line and 4 frigates. Three flags: Admiral, Vice and Rear; the Rochester and Chatham joined the fleet; repeated the signal to 8 sail on our larboard quarter still on chase.

Fresh gales and heavy squalls; at ½ past 2[pm] the Dorsetshire and Torbay began to engage the rear of the French fleet under sail; Soon after several of our head most ships began to engage; made signal for a general engagement; at 3 got round the Cardinal Rocks; at 55 minutes past 3 the French Rear Admiral struck to the Resolution; fired a shot at the Burford for her to make sail and engage the enemy; at 4 the ship [that] the Torbay was engaged with sunk; at 35 minutes after 4 we got up with 4 sail of the enemy ships who all wore and give us their broadsides, we there began to engage; at 41 minutes after 4 the French ship abreast of sunk; the French hauled their wind; at 5[pm] being dark made the signal to anchor; anchored in 15 fathoms [of] water; made the signal for all lieutenants; at 7am saw 2 French ships a shore near Crozie [Le Croisic] and 11 sail near Vilaine River; saw the Resolution ashore near the four bank with all her masts gone; made the signal to weigh but it blowing hard was obliged to wear away again. Made the signal for all captains and got down topgallant yards; made the Essex signal to cut or slip and chase leeward; at 9[am] the Essex ran ashore near the Resolution and made the signal of distress; the Rochester and 2 frigates and all boats went to the assistance of the Resolution and Essex.

On examining into damages sustained by the enemy found a pair of main shrouds shot away; 21 of the mizzen shrouds; 31 of four topmasts; shrouds of mast of our running rigging; our foresail much shattered, unbent it and bent another; 1 shot through the bowsprit and 1 through the mizzen mast; 1 lodged in the foremast; part of the main trussell truss shot away and 8 shot in the hull sound; the Swiftsure and the Revenge absent; at 11[am] sent our boats to take some men off from the French wrecks. Mastheads, made the Coventry signal to lay by the Formidable; in clearing the ship

DOC. 1 Log of the *Maidstone* 27 January 1758 to 31 October 1762.

throwed [threw] overboard 5 dead bullocks and a sheep just killed for the ships company.'

At around 5pm, with the onset of darkness, Admiral Hawke made the signal for the fleet to anchor, and the *Royal George* and several ships did so near the Isle of Dumet. As the morning of 21 November dawned, the results of the night's chaotic conditions became visible. The *Torbay* captain's log describes the scene:

> *'Two of the enemy's ships [the Héros and the Soleil Royal] that had anchored in the night were forced to run ashore near Croizie...; the Resolution being ashore with all her masts gone on the foursand [four shoal]; the admiral made the Essex's signal to go to her assistance who by not being acquainted with the sand likewise run aground...; saw 6 or 7 sail of the enemy's large ships and two or three frigates close in shore and as we supposed aground.'*

The enemy ships and frigates seen close in shore by the *Torbay* were attempting to retreat up the river Villaine and were jettisoning their guns and cargo to clear the sandbank at the river's estuary. One of the French ships, the *Inflexible*, did not successfully clear the sandbar and was wrecked. Eight French ships of the line managed to escape south to the port of Rochefort, whilst one, the *Juste*, was wrecked on rocks close to the river Loire.

Hawke's aggressive but risky strategy had paid off. The French fleet had been routed and the French invasion plans had literally been scuppered! This victory had a wider impact, affecting the course of the Seven Years' War (1756–63), as French ships could no longer resupply their territories and garrisons, leading to the collapse of French resistance in North America and Canada.

Hawke knew the risks involved that day, yet failure to engage the enemy could have been far more fatal to the security of Britain and his own career. In his dispatch to the Admiralty he wrote that, given '... *the hard gales on the day of action, a flying enemy, the shortness of the day and the coast we are on, I can boldly affirm that all that could possibly be done has been done. As to the loss we have sustained let it be placed to the account of necessity I was under of running all risks to break this strong force of the enemy.*'

DOCS. 2 & 3 Log of the *Royal George* 21 December 1756 to 27 February 1760.

216

Month Days	Days	Winds	Courses	Miles	Latitude	Longitude	Bearing & Distance at Noon	Remarks &c. on board His Majesty's Ship Royal George
Tuesday	Nov 13	NE / NW / NWbW					At Anchor in Torbay / Mewstone NE	
Wednesday	14	NW to NE					Mewstone N.E.b.N	
Thursday	15	NWbN ½S to SEbS		44	49-30 N	0-31 W	Start N.E.b.N ½ E League	
Friday	16	NE to SEbE / SEbS	SW	20	48-57	1-25	D.º N.E.b.N ½ N 30 Leag	
Saturday	17	SEbE to NE	NWbN	59	48-23	2-35	Ushant E.b.N 18 Leagues	
Sunday	18	SEbE to NEbE	SW	26	47-57	2-46	Penmarks E.b.N 30 Leagues	
Monday	19	SSE to NE / NE	ESEbS	74	47-22	1-10	Belle Isle E.b.N 23 Leag	
Tuesday	20	NE to NW			47-07		D.º W.b.N ½ N 5 Leagues	

Week Days	Month Days	Winds	Courses	Dist. in Miles	Latitude	Longitude	Bearings and at Noon
	Novem	WNW					At Single Anchor Isand Dumels NS of NoS Mile
Wednesday	21st	NW	" " " " " "				Cardenels WbS-
	1759	NWNW					
Thursday	22	SW to NNE	" " " " " "				Under Sail the Rocks SW3W 2 Le
Friday	23	ENE So SE	" " " " " "				At Anchor The Isle of Dum SbE Vilaine River The Cardinal Boc SW3W W
Saturday	24th	SE to SSE	" " " " " "				
Sunday	25th	SSE to SSW	" " " " " "				Winds varings as before
Monday	26th	SSW to SW	" " " " " "				
Tuesday	27th	SW to WSW	" " " " " "				
Wednesday	28th	WSW	" " " " " "				Under Sail the SbSo 2 Miles
Thursday	29th	WSW No NNE	" " " " " "				Moord the Cardinal Boc SW3W ½W S
Friday	30	NNE to NE	" " " " " "				

Remarks &c.ᵃ on board His Majesty's Ship Royal George

Agreed At Minutes after to the French Ship a Breast of Sunk the French Fleet hauled their Wind at 8 being dark made the Signal to Anchor ... ᵈ. fresh Water made the Signal for all Lieutenants at 7 AM Saw 2 French Ships a shore near Crozie and 11 Sail ... ... River ... Saw the Resolution a shore near the Four Bank with all her Masts gone made the Signal to ... It blowing hard was oblig'd to wear away again. Made the Signal for all Captains and got down Top G.t Yards made the Signal ... to cut or Slip and Schawls Leward at 9 the Essex was a shore near the Resolution and made Signal of Distress the Rochester and 2 Frigates ... sent went to the Assistance of the Resolution and Essex.

... into Damages sustained by the Enemy found a pair of Main Shrouds shott away 2 of Mizen Shrouds 3 of Fore Rigging ... much ... running Rigging our Foresail much Shatter'd ... boat 1 ... boat another 1 Shott thro the Arms ...chest, and 1 thro the Mizen Mast 1 Topsail in ... part of the Main Topsail Tore spott away and 8 Shott in the Hull found the Swiftsure and Revenge Absent at 11 sent ... boats ... ... one Man off from the French Packet. Mast heads, made the Coventry Sig.l to lay by the Torm...ble in Clearing Ship ... ... Bullocks and 3 Sheep just killed for the Ships Company.

... Signals at times at 2 Unmoor Top g.t t'ant masts, at 4 AM Got up Top G.t Masts and Yards at 7 made the Sig.l to Weigh the Portland & Chatham ... to burn their 2 Ships a shore near Crozie at 11 Weigh'd and came to Sail as did the Fleet.

... & t'anted at 1 PM more of the Ships on ... near Crozie was set on fire at 3 made the Sig.l to Anchor. the Namur ... Hercules and Temple ... ... bay in Chase of 2 Ships near Gueldon at 4 past came to an Anchor, 11 Sail of Ships got up Vilaine River. the Commodore with the rest ... to lat here was ordered to lay off Vilaine River at 7 AM made the Signal for all Lieutenants with Weekly Accounts at 9 made ... for all Longboats and Pinaces. the other Ships was set on fire near Crozie.

...hazey the Chatham and Portland was ordered to take their Stores &c. out of the Resolution and Essex, set the Ships on Fire that ... ... our time Lordship fired a Gun and made the Hercules Signal, made the Vengeance Signal for their Captain at Noon ... Signal and Mortal... each way.

... and t'angged th... fild here the Vengeance ... ... Camp bell ... made the Mars, Torbay, Kingston and Montague Sig. for ... ants at 7 AM made the General Sig. for Lieutenants ... came on board Capt. Lockhart and took Command.

...hazey their Frigate and Fireships Working to Vilaine River at 8 AM the Dunkirk Signal was made for an Officer the Mars Kingston and ... working up Anchor'd here the Swiftsure, Firm and Southampton Frigate.

...air at 2 PM Anchor'd here the Belliqueux at 7 AM made the Signal for all Weekly Accounts Sail'd here the Torbay Capt. Keppel with ... the Leward 3 Frigates at 11 the V. Admiral made the Sig. for all Captains Anchor'd here the Success and a bomb.

...hazey W. Pinsley's ... logging the Ship at ½ past 7 made the Sig. to Unmoor at Unmoored at ½ past 10 made the Sig. to Weigh at 11 ... Came to Sail.

...Wind & fair latter Squally with some Rain at 2 PM made the Sig. and Anchor'd with the Bt Bower in 14 f.m Water at ½ past made the Signal to Moor ... Scraping Sides heeling Ship and Boottopping. Anchor'd here the D.o ... ... Rochester and ... Torm...ble the V.e Admir... Sig. for all Captains Sail'd here the Coventry on a Cruize.

...fair Sail'd the Rochester on a Cruize. People Employ'd working in the Hold Received on board 8 Pipes of Wine at ... Signal for all Lieutenants. Anchor'd here the Saphire from Vilaine River.

The Battle of the Nile
ABOUKIR BAY, EGYPT ... 1798

In the early hours of 2 August 1798 a British fleet under Rear Admiral Sir Horatio Nelson completed what was arguably Nelson's greatest victory. The crushing defeat of the French fleet in Aboukir Bay re-established British control in the Mediterranean, ended any French hopes of taking the war to Britain in Asia and helped build the Second Coalition against revolutionary France.

Early in 1798 a young French general by the name of Napoleon Bonaparte petitioned the government to be allowed to lead an invasion of Egypt. French victories over the First Coalition had left only Britain holding out against the revolutionary forces. Napoleon decided to take the fight to the British by attacking them in Asia. He proposed the invasion of Egypt, with the eventual plan of linking up with Tipu Sultan, ruler of the Indian state of Mysore, in a grand alliance against Britain.

The French government approved this remarkable plan, and in May Napoleon left Toulon with his army, escorted by a French fleet of thirteen ships of the line. The French called in at Malta, besieging and capturing the fortress at Valetta before proceeding to Egypt. The fleet – in Nelson's words, '*a French Army of 40,000 men in 300 Transports with 13 Sail of the Line 11 Frigates, Bomb Vessels, Gun Boats &c*' – anchored at Alexandria, and Napoleon and his army disembarked unopposed. Victory over Egypt's Mamaluk rulers at the Battle of the Pyramids secured French control of the country and it looked as if Napoleon's plan was working.

The British, meanwhile, had known something was afoot and a fleet under Nelson had been sent to the Mediterranean. Nelson, however, guessed that the French would be heading to Egypt and sailed there directly. Napoleon's detour to Malta meant that the British arrived in Egypt to find the harbours empty. Nelson assumed that he had been mistaken and that the French were headed elsewhere. He proceeded to hunt all around the eastern Mediterranean for the French fleet. Eventually, intelligence reached him that the French were in Egypt after all, and

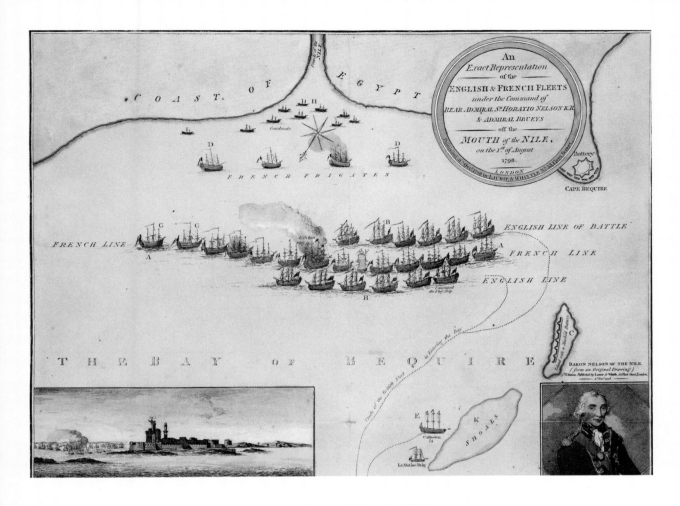

Map showing 'An Exact Representation of the English and French Fleets' at Abu Qir Bay on 1 August 1798. **ABOVE**

Nelson setting about a host of crocodiles with a club of 'British Oak' from a contemporary cartoon. **LEFT**

DOCS 1, 2, 3 & 4 Letter from Horatio Nelson to the Governor of Bombay written from his ship *Vanguard* at the mouth of the Nile, on 9 August 1798.

Vanguard, Mouth of the Nile 9th Augt 1798

Sir,

Altho' I hope the Consuls who are (or ought to be) resident [in] Egypt have sent you an Express of the Situation of Affairs here, as I know Mr Baldwin has some months left Alexandria, it is [possi]ble you may not be regularly informed, I shall therefore Calculate [state] briefly, That a French Army of 40,000 Men in 300 Transports [with] 13 Sail of the Line 11 Frigates, Bomb Vessels, Gun Boats &c [arr]ived at Alexandria on the 1st of July and on the 7th they left [it f]or Cairo where they arrived on the 22d — during the march [the]y had some Actions with the Mamalucks, which they call great Victories — As I have Buonapate's dispatches [befor]e me (which I took yesterday) I speak positively [H]e says, I am now going, to send off to take Suez & Damietta, [He] does not speak very favorably of either the Country or People, [bu]t there is so much bombast in his Letters, that it is
Difficult

difficult to get near the truth, and He does not mention India in these Dispatches. He is, what is called Organizing the Country, but you may be Assured He is master only of what His Army Covers.

From all the Enquiries which I have been Able to make, I cannot learn that any French Vessels are at Suez to carry any part of this Army to India; Bombay (if they can get there) I know is their first Object; but I trust Almighty God will in Egypt overthrow these Pests of the Human Race —

It has been in my power to prevent 12,000 Men from leaving Genoa and also to take 11 Sail of the Line and two Frigates in short only two Sail of the Line and two Frigates have escaped me: This Glorious Action was fought at the mouth of the Nile at Anchor. It began at Sunset Augt 1st and was not finished at 3 the next Morning, It has been severe but God blessed our Endeavours with a great Victory.

I am now at Anchor between Alexandria & Rosetta to
prevent

revent their Communication by Water, and nothing under a
Regiment can pass by Land; but I should have informed You
that the French have 4.000 men posted at Rosetta to keep
open the mouth of the Nile; Alexandria, both Town
and Shipping are so distressed for Provisions (which they can
only get from the Nile by Water) that I cannot guess the
good Success which may attend my holding our present
Position, for Buonaparte writes his distress for Stores, Artillery, Things for their Hospitals &c ———— All usefull
Communication is at an end between Alexandria and
Cairo —— You may be Assured I shall remain here as long
possible — Buonaparte had never yet to contend with
an English Officer and I shall endeavour to make him respect.
this is all I have to Communicate — I am Confident,
every Precaution will be taken to prevent in future any
Ships going to Suez which may be able to carry Troops

to India —— If my Letter is not so correct as might be expected I trust for your excuse when I tell you that my
Brain is so shook with the Wounds in my head that
I am sensible I cannot always be so clear as could be
wished — but whilst a Ray of reason remains my Heart
and my Head shall ever be exerted for the Benefit of
our King and Country ————

         I have the Honor to be

              Sir &c &c

       (Signed)   Horatio Nelson

The Officer Lieutenant Dewal who carries this Dispatch
Voluntary to You will I trust be immediately sent to
England with such Recommendations as his Conduct
may deserve ————

         To the Honble The Govr of Bombay

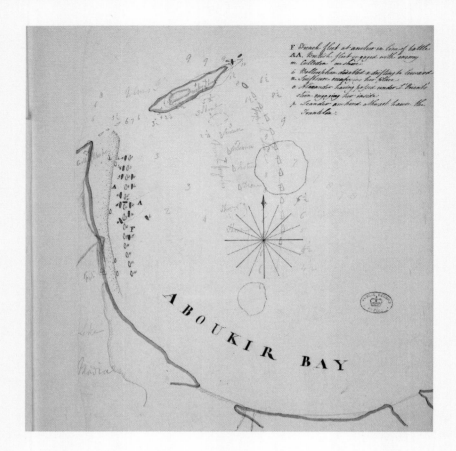

Two plans showing stages in the battle of Abukir Bay, 1798. **LEFT & RIGHT**

on the afternoon of 1 August the British sighted the French ships anchored in Aboukir Bay.

As the British closed in on their quarry, the Egyptian sun began to set. The French fleet was anchored in a line across the bay, protected at either end by shoals. The French admiral, François-Paul Brueys, was confident that the British would not risk a night-time battle and hoped instead to slip away and avoid combat. Nelson, however, had other ideas.

The British fleet proceeded into the bay and approached the front of the French line. As it did so, Captain Thomas Foley of HMS *Goliath* noticed that the French had left a gap between the ships and the shoal water which protected them. This enabled him to take the extraordinarily dangerous step of sailing inshore of the first French ship and engaging from the land side. Foley was followed by three more of the British ships, while Nelson in HMS *Vanguard* led a second column of British ships engaging from the seaward side. The French were ill prepared to face opponents on both sides, with many of their landward gunports blocked by stores and supplies.

Sandwiched between two enemy ships, the front of French line was

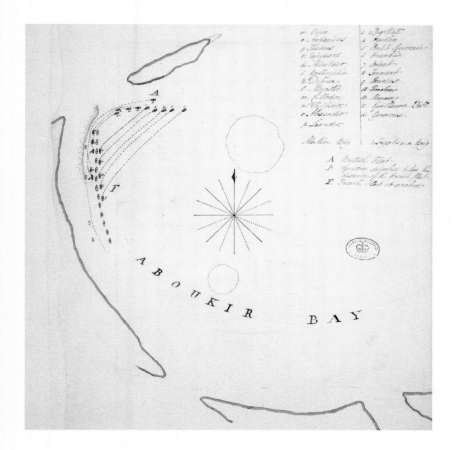

rapidly overpowered. Many of the ships were dismasted and all took heavy casualties. As the first French ships surrendered, the British moved down the line picking off ship after ship. The rear of the French fleet, prevented by the wind direction from coming to the assistance of their compatriots, could only watch and wait.

The battle reached its climax as the British began to engage the middle of the French line. *L'Orient*, the 120-gun French flagship, was comfortably the most powerful vessel in the battle and formed a rock at the centre of the line. She badly damaged a number of British ships, but a fire started on her lower decks and sustained gunfire hampered attempts to extinguish the flames. It took hold and spread to the masts and rigging. At 10pm the flames reached the ship's magazine and the ship blew up with such force that, briefly, silence fell over the battlefield.

The log from the *Goliath* paints this part of the battle in vivid detail:

'... *at 15 minutes past 6 the Goliath being the leading ship cross'd the bows of the van Ship of the Enemys line and commenced the action having cross'd anchored with the Sheet anchor out of the Gun room port and brought up alongside the second ship in the*

enemy's line about this time a French frigate run onshore and was dis-masted by our
ships as they came into action 50 minutes past six the Audacious cross'd ahead of the
ship we were Engaged with and brought up on her Larbd Bow, half past Eight ceased
firing the five van ships of the Enemy having struck their Colours — our main and
mizzen masts with the rigging of those masts were so much cut in several places that
there was much danger of loosing them — all the seamen emply'd stoppering and repairing
the rigging &c at 40 minutes past I observed the French Admls Ship L'Orient of 130
guns on fire at 10 she blew up, from 11 to 2 am a heavy cannonade in the Rear of the
fleets at day light six line of Battle ships had struck their colours ½ past 5 the Artemise
French frigate, fired from her broadside haul'd her colours down and the crew left her
after having set her on fire at 6 cut the cable and run further to leeward to engage the
Enemys rear ¼ past anchor with springs on the Cable and began to fire on the Enemy at
about 7 two ships onshore in the SS&S struck their colours at noon two of the enemy's
line of Battle ships and two frigate got under weigh and stood to the NE and one ship of
the line in the same direction whose foremast went overboard drifted further in shore and
was set on fire by the crew who left her in their boats she shortly afterwards blew up.'

Following frantic efforts to extinguish fires started by flying debris from the explosion on *L'Orient*, the battle recommenced. The British, now heavily outnumbering their opposition, proceeded to destroy or capture the remaining vessels in the centre of the French fleet. On both sides the combination of battered ships and exhausted men began to tell. The guns finally fell silent around 3am, with men falling asleep at their posts. By this point an extraordinary British victory was assured. Only a few ships at the rear of the French line had avoided the worst of the action. Sunrise saw a brief fight between the damaged British ships and the French rear. The French, realising the position was hopeless, tried to escape, but only two ships managed to do so.

Both sides had suffered heavy casualties, the British wounded numbering around 300 and the French approximately 3,000, with the same number of French taken prisoner. Nelson featured among the British wounded, being hit in the forehead by a metal splinter relatively early on in the engagement. This removed a large flap of skin above his right eye and left him unconscious for part of the battle.

On 9 August 1798, writing from HMS *Vanguard* stationed at the mouth of the Nile, Nelson informed the British government of the victory:

'... it has been in my power to prevent 12,000 men from leaving Genoa and also to take 11 Sail of the Line and two Frigates in short only two Sail of the Line and two Frigates have escaped me. This Glorious Action was fought at the mouth of the Nile at Anchor. It began as sunset Augt 1st, and was not finished at 3 the next morning. It has been severe but God blessed our Endeavours with a great Victory. I am now at Anchor between Alexandria and Rosetta to prevent their communication by water, and nothing under a regiment can pass by Land, but I should have informed you that the French have 4,000 men posted at Rosetta to keep open the mouth of the Nile. Alexandria, both Town and Shipping are so distressed for Provisions which they can only get from the Nile by water that I cannot guess the good success which may attend my holding our present Position, for Buonaparte writes his distress for Stores, Artillery, Things for their Hospitals &c – All useful Communication is at an end between Alexandria and Cairo – You may be assured I shall remain here as long as possible. Buonaparte had never yet to contend with an English Officer and I shall endeavour to make him respect us. This is all I have to communicate – I am confident every precaution will be taken to prevent in future any vessels going to Suez which may be able to carry Troops to India – If my Letter is not so correct as might be expected I trust for your excuse when I tell you that my Brain is so shook with the wounds in my head that I am sensible I cannot always be so clear as could be wished – but whilst a Ray of reason remains my Heart and my Head shall ever be exerted for the Benefit of our King and Country.'

The Battle of the Nile was one of the most complete victories in naval history. Nelson had entirely destroyed the French fleet. Of its thirteen ships of the line, only two escaped capture or being sunk. His own fleet, although badly battered, was intact and greatly augmented by the new French prizes. This guaranteed British control of the Mediterranean and left Napoleon and his army cut off in Egypt. It ended any French threat to India, and meant that the war in Europe would soon be reignited.

DOC. 5 Remarks in the log on HMS *Goliath*, August 1798.

DOC. 6 Page from a log on HMS *Vanguard* giving details of action in the battle of the Nile and injuries suffered by Admiral Nelson.

Remarks &c onboard His Majestys Ship Goliath

Fresh breezes and clear W^r at 2 saw Alexandria bearing S E b S up foresail & in stud^g sails
at 40 minutes past 2 the Zealous made the signal N° 23 and 45 minutes past she
made the signal N° 56 with the numeral signal 16 at 3 set the Courses having
discovered the French fleet in the E b N Employ'd clearing for Action as per
Signals 53 and 54 at 38 minutes past 4 PM the mutine bore up to reconitre
the Enemy who were 13 Sail of the Line and four frigates at anchor in Bequin
roads in Line of Battle from Van to Centre NNW and SS E and from Centre to Van
North and South 15 minutes past 5 the Vanguard made signals N° 45 & 46
and 55 minutes past 5 N° 31 at 3 minute past 6 N° 34 at 15 minutes past 6
the Goliath (being the leading Ship) cross'd the Bows of the van Ship of the Enemys
line and commenced the Action having cross'd anchors with the Sheet anchor
out of the Gun room port and brought up alongside the second Ship in the
Enemys line. about this time a french frigate run on shore and was dis-
-masted by our ships as they came into Action 50 minutes past six the
Audacious cross'd ahead of the Ship we were Engaged with and brought
up on her Larb^d Bow, half past Eight ceased firing the five Van
Ships of the Enemy having struck their Colours — our main and mizen
masts with the rigging of those masts were so much cut in several
Places that there was much danger of loosing them - all the seamen
Employ'd stoppering and repairing the rigging &c at 40 minutes past
8 observed the French Adm^{ls} Ship L'Orient of 130 Guns on fire at 10 she
blew up, from 11^h till 2 AM a heavy cannonade in the Rear of the fleets
at day light six line of Battle Ships had struck their colours ½ past
5 the Artemise french frigate fired her broadside haul'd her colours
down and ^{the crew} left her after having set her on fire at 6 Cut the cable
and run further to leeward to engage the Enemys rear ½ past anchor
with Springs on the Cable and began to fire on the Enemy at about 7
two Ships onshore in the BW struck their Colours - at noon two of the
Enemy's line of Battle Ships and two frigates got under weigh and
Stood to the NE and one ship of the line in the same direction whose
Foremast went overboard drifted further in shore and was set on fire
by *

Mens Names, Ages and Qualities.	When and where put on the Sick List.	Statement of the Case when put on the List.	Symptoms and Treatment while under Cure.	When discharged to Duty, Died, or sent to the Hospital.	REMARKS.
John Pullen	1st August Aft. of Nile	Wounded Thigh	1st. Applied a warm Cataplasm bis die. 2d. do. ... [daily entries through] ... 30th. d. 31. d. Sept. 1st. d. 2. d. 3. d. 4. d. 5. d. 6. d. 7. d. 8. d. 9. d. 10. d. 11th d. 12th d. 13 d. 14. d. 15. d. 16. d. 17. d. 18th d. 19. d. 20. d. 21. d. 22. d. 23. d. 24. d. 25. d. 26. d. 27. d. 28. d. 29. d. 30. d. Octr. 1st. d. 2. d. 3. d.	Discharg'd to Duty 5th October 1798.	
Jno. Dowland	1st August Aft. of Nile	Wounded Eye	1st. Applied a cold Cataplasm bis die. 2d. do. ... [daily entries] ... 21st d. 22. d. 23 d. 24. d. 25. d. 26. d. 27. d.	Discharg'd to Duty Sept 1st 1798	
Geo. Antram Midshipman Age 20	1st August Aft. of Nile	Wounded Thigh	1st. Applied a warm Cataplasm bis die. 2d. ... [daily entries] ... 16. d. 17. d. W. d.	Discharg'd to Duty 19th Sept. 1798.	
Sir Horatio Nelson Reed Admr. of the Blue &c. &c. &c. Age 40	K.B. 1st August Aft. of Nile	Wound on the Forehead over the Right Eye. The Examina... have been for more than an Inch; the wound three Inches long	[detailed daily treatment entries] ... 25. d. 26. d. 27. d. 28. d. 29. d. 30. d. 31. d.	Discharg'd 1st Sept.	The wound was perfectly heal'd on the first of September but as the integuments were much enlarg'd I applied every night a compress with a discutient embrocation for nearly a month which was of great service.

The Battle of Trafalgar
OFF CAPE TRAFALGAR, SPAIN ... 1805

The Battle of Trafalgar was the most significant British naval victory of the Napoleonic Wars, ending French hopes of invading Britain. On 20 August 1805 the French Grande Armée had massed near Boulogne to invade Britain. The English Channel was the only barrier, and more than 2,000 landing craft were to transport Napoleon's army across it. All Napoleon required was sufficient ships to protect the invading army, but his warships were blockaded by the Royal Navy in French and Spanish ports. His plan, therefore, was to distract the Royal Navy – Britain's protector – with his Mediterranean fleet, allowing his Channel squadrons to protect the invasion. The stage was set for the Battle of Trafalgar, the sternest test yet of Britain's resolve.

Nelson was Commander-in-Chief of the Mediterranean, and had joined HMS *Victory* in 1803. His mission was to prevent the French fleet at Toulon from joining their counterparts in Brest. The pressure on him was so immense that it had repercussions on his health, as revealed in his letter to the Admiralty of 16 August 1804, written on board HMS *Victory*, in which he requests permission to return to England for the sake of his health. He states:

> 'It is with much uneasiness of mind that I feel it is my duty to state to you for the information of their Lordships, that I consider my state of health to be such as to make it absolutely necessary that I should return to England to reastablish it, another Winter such as the last I feel myself unable to Stand against, a few months of quiet may enable me to serve again next Spring, and I believe that no officer is more anxious to serve than myself, no officer could be placed in a more enviable Command than the one I have the honor of being placed in, and no Command ever produced so much happiness to a Commander in Chief, whether in the flag officers, the Captains, or the good conduct of the Crews of every Ship in this fleet and the constant marks of approbation for my conduct which I have received from every Court in the Mediterranean leave me nothing to wish for, but a better state of Health'

Nelson riskily calculated not to closely blockade the French fleet at Toulon. On the contrary, he hoped it would escape and join the fleet at Brest, enabling him to annihilate the entire French fleet in one battle. This scenario became reality when the French fleet under Admiral Villeneuve escaped from Toulon on 30 March 1805. It was to join Admiral Ganteaume's fleet from Brest and attack the British fleet blockading the French and Spanish ships at Ferrol. This combined French fleet would then join Villeneuve in Martinique, a French island in the Caribbean. However, Ganteaume could not break the blockade of Brest, and he did not arrive in Martinique, Villeneuve was to intercept British convoys before returning to Cadiz. Six French and Spanish ships were already in Martinique, as well as

The British fleet at the battle of Trafalgar.

BELOW

Admiral Missiessy's fleet. Napoleon's plan was to unite them and direct them to Boulogne to aid Napoleon's invasion.

News of Napoleon's plan reached London in April 1805, but Nelson, who was at Toulon, was not informed. With Ganteaume unable to escape, Napoleon, who was advised that Nelson was pursuing Villeneuve's fleet, altered his plans. He ordered Villeneuve to capture British colonies in the West Indies before joining the Spanish ships at Ferrol. The joint force would then defeat the British blockade of Brest. This was asking a lot of Villeneuve, who decided to return to Europe.

In May 1805, Nelson discovered that Villeneuve's fleet had reached the West Indies. He pursued the French ships to Barbados, only to be told that Villeneuve had sailed towards Trinidad. In fact, he had sailed towards Martinique. Nelson had missed a golden opportunity, and returned to Europe on 20 July. It was the first time in nearly two years that he had set foot on land, and he declared himself mortified at not being able to get at the enemy.

On 22 August Nelson returned to Merton Place in Surrey, which he shared with his lover, Lady Emma Hamilton. He did not know that Villeneuve had in fact arrived at Cadiz two days before. Admiral Collingwood, commanding a blockading squadron off Cadiz, notified the Admiralty of the combined Franco-Spanish fleet's presence there. This news was relayed to Nelson on 2 September. He left Merton on 13 September, aware of his possible fate, as revealed by his diary entry:

> 'Friday night at half past Ten drove from Dear dear Merton where I left all which I hold dear in this World to go to serve my King & Country May the Great God whom I adore enable me to fulfil the expectations of my Country and if it is His good pleasure that I should return my thanks will never cease being offered up to the throne of His Mercy, If it is His good providence to cut Short my days upon Earth I bow with the greatest Submission relying that He will protect those so dear to me that I may leave behind. His Will be done amen amen amen'

Nelson rejoined HMS *Victory* on 14 September and sailed to Cadiz. On 27 September he took over Collingwood's squadron. The Franco-Spanish fleet remained there, and on 16 September Napoleon ordered it to sail to Naples. The senior officers refused, fearing the strength of the British fleet. Villeneuve, on hearing that six of Nelson's ships had reached Gibraltar on 18 October, gave the order to leave Cadiz. As it withdrew from Cadiz, the Franco-Spanish fleet was spotted by HMS *Euryalus*, and the British fleet was alerted.

Nelson did not attack immediately as he wanted to be certain of engaging all of the enemy ships. Instead he discreetly shadowed the Franco-Spanish fleet at a distance, keeping it under surveillance with his frigates. On 20 October 1805 the opposing fleets drew closer. At 4am on 21 October 1805 Nelson ordered a change of direction towards the enemy. He gave the order to prepare for battle at 6am. Owing to light winds, he knew that it would be several hours before his fleet would be able to engage the Franco-Spanish fleet in action. In the meantime, he finalised some private matters, requesting that the government take care of Lady Hamilton and his daughter, and writing in his diary what has become known as Nelson's prayer:

> *'May the Great God whom I worship Grant to my Country and for the benefit of*
> *Europe in General a great and Glorious Victory, and may no misconduct in any one*
> *tarnish it, and May humanity after Victory be the predominant feature in the British*
> *fleet, for myself individually I commit my Life to Him who made me…'*

At 11.48am Nelson made the famous signal 'England expects that every man will do his duty' to his fleet of thirty-three ships and 18,000 personnel. At around midday, off Cape Trafalgar, his fleet formed into two columns. One was led by HMS *Victory*, the other by HMS *Royal Sovereign*, commanded by Collingwood. They sailed towards a single line of thirty-three French and Spanish ships on which nearly 30,000 men served.

Traditionally, naval fleet battles at sea consisted of two opposing parallel lines of ships firing broadsides at each other. Such tactics were found in the Royal Navy's first publication on this subject, *Sailing and Fighting Instructions*, published in 1673. This book stressed the importance of maintaining the line in battle. It was a tactic that had been employed virtually unchanged until Nelson's day. However, by using a different tactic and splitting his fleet into two columns,

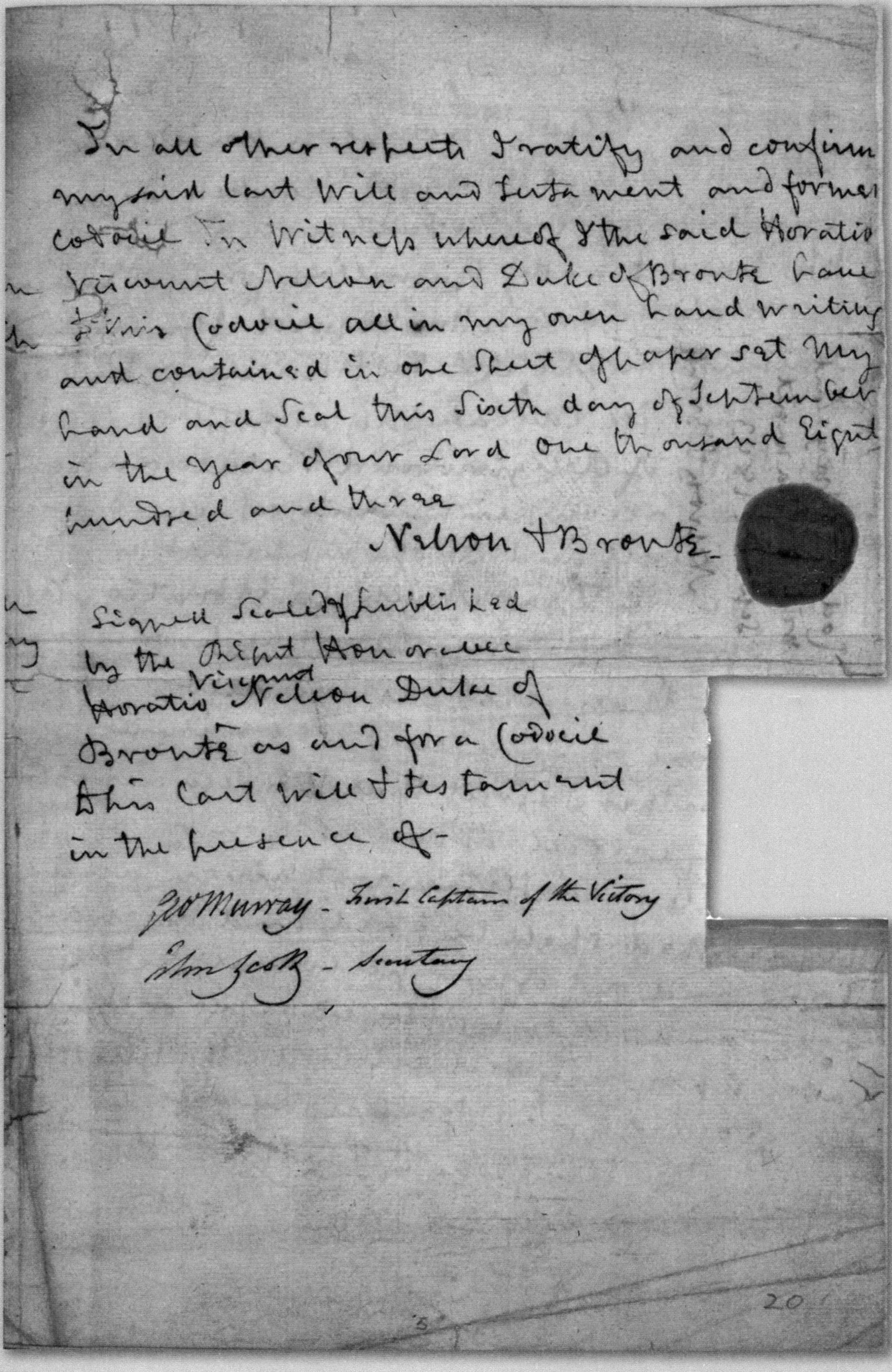

In all other respects I ratify and confirm
my said last Will and Testament and former
codicil In Witness whereof I the said Horatio
Viscount Nelson and Duke of Bronte have
this Codicil all in my own hand writing
and contained in one sheet of paper set my
hand and seal this Sixth day of September
in the year of our Lord one thousand Eight
hundred and three

Nelson & Bronte

Signed Sealed & published
by the Right Honourable
Horatio Viscount Nelson Duke of
Bronte as and for a Codicil
& his Last will & Testament
in the presence of —

Geo Murray — First Captain of the Victory

John Scott — Secretary

234

Nelson was intent, daringly and innovatively, on concentrating his ships' attack on breaking the enemy line at several strategic points. This tactic was known as the 'Nelson Touch', and it would surprise the enemy, causing what he referred to as a '*pell-mell battle*'. This favoured the superior gunnery and seamanship of the British fleet, though it was a dangerous tactic as the leading ships of the two

DOC. 1   The last page of Admiral Nelson's will, signed on 6 September 1803.

Map showing the position of the British fleet at the battle of Trafalgar on 21 October 1805.   LEFT

AN ACCURATE PLAN of the THREE POSITIONS of the BRITISH FLEET.

Before Lord Nelson Commenced the Action with the Combined Squadrons of France & Spain on the 21st Octr. 1805. Cape Trafalgar bearing E.SE 4 leagues, Drawn by Mr. Jonas Toby, Purser of H.M.Ship Euryalus who was a Spectator of this Glorious Victory.

British divisions were raked head-on with enemy gunfire from about noon without being able to return fire until they closed in on the enemy line, as HMS *Victory* did at about 12:30pm. Although these tactics had been used before – for example, at the Battle of St Vincent in 1797 – they had never had such a devastating effect as at Trafalgar.

HMS *Victory* fired her first broadsides at the *Bucentaure*, the French Admiral's flagship. Alongside HMS *Victory*, other British ships began to engage French and Spanish ships, breaking through the enemy line. In his log, Captain Thomas Hardy of HMS *Victory* described the ships in their proximity to each other as '*closed like a forest*'. HMS *Victory* then collided with *Redoutable*, becoming entangled with her rigging.

At about 1.15pm, Nelson was hit by a musket ball fired by a sharpshooter on *Redoutable*. It passed through his left shoulder and a lung and lodged in his spine. Nelson was carried to the cockpit, knowing his backbone had been shot through and that he was close to death. In his eyewitness account of the carnage of battle, Hardy describes Nelson's fatal wounding:

'Tuesday, Oct 22, 1805 Light airs and cloudy, standing towards the Enemy's van with all sail set. At 4 minutes past twelve opened our fire on the Enemy's van, in passing down their line. At twenty minutes part 12, in attempting to pass through the Enemy's line, fell on board the 10th and 11th ships, when the action became general. About 15 minutes after one, the Right Hon. Lord Viscount Nelson, and Commander in Chief was wounded in the shoulder. At 1h 30m the Redoubtable having struck her Colours, we ceased firing our starboard guns, but continued engaging the Santissima Trinidad and some of the Enemy's ships on the larboard side. Observed the Temeraire between the Redoubtable and another ship of the line, both of which had been struck. The action continued general until three o'clock, when several of the Enemy's ships around us had struck... at 4.15 the Spanish Rear Admiral to Windward struck to some of our Ships, which had Tacked after them, observed one of the Enemy's Ships blow up and 14 Sail standing towards Cadiz and 3 standing to the Southward, partial firing continued until 3.40 when a Victory having been reported to the Admiral Right Hon[oura]ble Lord Visc[oun]t Nelson KB [] and Commander in Chief, he died of his Wounds, at 5 the Mizzen Mast fell about 10 feet above the Poop, the lower Masts,

DOC. 2 Log from Admiral Nelson's ship, HMS *Victory*, 16–22 October 1805.

DOC. 3 Log from Admiral Nelson's ship, HMS *Victory*, 22–24 October 1805.

132

Week Days	Mo Days	Winds	Courses	Dist.	Lat.	Long.	Bearg & Dist at Noon	Remarks &c
October Tuesday	16	NWbN South	N 23 W	5	36. 20	7. 20	Cadiz N 78 E 18 Leags	P.M. Moderate Breezes and cloudy, L'Aimable & Renommée parted Company with Convoy. A.M. Ditto. Exercised great Guns and small Arms
Wednesday	17	WbS	N 7 W	16	36. 36	7. 22	Do S 84 E 18½ Leags	P.M. Fresh Breezes and cloudy. Donegal & Naeegle parted Company.
Thursday	18	WSW	North	3	36. 39	7. 22	Do S 81 E 19 Leags	P.M. Ditto Wr. Employd variously. at Noon light Airs the high land of Cape St. Mary's bore NbW 10 Leagues, Fleet in Company.
Friday	19	ESE	S 10 E	8	36. 32	7. 19	Do S 89 E 17 Leags	P.M. Light Airs shifted the Maintopsail. employd occasionally
Saturday	20	SEbS	N 25 E	4	36. 36	7. 16	S 88 E 16 Leags.	P.M. Light Breezes and Calm tried for soundings, every two hours with 160 furs of line, performed Divine Service. Squally with Rain lowered the Topsails on the Cap, Fleet in Company—
							Do N 39 E	P.M. Light Breezes and squally with Rain at 2 taken aback, came to the wind on the Starboard Tack. at 4 wore Ship sup Topgallant Yards lookout Ships making Signals of the Enemy's Position. at 8.40 wore Ship at 12 ditto Wr. at 4 wore Ship at 6 observed the Enemy bearing SbE 10 or 11 Miles bore up out all Reefs Topsails, set steering Sails & Royals cleared for Quarters. at 8 Light Breezes and cloudy Body of the Enemy's Fleet EbS 9 or 10 Miles still standing for the Enemy
Sunday	21	SSW SWbS	W	28	36. 10	6. 18	9½ Leagues Cape St. Mary's N 49 W 26½ Leagues	on the Royal Sovereigns other Line of Battle steering for the centre of the Enemy's Line— The Enemy's line extending about NNE & SSW at 11.40 the Royal Sovereign commenced firing on the Enemy, they having begun on her at 11.30 —
Tuesday	22	NNW W SSW						P.M. Light Airs and cloudy, standing towards the Enemy's Van with all Sail set. at 4 minutes past 12 opened our fire on the Enemy's Line in passing down their Line at 12.20 in attempting to pass through their Lines, fell on board the 10th & 11th Ships, when the Action became general. about 1.15. Admiral, the Right Honble Lord Visct Nelson K.B. &c— and Commander in Chief was wounded in the Shoulder at 1.30 the Redoubtable having struck her colors we ceased firing our Starboard Guns, but continued engaged with the Santissima Trinidada, and some of the Enemy's Line on the Larboard side observed the Temeraire between the Redoubtable and another Enemy Ship of the Line, both of which had struck. The Action continuing general until 3 O'Clock when several of the Enemy's Ships around us had struck. observed the Royal Sovereign with the loss of her Main and Mizen Masts and several of the Enemy Ships around her dismasted. at 3.30 observed 4 Sail of the

Week Days	Mo Days	Winds	Courses	Dist.	Lat	Long.	Bear at No
October							
Tuesday	22	NNW W SSW					
Wednesday	23	SSE W SWbS			36.19	6.38	Cape Tra S72 E 10" Lea Cadi N57 E 72 Lea
Thursday	24	SbW SSW SWbS					The heigh of Notar E½ S Cape 70 N 22½ Le

238

Remarks &c ~

133

...y; ...tian Tack and stand along our Wr. Line to windward, fired our
...oard Guns at those they would reach at 3.40 made the Signal for our
... to keep their Wind and engage the Enemy; then coming along our
...ther Line, at 4.15 the Spanish Rear Admiral to Windward struck to
... of our Ships, which had Tacked after them, observed one of the Enemy's
... blew up and 14 Sail standing towards Cadiz and 3 standing to the
... tward, partial firing continued until 3.40 when a Victory having
... reported to the Admiral Right Honble Lord Visct Nelson KB the
... commander in Chief, he died of his Wound, at 5 the Mizen Mast
... bout 10 feet above the Poop, the lower Masts, Yards & Bowsprit all
... killed, rigging and Sails very much cut, the Ships around us very
... h crippled, several of our Ships pursuing the Enemy to Leeward
... vice adml Collingwoods Flag flying onboard HMS Euryalus
... one of our Ships taking possession of the Prizes, struck Top Gt.
... ts got up runners and Tackles to secure the Masts, emp'd
... ing the Wreck of the Yards & Rigging, wore Ship and sounded
... f ms sandy Bottom, stood to the Southward under the remnants,
... sail and maintopsail, sounded from 13 to 19 fms at 2 wore Ship
... y Light saw our Fleet and Prizes 43 Sail, still closing with them
... ape Trafalgar bore SEbE 4 or 5 Leagues, 6.30 saw 3 of the Enemy's
... s to Leeward standing towards Cadiz ~ Fresh Breezes and cloudy
... loyed Knotting the Fore and Main Rigging & fishing and
... ring the Lower Masts, struck the Fore Topmast for a fish for
... foremast, which was very badly wounded, at Noon fresh Breezes and

...u. fresh Breezes and cloudy, employed Knotting and splicing the
... ing, fishing the Fore and Mainmast & bent a Foresail for a Main
... the old Mainsail shot all to pieces, at 11.30 wore Ship, watch emp'd
... ding the lower Masts &c &c &c bent a Maintopsail the old one shot
... ieces, got a Jibboom up & Rigged for a Jury Mizen Mast. Emp'd
... ring the Masts, Yards & Rigging, Carpenters stopping the shot

...u. Fresh Breezes and cloudy Employed clearing the Wreck of the Mizen
... sounded every Hour with 100 fms Line, no bottom, strong Gales and
... Squalls with Rain and a heavy Sea from the Westd at 4 more
... erate sounded in 70 fms mud, Emp'd knotting and splicing the
... ing & woulding the fishes on the lower Masts, Mustered the Ships
... any, Polyphemus took us in Tow

Remarks &c. Victory —

and engage the Enemys van coming along our Weather
Line — At 4.15 The Spanish Rear Admiral to Windward
struck to some of our Ships, which had Tacked after them —
Observed one of the Enemys Ships blow up and 14 Sail of
the Enemys Ships standing towards Cadiz — And 3 Sail
of the Enemys Ships standing to the Southward — Partial
Firing continued untile 3.40 when a Victory having
been reported To the Right Honble. Lord Viscount Nelson
K. B. and Commander in Chief he died of his Wound
At 5 the Mizen Mast fell about 10 feet above the Poop
The Lower Masts, Yards and Bowsprit all crippled
Rigging and Sails very much cut — The Ships around us
much crippled — Several of our Ships pursuing the Enemy
to Leeward — Saw Vice Admiral Collingwoods Flag
flying on Board H. M. Ship Euryalus and some of our
Ships taking Possession of the Prizes — Struck Top Gallt.
Masts, Got up runners and Tackles to secure the Lower
Masts — Employed clearing the Wrecks of the Yards and
Rigging — Wore Ship and Sounded in 32 fm Sandy
Bottom — Stood to the Southward under the Remnants
of Fore Sail & Main Top Sail — Sounded from 13 to 19
fm. At 2 Wore Ship — At Day Light Saw our Fleet and
Prizes 43 Sail in Sight Still closing with our Fleet
At 5 Cape Trafalgar bore S E b E Dist 4 or 5 Leagues — At 6.30
Saw 3 of the Enemys Ships to Leeward Standing
towards Cadiz — Fresh Breezes and Cloudy — Employed
Knotting the Fore and Main Rigging, and Fishing
and Securing the Lower Masts — Struck the Fore
Top Mast for a Fish for the Fore Mast, which was
very badly Wounded — At Noon Fresh Breezes and
Hazy ———

Yards & Bowsprit all crippled, rigging and Sails very much cut, the Ships around us very much crippled, several of our Ships pursuing the Enemy to Leeward Saw Vice Adm[ira]l Collingwoods Flag flying onboard HMS Euryalus and some of our Ships taking Possession of the Prizes...'

DOC. 4 Captain Hardy's log entry recording the death of Admiral Nelson on 21 October 1805.

The funeral barge of Admiral Nelson, 8 January 1805. BELOW

As Nelson lay dying, news arrived from Hardy that between twelve and fourteen enemy ships had been captured. The destruction of the French ship *Achille* at 5:45pm marked the end of the battle; nineteen French and Spanish ships were lost, with 6,953 casualties. Britain suffered 1,690 casualties, but no British vessels were lost.

With this victory, the Royal Navy had established mastery at sea that would last for over a century. It was an emphatic naval victory, but one overshadowed by the death of Nelson, a popular British national hero.

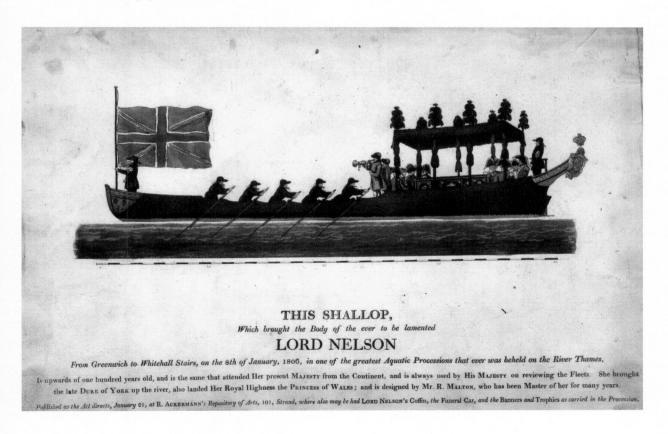

THIS SHALLOP,
Which brought the Body of the ever to be lamented
LORD NELSON
From Greenwich to Whitehall Stairs, on the 8th of January, 1806, in one of the greatest Aquatic Processions that ever was beheld on the River Thames,
Is upwards of one hundred years old, and is the same that attended Her present MAJESTY from the Continent, and is always used by His MAJESTY on reviewing the Fleets. She brought the late DUKE OF YORK up the river, also landed Her Royal Highness the PRINCESS OF WALES; and is designed by Mr. R. MALTON, who has been Master of her for many years.
Published as the Act directs, January 21, at R. ACKERMANN's Repository of Arts, 101, Strand, where also may be had LORD NELSON's Coffin, the Funeral Car, and the Banners and Trophies as carried in the Procession.

The Battle of Navarino Bay
SOUTH-WESTERN GREECE ... 1827

On 20 October 1827 a combined British, French and Russian fleet sailed into Navarino Bay in Greece, lining up alongside the joint Ottoman and Egyptian fleet. The tension between the two sides soon led to all-out battle, and the superior firepower and professionalism of the allied force quickly began to tell. By evening the smoke cleared, revealing the remnants of the shattered Turkish forces. Little did anyone know, but that battle would be the last fought between two sailing fleets, marking the end of a millennia-long era of wood and canvas.

The events that led to the allied fleet sailing into Navarino Bay began six years earlier, with a rebellion by the Greeks against their Ottoman overlords. The Greek cause was very popular with the public throughout Europe, many people wanting to show their support for their Christian brothers against Muslim oppression. Their ranks were swelled by those inspired by a love of Greek culture and history to form a powerful philhellenist movement. Driven by this popular support, the governments of Britain, France and Russia stepped in to prevent the

Simplified map showing the ships' formations prior to the battle of Navarino Bay. **BELOW LEFT**

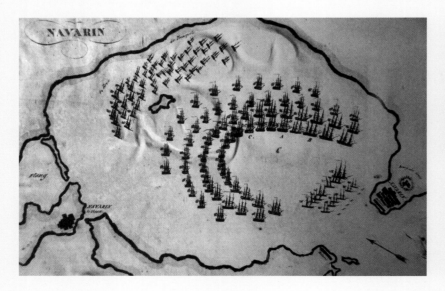

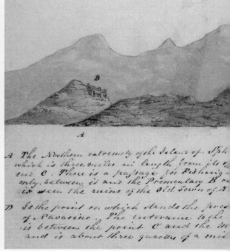

Ottomans from crushing the rebellion. The Treaty of London, signed in 1827, called for an end to hostilities and the establishment of an effectively independent Greek state. When the Ottoman Turks rejected this, Britain, France and Russia sent naval forces to the region to enforce the wishes of the Great Powers.

Attempts at a ceasefire between the Greeks and Ottomans soon broke down and accounts of atrocities committed by the Turks were rife. The Ottoman offensive was facilitated by their superior naval power and it became clear that their fleet posed a major threat to the fledgling Greek state.

Vice-Admiral Sir Edward Codrington, commander of the British fleet, was inspired by the philhellenist movement and had good relations with many of the former Royal Navy officers fighting on the side of the Greeks. By the middle of October his patience with the Ottomans had worn thin and he decided to act. Together with his French and Russian colleagues, Codrington decided to sail into Navarino Bay, where the Turkish fleet was anchored, in a show of force. The allied fleet comprised eleven ships of the line and a number of frigates. The Ottoman fleet was much larger, but had only three ships of the line in total, the remainder being frigates and smaller vessels.

Thus at 1.30pm on 20 October 1827, on a moderate breeze Codrington's flagship HMS *Asia* sailed into the bay, anchoring alongside the Turkish flagship.

Sketch of the entrance of Navarino Harbour seen from a distance of c.seven or eight miles from the Island of Sphazia. It was drawn by Lieutenant E St L Cannon on HMS *Wolf* on 31 January 1828. BELOW

The rest of the allied fleet followed him in, anchoring next to the respective Ottoman ships. Codrington would later argue that entering Navarino Bay was simply a display of force and did not necessarily have to result in violence. In truth, however, it was a highly provocative act, and the decision to anchor so close to the Turks and in fighting order made any other outcome highly unlikely.

For a short while there was an uneasy standoff, with both sides expecting battle, but neither willing to fire the first shot. The spark came when HMS *Dartmouth* sent a boat to guard an as yet unlit Turkish fireship. The Turks, believing the British intended to seize the ship, opened fire on the British sailors. The sailors responded, soon supported by *Dartmouth*. The action spread and the two fleets were fully engaged by 3.00pm.

Edward Curzon, captain of HMS *Asia* took up the story in the captain's log:

'…at 3.15 having completely silenced the Capt Bey hove on the spring and got the starbd Broadside to bear on Moucharem Bey's double tier frigate & some other Vessels that were raking us. At 4.40 the mizzen mast went by the board & the rigging together cut to pieces by the raking fire we were exposed to. at 5.30 having silenced every Vessel our Guns could reach, ceased firing entirely some of the Enemy's Ships on fire ran a hawser to the Genoa, in readiness to haul of a Frigate burning close on our larbd bow, at 5.50 PM she blew up, the firing had then ceased along the whole line, the Turkish fleet being the most part destroyed…'

When HMS *Asia*, the most powerful of the British ships, destroyed the flagship of the Turkish admiral, *Capitana Bey*, inside 30 minutes, she then turned her guns on the frigate leading the Egyptian squadron. While doing so, *Asia* was quite badly damaged by fire from other Ottoman vessels, including a shot which carried away her mizzenmast and killed a number of men. Gradually, however, the greater allied firepower told and the Ottoman ships were silenced one by one. By 5.50pm, as Curzon's log confirms, firing had ceased, and Navarino Bay was littered with the burning wrecks of Turkish ships, a number of which proceeded to blow up.

The allied casualties numbered around 650, among them, according to Curzon: '*Captain Bell of the Royal Marines, Mr Wm Smith Master, Mr J Lewis Boatswain. Mr Peter Mitchell Pilot, and 15 Seamen & Marines: wounded severely, 32 Seamen & Marines; slightly wounded, 25 Seamen & Marines.*' The Ottoman toll, however, was much higher, reported to be approximately 4,000, with lurid, if uncorroborated, stories circulating of doomed convicts and Greek prisoners chained to the sinking and burning Ottoman ships.

The reaction to the battle in Britain was mixed. Many rejoiced that an old enemy had been defeated and the flame of Greek independence kept alight. Others, however, felt that Codrington had far overstepped his instructions and engaged in a conflict which was not in Britain's best interests. King George IV lamented to Parliament that the battle was an '*untoward event*', and the resulting

View of Navarino Harbour, showing the situation of the combined squadrons of England, Russia and France, with the remaining vessels forming part of the Turkish and Egyptian fleets, on 21 October 1827. **ABOVE**

H	K	F	Courses	Winds	Sea lry	Sig

Remarks &c H. M. S. Asia Saturday 20 Octr. 1827

P M — of the Harbour, at 2.30 observ'd Dartmouth
which Ship had anchored close to a fire Vessel, send
her boats to board the fire ship who opened Musketry
on the Boats, which was returned by the Dart-
-mouth &c irons;— sent a boat with a flag of Truce
to the Moucharem Bay, on coming away Mr. Mit-
-chell the Pilot was shot in the breast, by a man in the
Frigate while her Capt. was speaking to Lt. D. Ilben
the Gangway;— at 2.40. observed a bruist to be fired,
about this time, a shot was fired into the Sirene,
which being returned, the Action soon became
general;— Having hove in our Larbd. spring, we o-
-pened our Starbd. broadside on the Capt. Bay, &
some of the after St. Guns on a Frigate ahead of
Moucharem Bay's Ship. at 3.15 having completely
silenced the Capt. Bay, hove on the spring & got the
starbd. Broadside to bear on Moucharem bay's dou-
-ble tier frigate & some other Vessels that were raking
us. at 4.40. the mizen mast went by the board &
the rigging   together cut to pieces by the
raking fire we were exposed to. at 5.20. having silenced
every Vessel our Guns could reach, ceased firing entirely
some of the Enemy's Ships on fire ran a hawser to the
Genoa, in readiness to haul of a Frigate burning
close on our larbd. bow, at 5.50. P. M. she blew up, the
firing had then ceased along the whole line, The
Turkish fleet being the most part destroyed, Return
Killed, Capt. Bell of the Royal Marines, Mr. Wm.
Smith Master, Mr. J. Lewis Boatswain, Mr. Peter
Mitchell Pilot, and 15 Seamen & Marines;
Wounded severely, 32 Seamen & Marines; slightly
Wounded, 28 Seamen & Marines; Employed clearing
the wreck, threw the Main Yard overboard
being rendered useless— Committed the bodies of
the deceased to the deep, Guard Boats rowing
round the Ship and People at Quarters
            Turkish Ships blowing up oc-
-casionally.

hostilities between Russia and the Ottoman Empire presented Britain with a major strategic problem.

DOC. 1 Log entries from HMS *Asia*, 20 October 1827.

In a letter to the Lord High Admiral, the Duke of Clarence, written from Navarino while on board HMS *Asia* on 21 October 1827, Codrington described the '*bloody and destructive battle [that] was continued with unabated fury for four hours: and the scene of wreck and devastation which presented itself at its termination, [that] was such as has been seldom before witnessed*'. He went on to praise his fellow officers, including those who lost their lives or sustained serious injuries:

> '*It is impossible for me to say too much for the able and zealous assistance I which derived from Captain Curzon throughout this long and arduous contest: nor can I say more than it deserves for the conduct of Commander Baynes, and the Officers and crew of the Asia, for the perfection with which the fire of her guns was directed: each Vessel in turn to which her broadside was presented, became a complete wreck. His Royal Highness will be aware that so complete a Victory, by a few however perfect against an excessive number however individually inferior, cannot be acquired but at a considerable sacrifice of life. Accordingly, I have to lament the loss of Captain Bathurst of the Genoa, whose example on this occasion is well worthy the imitation of his survivors. Captain Bell commanding the Royal Marines of the Asia, an excellent Officer, was killed early in the action in the steady performance of his duty; and I have to mourn the death of Mr William Smith, the Master, admired for the zeal and ability with which he executed his duty, and beloved by all for his private qualities as a Man. Mr Henry S Dyer my secretary having received a severe contusion from a splinter I am deprived temporarily of his valuable assistance in collecting and keeping up the general returns and communications of the Squadron. I shall therefore retain in my Office Mr E I J White his first Clerk, whom I have nominated to succeed the Purser of the Brisk. I feel much personal obligation to the Honorable Lieutenant Colonel Cradock, for his readiness during the heat of the battle in carrying my orders and messages to the different quarters after my aid-du-camps were disabled. But I will beg permission to refer His Royal Highness for further particulars of this sort, to the details of the killed and wounded; a subject which it is painful for me to dwell upon*'

He then went on to attempt to justify the battle and the resulting carnage, and shift the blame to the enemy, whose losses, he claimed, '*must have been immense*':

> '*When I contemplate as I do with extreme sorrow, the extent of our loss, I console myself with the reflection that the measure which produced the battle, was absolutely necessary for obtaining the results contemplated by the Treaty, and that it was brought on entirely by our opponents.*
>
> *When I found that the boasted Ottoman word of honor was made a sacrifice to wanton, savage devastation, and that a base advantage was taken of our reliance upon Ibrahim's good faith, I own I felt a desire to punish the offenders. But it was my duty to refrain, and refrain I did; and I can assure His Royal Highness, that I would still have avoided this disastrous extremity if other means had been open to me.*'

Despite the major doubts in Britain about the political wisdom of the battle, it is clear that it was a major turning point. By ending Ottoman hopes of retaining control of Greece it ushered in a new era in the long history of the eastern Mediterranean. Ottoman Muslim domination, dating back almost 400 years, had been swept aside by the Greeks and their Christian Great Power allies. It also marked a watershed in naval history. Never again would two sailing fleets line up against each other. Steam and iron would come to replace wood and canvas as the backbone of naval power.

DOC. 2   Admiralty chart of Navarino Bay in 1830, showing the town and castles, soundings, the island of Sphagia, rivers, hachures and roads.

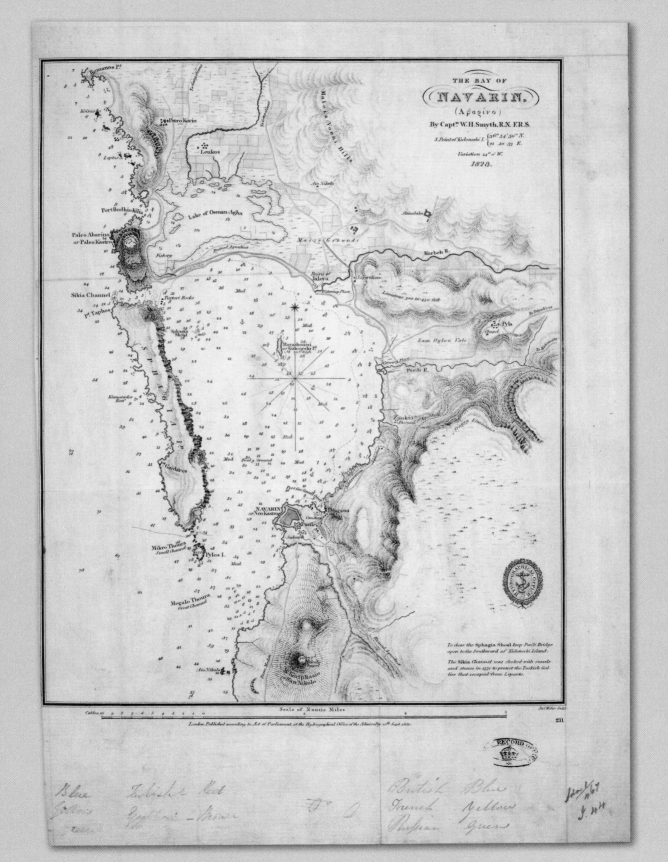

5

Emigration & Transportation

Emigration to the Americas
SEVENTEENTH TO NINETEENTH CENTURIES

Britain, in common with other European countries, has always had a mobile population, but with the discovery of the Americas and the opening up of trade routes to sub-Saharan Africa and the Orient, whole new vistas were created. Emigration to the New World was driven by the opportunities it offered to seek wealth and start over, to expand boundaries and to get rid of undesirables. The early colonists were merchants, pirates, buccaneers and adventurers, but it was not too long before large-scale free migration was encouraged to develop the land and build the economy. Since 1607 it is estimated that Great Britain and Ireland have sent well over ten million emigrants to the USA alone, along with four million to Canada. In the six-year period between 1845 and 1851 alone,

A perspective view of New York across the North River in 1765 showing the position of HM ships. **BELOW**

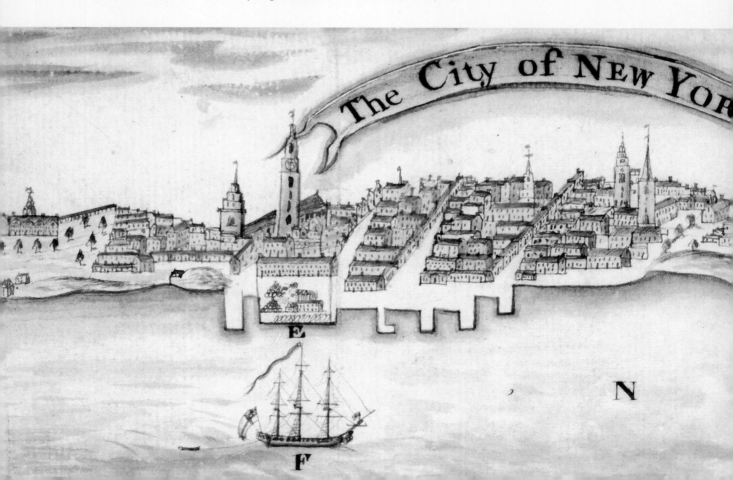

there were over one and a quarter million Irish emigrants to the USA as a result of the potato famine.

Colonial populations were not static, however. After the defeat of Britain in the American War of Independence in 1783, loyalists left America for Canada (in particular Nova Scotia), the Bahamas and England. Also, after the abolition of slavery, emigrants from the Indian sub-continent were encouraged to migrate to the West Indies to help with local labour problems, as indentured labour.

As with every phase of migration, there were various types of motivation, some pushing people out of their native country and others pulling them towards the new country. Interest in emigration to the British colonies increased following the end of the Napoleonic Wars in 1815, as did the demand for immigrants, as a result of heightened levels of economic and political uncertainty in Britain. The British government was keen to foster emigration and devised experimental programmes to assist in the settlement of

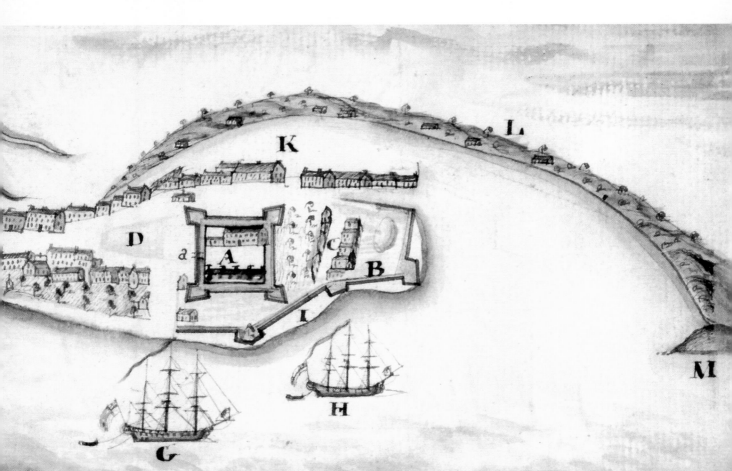

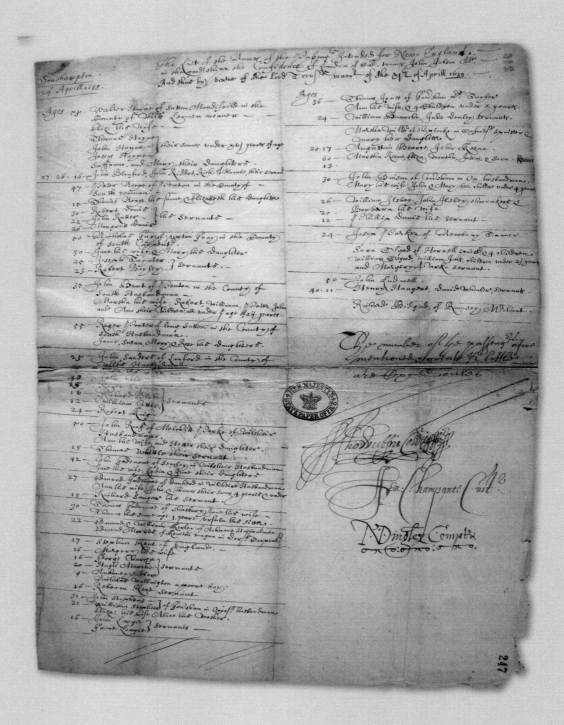

people overseas, especially in its expanding empire.

In the eighteenth and nineteenth centuries, former officers and soldiers of the British Army were given free grants of land if they would migrate to British North America (Canada). This helped build up strong communities of loyalists, largely civilian but some military, following the loss of America. If anything, this loss led to an increase of emigrants to North America, in newly created colonies. Loyalists were important for the preservation of British trade and defence interests. Scottish Highland regiments were disbanded and given lands in Nova Scotia and Quebec, in accordance with the government's plans for military defence. New Brunswick was created as a separate colony in 1784 and attracted 13,000 loyalists, who formed a reliable workforce and a useful defence.

In parallel with this, in the 1820s, Parliament agreed to allow free passage to the Canadian colonies for paupers with much-needed agricultural skills. At the same time, several boards of guardians actively sought and dispatched those seeking parish relief, reducing the levels of economic stress being experienced at parish level. Typically, applications for these schemes, and those ultimately selected, came from active labourers in areas where there were high levels of unemployment. In 1826 and 1827 these experiments gave select committees ample evidence to support their recommendations of state-aided and -directed emigration schemes as a means of providing social stability and prosperity across the empire. Destinations in Ontario, New Brunswick, Nova Scotia and Prince Edward Island were quickly established to lure skilled labour from Britain.

Michael Cronin emigrated from Mitchelstown in County Cork to Upper Canada in July 1823 with his wife, Mary, and another 287 emigrants on board the *Flebe*. Along with twenty-nine other settlers, he was awarded a lot of land in the township on Huntley, and his experience, as recorded in a letter to his mother dated 26 October 1823, was typical of that of most free emigrants from Ireland at that time:

> *'My Dear Mother*
> *I take the opportunity of writing you these few lines hoping to find you and the rest of*
> *the family in as good health as I am at present thanks be to God. We sailed from the*

DOC. 1 Passenger list for *The Confidence* of London bound for New England on 24 April 1638.

255

16 *General List of Settlers Inrolled for Canada Under the*

No. of Receipt	Date of Certificate.	Names of Applicants.	Names of the Relations of Applicants.	Trade, Profession, or Occupation.	Former Trade, if Changed.	Present Place of Residence.	Applicants' Ages, and where Born.		
							Scot.	Eng.	Ire.
							479	17	1
104/2	Apr¹ 1	Duncan McLaren	"	Husb⁴ Weaver	Labourer	Willin	37	"	"
"	"	"	Annabella McDiarmid Wife	"	"	"	33	"	"
"	"	"	John McLaren Son	"	"	"	11	"	"
"	"	"	Mary McLaren Dr	"	"	"	9	"	"
"	"	"	Katharine McLaren Dr	"	"	"	7	"	"
"	"	"	Duncan McLaren Son	"	"	"	4	"	"
"	"	"	Donald McLaren Son	"	"	"	3	"	"
105/2	" 14	Donald McPhee	"	Husb⁴ Wright	Labourer	Ardgour	40	"	"
"	"	"	Catharine McLean Wife	"	"	"	40	"	"
"	"	"	Alexr McPhee Son	"	"	"	15	"	"
"	"	"	Allan McPhee Son	"	"	"	10	"	"
"	"	"	John McPhee Son	"	"	"	6	"	"
"	"	"	Catharine McPhee Dr	"	"	"	12	"	"
"	"	"	Ann McPhee Dr	"	"	"	7	"	"
"	"	"	Mary McPhee Dr	"	"	"	14 m	"	"
106/2	April 15	Andrew Donaldson	"	Husb⁴ Farmer	"	Kinglassie	59	"	"
"	"	"	Margaret Richardson his Wife	"	"	"	58	"	"
"	"	"	Betty Donaldson Dr	"	"	"	15	"	"
107/2	" 15	David Donaldson	"	Susten Farmer	"	Ditto	30	"	"
"	" 15	"	Margaret Donaldson Sister	"	"	"	21	"	"
108/2	" 15	Thomas Donaldson	"	Farmer	"	Ditto	28	"	"
"	"	"	Isabella Donaldson Sister	"	"	"	17	"	"
109/2	" 15	Andrew Donaldson	"	his Brother Blacksmith	"	Ditto	36	"	"
110/2	" 15	John Donaldson	"	his Ditto Millwright	"	Ditto	25	"	"
111/2	" 15	James Donaldson	"	his Ditto Farmer	"	Ditto	23	"	"
112/2	"	David Duncan	"	Brother in law Farmer	"	Ditto	25	"	"
"	"	"	Jean Donaldson his Wife	"	"	"	20	"	"
113/2	June 5	Thomas Jeffryes	"	Husb⁴ Farmer	Account¹	Edinburgh	22	"	"
"	"	"	Isabella Wilson his Wife	"	"	"	19	"	"
"	"	"	Mary Jeffryes his Dr	"	"	"	1	"	"
114/2	" 5	Joseph Jeffryes	"	Bro³ Ditto	Ditto	Ditto	20	"	"
115/2	" 2	Duncan McDonell	"	Husb⁴ Labourer	Lab	Ft Augustus	38	"	"
"	"	"	Isobel McPhee his Wife	"	"	"	26	"	"
							512	17	1

Cove of Cork on the 8th of July and arrived in Quebec on the first of September. We had as favourable a voyage and as pleasant as ever was performed to this Country and as good usage as any person could expect. Then from Quebec to Montreal we came on the steam boat, that is as I am informed 180 miles and from Montreal we came in waggons to a barrack called La Chine only 9 miles from Montreal and from thence to Prescott in boats which is 130 miles and from Prescott to the place which we are all encamped there this month back. The whole crew of settlers which came in both ships was sent out from this place in squads in numbers from 6 to 30 in a number to look for their lands with a pilot to show them their respective lots and it was on Thursday last I made out my own farm which was 23 of October and as to my own judgment I take it to be as good a farm as any in the Country. Mr Robinson our Superintendent is uncommonly humane and good to us all. He at first served us out bedding and blankets

DOC. 2 Page showing list of emigrants to Canada from Edinburgh in 1815.

The town of Stanley, New Brunswick in August 1835. **BELOW**

and all kinds of carpenter's tools and farming utensils and sending people which are in the habit of building houses with the whole of us and each man's house is built in the course of two days. And Mr Robinson promises us a cow to the head of any family next Spring and several other things which I have not mentioned now. Since we came on shore, each man is served out in the day with one pound of bread or flour and the pound of beef or pork and each woman boy and girl the same. I do recommend to you my dear Mother and to Denis and Mary and Jude to get yourselves ready early next Spring to come here. Mr Robinson tells me he is to go back to Ireland very early next Spring to bring a good many more settlers.

I do recommend to you all to get yourselves in readiness and come here and not to forget to bring William and to tell he is fourteen years of age and to bring as many pots as you can with you here and cloathing and to have Denis go to my Uncle's son Michael Cronan and sister and show them the letter and perhaps it might encourage them to come here.

This is as good and as free a country as any in the world and each man is paid 12 dollars a month throughout all America and each woman six dollars, each dollar is five shillings here.

Jeremiah Ryan which came with me in place of my brother Denis is hired in Prescott at £24 a year and Peggy Carey is hired in the same place at six dollars a month and send her Mother an account that she is in as very good place and is very well and remember me etc. etc. etc.

Michael Cronin

DOCS. 3, 4 & 5 Letter from Superintendent Robinson to the Land and Emigration Commission in 1823.

Such letters were used by the Land and Emigration Commission to foster and promote further migration, which it championed as a remedy for poverty and unemployment at home, and as a means of providing labour and value to undeveloped areas in North America and, later, South Africa and Australasia. Both themes, it claimed, would unite to help create a vibrant, living empire. The colonies did, however, need a steady supply of skilled tradesmen and labour in order to fully develop over time.

Social conditions affected where the migrants came from within the UK. Some push factors are well known, such as the Irish potato failure of 1822, and

10.

strictly inspected, and they were in
every respect as well found as if they
had been fitted out by a Company of
passengers for their own convenience,
safety and comfort.

Thus in rather less than a
month from the time of issuing the
proposals the emigrants were on board
and the ships ready to sail, such was
the promptness of Government in making
its arrangements, and the active exertions
of the Nobility and Magistrates in enabling
one to select the requisite number — For
their kindness in thus forwarding the
object of my journey to Ireland, as
well as their attentions to myself, I feel
exceedingly grateful.

During the voyage nothing
happened of importance, the rations
were abundant and comfortable, the
men were allowed Cocoa for breakfast
and nearly half a pint of spirits which
was perhaps not too much — The Women
and Children were allowed Tea and
Sugar — The best proof of the attention paid

to

to them on the voyage arises from the
good health which they enjoyed as only
one woman and eight children died on
the passage, and these from the small
pox, which had unfortunately got into
both ships, and not from any causes
that could be attributed to their change
of circumstances or situation

    It may be worth remarking as
it is so characteristic of the fondness of
the Irish people for potatoes, that the
men preferred them to the cocoa, which
they refused for several days to taste till
they saw the Officers of the ship repeatedly
breakfasting upon it – The children during
sickness called constantly for Potatoes,
refusing arrow root or any other aliments
more congenial to their situation & nothing
could prevail on Man Woman or Child
to eat plumb pudding, which as is
usual on ship board was part of the
Sunday's dinner.

    Few of them would eat the best
english cheese and when it was served
out as part of their ration it was most
        commonly

12.

commonly thrown overboard.

We arrived at Quebec in the Wakesby
on the 2nd of September after a passage of
eight weeks, the Hebe had been in port
two days — I shipped the people from the
transport on board the steam boats without
landing them and proceeded to Montreal
on the 4th having been detained only two days—
We were much facilitated in our progress
by the orders which His Excellency Lord
Dalhousie had given before our arrival
to the Quarter Master General to find
provisions and transport as far as Prescott
in Upper Canada a distance of about
320 Miles.

We reached Montreal on the sixth
and finding the means of transport ready
I forwarded the emigrants by land immediately without stopping in Montreal, to
La Chine distant ten miles — Here we
remained two days and then set out in
boats to Prescott the crews of each con-
-sisting chiefly of emigrants with two
Canadians to guide & steer — Notwithstanding
the rapidity of the River and unskilfulness

does not
mention the
depredation
committed at
Lachine
by those emigrants

of

later the full-scale epidemic in the 1840s. Similarly, the distress of the Scottish crofters in the 1830s and the failure of the kelp manufacturing industry and the herring fisheries of the Highlands and Islands helped to lure more people overseas from well-established local vibrant communities.

The voyage to a new land in itself presented new experiences for most settlers like Michael Cronin, as Superintendent Robinson recorded in his letter to the Commission in 1823:

> *'During the voyage nothing happened of importance, the rations were abundant and comfortable, the men were allowed cocoa for breakfast and nearly half a pint of spirits which was perhaps too much. The women and children were allowed tea and sugar. The best proof of the attention paid to them on the voyage arises from the good health which they enjoyed as only one woman and eight children died on the passage, and these from the smallpox, which had unfortunately got into both ships, and not from any causes that could be attributed to their change of circumstances or situation.*
>
> *It may be worth remarking as it is so characteristic of the fondness of the Irish people for potatoes, that the men preferred them to the cocoa, which they refused for several days to taste till they saw the Officers of the Ship repeatedly breakfasting upon it. The children during sickness called constantly for potatoes, refusing arrow root or any other ailments more congenial to their situation and nothing could prevail a man, woman or child to eat plumb pudding, which as is usual on ship board was part of the Sunday's dinner. Few of them would eat the best English cheese and when it was served out as part of their ration it was most commonly thrown overboard.'*

The 1830s saw a significant increase in the annual number of emigrants to North America, which led to accounts of overcrowding on ships, shortages of food and water, and the subsequent spread of disease. The decade would see an examination of emigration facilities, resulting in the introduction of ship inspections. This coincided, in 1834, with the new Poor Law Act, which, for the security of the parishes, required those paying rates to raise money to finance sending the poor of the parish away, mainly through emigration overseas. It was during this time that the Emigration Office of the Colonial Office expanded, appointing in 1836 the first Agent-General for Emigration, Thomas Elliot. The Emigration Office became semi-independent from the Colonial Office, enjoying its own budget, paid directly from the Treasury.

During the 1830s, the average annual migration to British North America was just over 32,000, compared with nearly 30,000 to the United States. Many emigrants were more strongly attracted to the United States, particularly those who were not politically inclined. To the common man, the United States and Britain had so much in common, most notably the language, economic prosperity and culture.

Map of Manhattan Island, New York, c.1776. **ABOVE**

263

Convict ships to Australia
TRANSPORTATION AS PUNISHMENT ... 1787–1867

Between 1787 and 1867 over 160,000 convicts were transported to Australia and Van Diemen's Land (now Tasmania). Transportation was both an alternative punishment for criminals who would otherwise have been executed and a sentence in its own right. While the term of transportation might be limited to a set number of years, most transportees had little prospect of returning home, and a sentence effectively meant leaving behind their family and friends for the rest of their lives.

The First Fleet, the name given to the first convoy of six convict transports with five supply and naval ships, left Portsmouth for New South Wales in 1787. Some 600 male convicts and 250 convicted women undertook that first voyage under the command of Arthur Phillip, who was to become the colony's first governor. Their journey took a long seven months, with stops at Tenerife, Rio de Janeiro and Cape Town for supplies and repairs.

While the Royal Navy organised and fitted out the First Fleet, later transports were more likely to be operated by private contractors who worked to requirements set out by the Navy Board. This arrangement led to wide variations from ship to ship in how convicts were handled, largely depending on the inclination of the transport's master.

Many early voyages to Australia were characterised by debauchery, rebellion among the convicts and corruption. Contractors were known to illegally load ships with goods for sale in New South Wales, restricting prison space for convicts, or to stint on rations so that any surplus could be sold on arrival. From 1815 conditions improved markedly with the appointment of a Royal Navy surgeon on board every transport ship. This change ensured the presence of a government representative on each voyage who could enforce procedures and report back on conditions on board.

The logs kept by these Royal Navy surgeons provide some of the most detailed records of life on board the convict transports. The surgeons were not

A convict in chains bids farewell before he is rowed out to join a convict ship bound for Australia.

only responsible for treating convicts, crew and guards, their duties also included setting and enforcing rules and regulations governing convict behaviour on board, controlling rations, ensuring the prison quarters were hygienic and well ventilated, and schooling prisoners.

George Thomson, surgeon superintendent on the *England* transport ship in 1826, kept a particularly detailed daily log of his ship's passage to New South Wales. Introducing his log, Thomson remarks that '*the medical duties of this ship have been trifling*': all 148 convicts who boarded the ship arrived and there was no sickness, accident or scurvy. In the absence of any medical cases to note, Thomson used his log to record in minute detail life on board the convict transport. Thomson joined the ship on 18 March 1826 and his account spans more than six months, encompassing both the mundane aspects of his job (such as inspecting the opening of every barrel or cask of food or drink, and giving the prisoners their daily sherbet mixture of lime and sugar to stave off scurvy) and the more dramatic prospect of mutiny and murder.

The early pages of Thomson's log give no indication of the trouble to come. The crew, Thomson, and a guard of thirty-one men from the 39th Regiment, were on board by mid-March, with a small number of wives and children. Stores were loaded and preparations continued to be made until the convicts began to arrive on 15 April. Thomson examined each man for fitness to be received on board. Any convicts with infectious diseases or whose health suggested that they might not survive or that they could endanger others could be refused embarkation.

Following their examination, convicts were shown to their berths in the prisons below deck and issued with a bed, blanket and pillow. Before departure, each man also received a pair of trousers and shirt so that they might rotate their clothes and wash them. The next day began a daily ritual that would continue for the rest of the convicts' time on board: their beds were rolled up and stowed on deck so that the prisons, berths and decks could be cleaned and ventilated. The convicts themselves were also washed and mustered on deck and their leg irons inspected. As was common practice on convict ships, leg irons were only removed when the ship was safely away from port. While awaiting departure, the men were free to move between decks and could even receive any last visitors on board before they left.

Once all the convicts had been received on board, Thomson assigned to them individual responsibilities. His log for 22 April 1826 details the convicts' role in keeping the ship clean and efficient:

> '*Soon after Daylight, Beds stowed on Deck, Convicts washed, Prison Decks and Sleeping Births [sic] cleaned and ventilated as usual. Mustered and inspected convicts' irons, clothes, etc. Appointed Two Captains for the Prison Decks, and two for the upper Deck. Likewise a Captain for every Division of Twenty-five convicts, Superintendent of the Hospital, and Surgeryman, Cook and Mate, a Nightman for each water closet, and to keep the air conductor clean. Appointed a Schoolmaster for the Boys. Directed each mess of six convicts to appoint one of their messmates caterer, and the members of each sleeping birth to appoint one of their number to take charge of, and be responsible for the order and cleanliness of the birth. Guard and convicts healthy. Allowed to pass and repass to, and from the Deck, from daylight till sun-set.*'

The division of responsibilities, and the daily cleansing and ventilation of the ship as described here, kept the convicts busy in an attempt to maintain discipline, and also helped to prevent disease, which perhaps was the surgeon's overriding concern. Thomson's journal is particularly illuminating in terms of steps taken to prevent disease. On 16 May, for example, he made the following entry:

> '*Weather moderate and fine. Convicts to have their meals on deck when the weather is dry – half an hour at breakfast, an hour at Dinner, and half an hour at Supper. The better to preserve cleanliness in the prisons. The use of the fixed stove discontinued. Convicts allowed to pass and repass to and from the deck during the day. Soon after daylight, beds stowed on deck as usual. Prisons scraped and dry swabbed; sleeping births cleaned; air conductors cleared; water closets scrubbed out with a half worn broom and every thing passed through the soil pipe – morning noon and evening. Prisons ventilated by windsails and airing stove; scuttles opened whenever the weather will permit… Convicts on deck to wash and scrub clothes in rotation, by division as usual.*'

As the *England* continued on to hotter climates the convicts appear to have become more unruly. On 18 May four convicts were flogged for theft. On the evening of 29 May the convicts were ordered below deck early because of further petty thefts and '*irregularities*'. The men did not take this well and upset a fixed stove below decks in response. The next day, with the weather humid and close and the thermometer showing 86°F, Thomson notes the mood had soured further:

> '*Convicts very disorderly, and disposed to be mutinous; very clamorous to have their irons taken off. Several evil disposed convicts berthed on the starboard side of the prison, make a habit of going about the prison at night and disturbing the other convicts, and although repeatedly challenged by the sentries, have hitherto eluded detection.*'

On 31 May an alarming report reached Thomson:

> '*At seven am received a letter from Walter E Taylor [convict superintendent of the hospital and captain of a convict division] requesting me to send for him as soon as possible, stating that he had something to communicate to me privately of the utmost importance. I immediately sent for him to come to my cabin, when he informed me that John George Munns [convict] had that morning come to him at the Hospital very early before he, or the other convicts were out of bed, and told him privately, that there was a conspiracy formed to murder him (W.E.T.) to prevent him giving any alarm, and then to murder me and all who would not assist them to seize the ship, and run her into South America. That Robert Hughes, and Thomas Jones were at the head of it, and it was their intention to carry it into effect, the first time the Ship was in a squall.*
>
> *In consequence of this information, the following memorandum, in the form of a protection was given by me to Walter E Taylor, to be shewn to such men as he could trust; as two thirds of the convicts are the most depraved and desperate of characters, and robust athletic men, in order to prevent their taking any alarm, and assassinating in the prison during the night, as they had threatened to do, or at any future period, however distant, those convicts who dared to divulge their wicked intentions, every necessary precaution was privately taken, until the ringleaders could all be discovered, and safely secured without violence.*
>
> *Memorandum: Dr Thomson will thank W E Taylor and other well disposed men to be on their guard, and if possible to get such evidence as will enable Dr T to act against the malcontents. Dr Thomson promises protection, and his best services with the Governor of N S Wales, to such men as may appear to him to deserve it.*'

DOC. 1 Pages from the journal of the *England*, 30–31 May 1826.

Log and *Proceedings, of the Male Convict Ship Englar*

Date.	Wind.	N. Latitude	Ther:	Baro:	Remarks. Tuesday, 30th May 1826.
May 30	V.	9.21	86	30	Moderate Weather and light Breezes. Atmosphere close, humid. Soon after daylight, the Beds stowed on Deck, Berths and Decks cleaned and ventilated as usual. Co on Deck by Divisions, in rotation to wash and scrub ce After which, three fourths were permitted to remain on two hours in rotation, during the day. Two of the Gu Three of the Crew, and Nine of the Convicts, taking Med chiefly for Head aches, constipation, and Bowel Comple Convicts very disorderly, and disposed to be Mutinous; clamorous to have their Irons taken off. Several evil a Convicts Berthed on the Starboard side of the Prison, mak habit of going about the Prison at night, and disturbing other Convicts, and although repeatedly challenged by th tries, have hitherto eluded detection. Issued Sherbet to the Convicts, as usual.
May 31.	V.	7.53	82	30	Remarks. Wednesday, 31st May 1826. Weather moderate and fine, with light Breezes. Beds stow Deck soon after daylight. Prison, Berths and Decks clea and ventilated as usual. The Officer of the Guard, One of Crew and Four Convicts, taking Medicines. In consequen the insubordinate state of the Convicts, one half only ac on Deck at a time, four hours in rotation, during the a At Seven A.M. received a Letter from Walter C. Fay requesting me to send for him as soon as possible, stating he had something to communicate to me privately of th utmost importance. I immediately sent for him to c to my Cabin, when he informed me that John George had that morning come to him at the Hospital very ea before he, or the other Convicts were out of Bed, and told th privately, that there was a Conspiracy formed to Murd (W.C.F.) to prevent his giving any alarm, and then to me and all who would not assist them to Seize the Ship

Voyage to *New South Wales*, in the year Eighteen Hundred & Twenty Six. 13

c.	Wind.	N. Lat.d	Ther.	Bar.	Remarks. Wednesday, 31st May 1826.
y 31. inued	W.	7.53	82	30	

and run her into South America. That Robert Hughs, and
Thomas Jones were at the head of it, and it was their intention
to carry it into effect, the first time the Ship was in a Squall.
In consequence of this information, the following Memorandum,
in the form of a Protection was given by me to Walter E. Taylor,
to be shewn to such men as he could trust; As two thirds of
the Convicts are the most depraved and desperate of Characters,
and robust athletic men, in order to prevent their taking
any alarm, and afassinatingin the Prison during the night,
as they had threatened to do, or at any future period, however
distant; those Convicts who dared to divulge their wicked
intentions, every necefsary precaution was privately taken, untill
the ringleaders could all be discovered, and safely secured
without violence.

    Memorandum.   Dr Thomson will thank W. E. Taylor
and other well disposed men to be on their guard; and if pofsible
to get such evidence as will enable Dr T. to act against the
Malcontents. Dr Thomson promises protection, and his best services
with the Governor of N. S. Wales, to such men as may appear
to him to deserve it.

    Memo.   Major D'Arcy, who is at present indisposed;
likewise promises his protection, and intercefsion with the Gov-
-ernor of N. S Wales, to such as may deserve it.
    Ship England at Sea, May 31st 1826. —

    On the evening of the Thirtieth Inst (last night) after all the
other Convicts had gone below, Charles Powell stated to John Herbert,
one of the Guard, that from something he had heard in the Prison,
he was afraid they would soon have to use their Muskets against
the Convicts, — which Serjeant Williams reported to me.
    Opened a Barrel of Pork, Containing Eighty pieces of four
Pounds each, is Three hundred and Twenty Pounds.

The next day Thomson interviewed Robert Hughes and other convicts, on the pretext of following up an earlier allegation of assault on another prisoner. Thomson had ordered the captains of the decks and divisions to investigate this report but Hughes and his confederates had so effectively intimidated any witnesses that none of them had wanted to give evidence. Now Thomson, the ship's master (who was also the chief officer) and an officer of the guard took evidence under oath. Sadly the evidence has been lost from the log, but in response to his investigations, Thomson ordered that Hughes, whose leg irons had been removed to allow him to perform his duties as captain of a division, be double ironed and handcuffed. Hughes was placed under the sentry's charge on the quarter deck and was not allowed to communicate with anyone, except whoever was on duty. The next day a further four men were identified as would-be mutineers. They too were handcuffed and ordered to sleep on deck, away from the other prisoners. We can well imagine the tense atmosphere on board from Thomson's log of 2 June. Writing of the mutineers, he noted:

> 'Their handcuffs to be taken off at their meals, and when they wished to go to the head [where they washed], likewise to walk under charge of the sentry, one hour and a half every morning, and evening. Major D'Arcy gave the necessary order to the Guard how to act in case of an alarm, and [Captain Reay] to the crew, whom he armed with cutlasses. At 8pm I proceeded to the men's prison accompanied by Sergeant Wilson, the sentry and the orderly, and stated to the convicts that if any violence was offered to the convicts in the prison in the night, or any attempt made to rescue the prisoners during the day or night, I would instantly direct them to be put to death; and that whenever the convicts on deck were ordered below during the day, if they did not instantly obey, after a reasonable time had been allowed for them to get down, the Guard would be ordered to act against them as Mutineers; but that in the event of being obliged to proceed to this extremity, protection would be given to such convicts as obeyed orders, and remained quiet in their berths.'

From this time on, during the day, only fifty convicts were allowed on deck at any one time, in rotation, for two hours at a time, greatly reducing opportunities for them to exercise and breathe fresh air. Over the next month further associates of

Hughes and his fellow would-be mutineers were identified and imprisoned separately in the boys' prison ward to keep them apart from the other prisoners. Nonetheless, Thomson's log notes further outbursts of rebellion and frustration among the convicts. On 12 June, he records:

'At 6am Thomas Phillips the elder was excessively insolent, mutinous and contemptuous to the Corporal of the Guard and me, in consequence of his wine being stopped for his misconduct. When ordered on deck he asserted in a violent, menacing manner and attitude that he was entitled to his rights, and would have them, and when repeatedly ordered by me or any person, that he had a right to speak, and he would speak. He was handcuffed and placed under charge of the sentry in the main hatchway. James Griffiths, who was already in handcuffs for insolence to me on the sixth was likewise excessively mutinous, and stated that I did as I pleased now, but that he would have me at Sydney.'

Convicts at work, 1836. BELOW

By mid-July the ship was past the tropics and the cooler weather appears to have cooled tempers, as did the rough seas which the ship endured for the rest of its passage. As the temperature dropped, the convicts were issued with flannel drawers to keep them warm, and even Robert Hughes and his confederates were allowed their wine ration again '*as a medical comfort, in consideration of the cold and boisterous weather*'.

On 18 September the *England* finally made the lighthouse at Sydney and anchored at Port Jackson that morning. The convicts remained on board for a further eleven days, during which time they were issued with fresh provisions and vegetables, as well as with a cap, a neck handkerchief, a jacket, a waistcoat, a shift, a pair of trousers and a pair of shoes for their new lives in the colony. They were inspected by the colonial secretary on arrival and by the governor and the colonial secretary on landing to assess their health and fitness. The governor was pleased with the health of the men but directed a court of inquiry to be held on the twenty-four convicts whose names are noted in the log for mutinous and insubordinate conduct. The master of the ship, Captain Reay, was reprimanded for not better supporting Thomson's authority during the attempted convict mutiny.

A northern view of Sydney, in New South Wales, sketched in watercolour on canvas by J Lycett, 1820.

Emigration to Australasia
THE NINETEENTH CENTURY

European settlement of Australia began with the establishment of the penal colony at Botany Bay on the east coast of Australia in 1787, following the loss of America and the need for Britain to find a new destination for transported criminals. It is estimated that more than 162,000 men, women and children were transported to Australia, to locations in New South Wales, Western Australia and Tasmania (then known as Van Diemen's Land), between 1787 and 1867, but Australia also attracted free settlers through the Colonial Office, as did New Zealand, which was never used as a penal colony.

The journey to Australia was perilous and lengthy, especially in the early period of settlement. The First Fleet voyage of 1787, comprising six vessels carrying the first transported convicts (plus two Royal Navy vessels and three store ships), would last eight months, travelling across the Atlantic and Indian Oceans

Emigrants on deck on a ship bound for Australia, published in the *Illustrated London News*, 20 January 1840. BELOW

and stopping at Tenerife, Rio de Janeiro and Cape Town en route, before arriving at Botany Bay in January 1788. The ships carried nearly 1,000 souls — 558 male and 192 female convicts, 197 marines and nineteen officers, and a further forty-five family members of some of the crew, including wives and children. Across the Atlantic the weather was stormy, but it was the extreme heat of the tropics that brought vermin, rotting food, sickness and diarrhoea, resulting in the deaths of six convicts. It was a miracle that as few as twenty males, three females and five children died on the voyage and that it was without incidents of shipwreck and mutiny. The Second Fleet , that set off later in 1788, would fare much worse, with the deaths of some 256 men and eleven women, resulting from

Map of New Holland or Australia in 1820 with insets showing Van Diemen's Land (Tasmania) and the environs of Port Jackson (Sydney). **BELOW**

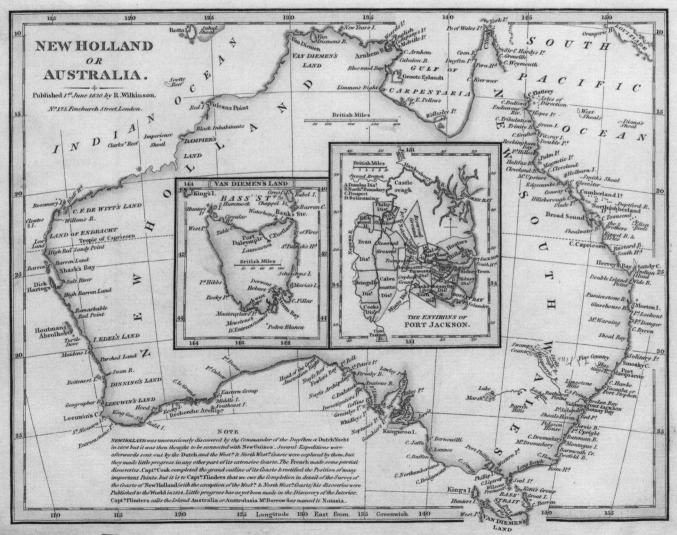

STRALIA 7

appalling conditions of squalor and disease and from the brutal treatment of the convicts by the officers and crew.

Marines on board vessels of the First Fleet were aggrieved to learn that they were not to be allowed wines and spirits once they reached Botany Bay, writing in letter to the Admiralty from the transport *Scarborough* dated 7 May 1787:

> '*We the Marines embarked on board the Scarborough who have voluntarily entered on a dangerous expedition replete with numberless difficulties which in the faithful discharge of our duty we must necessarily be exposed to, and supposing ourselves to be on the same footing as if embarked on board any of His Majesty's Ships of War or as the seamen and marines on the same indulgences now concern ourselves sorely aggrieved by finding the intentions of Government to make no allowance of spirituous liquor or wine after our arrival at the intended Colony in New South Wales. A moderate distribution of the above mentioned article being indispensably requisite for the preservation of our lives which change of climate and the extreme fatigue we shall be necessarily exposed to may probably endanger. We therefore humbly entreat you will be pleased to convey these our sentiments to Major Ross presuming sir that you will not only be satisfied that our demand is reasonable but will also perceive the urgent necessity there is for a compliance with our request, flatter ourselves you will also use your influence to cause a removal of the uneasiness we experience under the idea of being restricted in the supply of one of the principal necessarys of life without which or the reasons above stated we cannot expect to survive the hardships incident to our situation, you may depend on a cheerful and ready discharge of the service duties that may be enjoyned us, the design of Government is we hope to have a feeling for the calamities we must encounter as to induce them to provide in a moderate and reasonable degree our maintenance and preservation, we beg leave to tender our most dutiful appearances of executing to the utmost of our power our several abilities in the duty assigned, so that we remain in every respect loyal subjects to our King and worthy members of society.*'

Initially, the British government showed no interest in promoting free migration, although this stance shifted from the start of the nineteenth century, when it provided the means for people to emigrate particularly to destinations in New South Wales and Victoria, the latter never accepting convicts. New Zealand, initially part of the colony of New South Wales before it became a separate colony in 1840, was also a destination for free settlers.

Colonial Office returns of deaths at sea reveal how treacherous the travelling conditions were for emigrants, particularly in the cheapest class of accommodation, known as steerage, in which most of them travelled. The accommodation was frequently overcrowded, and with poor ventilation, diseases such as cholera and typhus reached epidemic proportions. Many emigrants died as a result, particularly prior to the 1870s, after which time virtually all emigrants to North America and most to Australia travelled by steamship, which helped to cut journey times considerably. From about 1900, third-class cabins replaced steerage accommodation, and although they were spartan, they were a considerable improvement.

Ironically, the conditions for convicts were often better than those of free emigrants. Contractors were paid to transport convicts to their destination, and their services were likely to be used again if the convicts arrived alive, safely and relatively fit. This helped persuade them to employ surgeon-superintendents who would be responsible for medical welfare and discipline on board the ships. Such appointments proved successful as death rates began to fall to as low as 1 in 122 by the 1820s, and free-emigrant ships would also appoint surgeon-superintendents in due course.

Seven-year-old John Dempsey sailed on the emigrant ship Susan from Londonderry, Ireland, to Sydney New South Wales, on 10 October 1838. Sadly, he never reached Australia, having developed an abscess on 17 October 1838, and ultimately succumbing to tuberculosis and dying on 5 November 1838, as Surgeon-Superintendent Charles Kennedy noted in his medical log:

'John Dempsey was put on the sick list having suffered severely from seasickness, that he had been unable to retain anything upon his stomach, producing great debility and emaciation has been so ever since the ship left port is of a delicate and scrofulous habit of body at present he complains of headache and soreness over the region of the stomach foul and small and frequent tongue, white skin moist, thirst, bowels constipated.'
November 1838

DOCS. 1 & 2 Record of the Scarborough Transport, 7 May 1707.

(Copy)

Scarborough Transport May 7th 1787

We the Marines embarked on board the
Scarborough who have voluntarily entered on a
Dangerous expedition replete with numberless
Difficulties which in the faithful discharge of
our Duty we must necessarily be exposed to, &
supposing ourselves to be on the same footing as
if embarked on board any of His Maj.y Ships of
War or as the Seamen & Marines on the same
expedition with us we hope to receive the same
Indulgence – Now conceive ourselves sorely aggrieved
by finding the intentions of government to make
no allowance of Spiritous Liquor or Wine – after
our arrival at the intended Colony in New
South Wales – A moderate distribution of the
above ment.d article being Indispensibly Requisite
for the preservation of our lives which change of
climate & the extreme fatigue we shall be
necessarily exposed to may probably endanger –
We therefore humbly entreat you will be pleased
to convey these our Sentiments to Major Ross
Presuming Sir that you will not only be
satisfied that our demand is reasonable but will
also perceive the urgent necessity there is for a
compliance with our request, flatter ourselves you
will

will also use your influence to cause a
removal of the uneasiness we experience under
the Idea of being restricted in the supply of
one of the principal necessarys of life without
which or the reasons above stated we cannot
expect to survive the Hardships incident to
our situation, you may depend on a chearful
and ready discharge of the service duties that
may be enjoyned us, the design of Government
is we hope to have a feeling for the Calamities
we must encounter as to induce them to
provide in a Moderate & reasonable degree
for our Maintenance & preservation, we
beg leave to tender our most dutiful assurances
of executing to the utmost of our power our
several abilities in the duty assign'd, so
that we remain in every respect loyal
subjects to our King & worthy members of
Society.

(signed by the Detachment)

9

Nature of the disease, time when and where taken ill how disposed of	Names, ages, history symptoms treatment & daily progress of the Disease or hurt &c
Abscess Supervening upon Sea Sickness Octr 17th 1838 at Sea Novr 5 1838 Died Case No 1	John Dempsey Ætat 7 — was put on the Sick List having suffered severely from Sea sickness, that he has been unable to retain any thing upon his sto- mach, producing great debility and emaciation has been so eversince the Ship left port is of a delicate and scrofulous habit of body at- present he complains of headache and soreness over the region of the stomach, pulse small and frequent tongue white skin moist thirst bowels constipated Calomel grii Stat. Sumend et postea Haust Salin ⁿ ℞ Opii gtts x 11th quaque h. S. Vesp — vomited after taking the Calomel and likewise the draught two purgative Pills were given and were rejected imme- diately, bowels not opened. mema —

Some of the early 'free' settlers were in fact wives of transported convicts, as letters received by the Home Secretary during the convict years, show. One such letter, written on 7 August 1835, was from Ann Adams from near the Griffin Inn, Belgrave Park, Leicester, pleading for a free passage to Van Diemen's Land to join her husband and son:

> 'I take liberty of writing to your Honour wishing to know if I could go to Van Diemen's Land at Government expense under the following circumstance. My husband by the name of Edward Adams was a convict from Leicester and sentenced to 7 years transportation which he served and is now free as a settler and also my son Thomas Adams was convicted of sentence the same, he is also free and they are both settled at Ho Cart Town Van Diemen's Land — as they have sent for me to come and thank you for your advice which way I must act by what means I must get there...'

DOC. 3 Medical report on John Dempsey, November 1838.

One of the biggest problems Australia faced was a lack of women. The number of female convicts sent to Australia between 1787 and 1868 was only 20 per cent of the number of males transported. The granting of permission for wives to join convict husbands partially helped to address this, but there were also separate schemes to provide incentives for women to migrate freely to address the immense need for female labour, especially in domestic employment and the textile industry.

Colonial Office records contain a wealth of information relating to free emigrants to Australasia. For each family member, their application for free passage provides their previous address, their age and their relationship to the main applicant, together with their employment skills and character references.

In the 1830s, the politician Edward Gibbon Wakefield devised a scheme to replace free land grants. In what became known as the Wakefield Scheme, land was sold for a substantial price in the colony, and the funds thus generated were used to ship emigrant labourers from Britain to work the land. Those purchasing the land were assured of an adequate supply of labour of the right type, since labourers were vetted before being given passage. The labourer was promised a new and more prosperous life in a colony where labour was in demand, while prospects were poor at home. The scheme proposed to set up a colony along approved lines and, at the same time, to further relieve unemployment and pauperism at home. This also helped to end speculative buying and forced labourers to work for some time before they could purchase land for themselves. A steady supply of labour to the colonies was created by proceeds from the sale of the land. As more land was sold, more people would migrate and develop the land, helping to establish a more robust, well-balanced society in the colonies. Wakefield's theory proved successful, allowing for further colonisation across the British Empire.

In 1831, a plan for the new colony of South Australia emerged. In order for the land grant scheme advocated by Wakefield to be practised fairly, there was a desire that the government of the colony and its officials should be appointed by the Crown. This became the provisions of an Act passed in 1834, and in 1835 there emerged a board of ten commissioners who would work with a resident agent in the colony to administer its affairs.

As happened in the Americas, migration to Australasia would begin to increase in the 1840s as opposition to the policy of transporting convicts grew, making the prospect of migration to Australia more attractive. Nearly 165,000 convicts had been transported to Australia between 1787 and 1867, when it finally ended, but numbers of newly arrived convicts began to fall significantly from the 1840s, when free settlers began to outnumber convicts, thanks in many respects to government incentives such as the Wakefield Scheme, and the discovery of gold in 1851.

Map of the Bay of Islands, New Zealand, 1830. RIGHT

DOC. 4 Register of cabin passengers on the *Bolton*. The register runs from 1839–50.

DOC. 5 Peculiar Land Order, South Australian, 1839 recording the purchase of eighty acres of rural land and ten acres of town land and the gift of a grant to help him develop those lands.

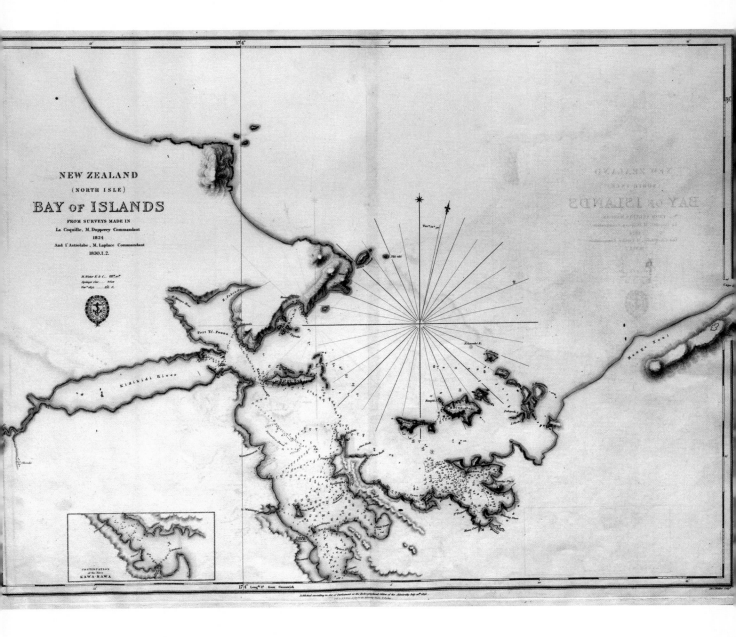

"Bolton" 540 Tons O.M. John Percival Robinson Com.ᵈʳ
Sailed ft Gravesend 19ᵗʰ Novʳ — Off the Isle of Wight 22ᵈ Novʳ

	Name	age	Adults		Children	
			M.	F.	M.	F.
5 Co.	Churton, Reo: John Frederick					
	Wrexham Denbigh	41	1			
	Churton, Mary					
	Wife of above	38		1		
	Churton, Alexander Knowls	11			1	
	do Catharine Letitia	9				1
	do Alice Sarah	7				1
	do Jane Frederica	5				1
	do Marion	3				1
	do Dorothy	2				1
	do Charles April George	Inft			1	
	Children of the above					
2 Co.	Falwasser, Miss Sarah					
	Wrexham, Denbigh	40		1		
	Hargreaves, Miss Eliza					
	Wrexham Denbigh	17		1		
	Hargreaves, Winter					
	Wrexham, Denbigh	11			1	
2 Pr. 10 Co.	Harrison, Henry Shafto					
	Wakefield	29	1			
	Harrison, Henrietta					
	Wife of above	29		1		
	Harrison, Louisa Adelaide	6				1
	do John Shafto	5			1	
	do Henry Nevinson	1			1	
	Children of the above					
	Harrison, Miss Isabella					
	Wakefield	22		1		
	Harrison, Robert John					
	Wakefield	20	1			

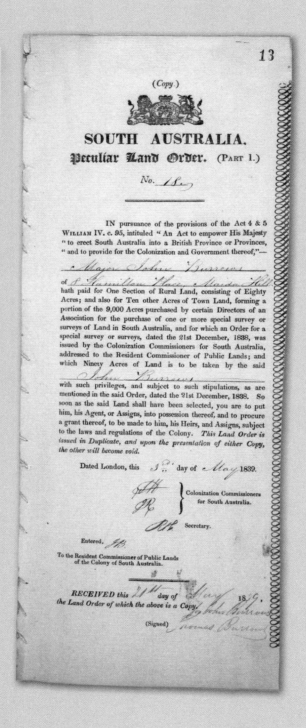

13

(Copy.)

SOUTH AUSTRALIA.
Peculiar Land Order. (Part 1.)

No. *18*

IN pursuance of the provisions of the Act 4 & 5
WILLIAM IV. c. 95, intituled "An Act to empower His Majesty
"to erect South Australia into a British Province or Provinces,
"and to provide for the Colonization and Government thereof,"—

Major John Burrows

of *8 Hamilton Place, Maida Hill*
hath paid for One Section of Rural Land, consisting of Eighty
Acres; and also for Ten other Acres of Town Land, forming a
portion of the 9,000 Acres purchased by certain Directors of an
Association for the purchase of one or more special survey or
surveys of Land in South Australia, and for which an Order for a
special survey or surveys, dated the 21st December, 1838, was
issued by the Colonization Commissioners for South Australia,
addressed to the Resident Commissioner of Public Lands; and
which Ninety Acres of Land is to be taken by the said

John Burrows

with such privileges, and subject to such stipulations, as are
mentioned in the said Order, dated the 21st December, 1838. So
soon as the said Land shall have been selected, you are to put
him, his Agent, or Assigns, into possession thereof, and to procure
a grant thereof, to be made to him, his Heirs, and Assigns, subject
to the laws and regulations of the Colony. *This Land Order is
issued in Duplicate, and upon the presentation of either Copy,
the other will become void.*

Dated London, this *3rd* day of *May* 1839.

} Colonization Commissioners
   for South Australia.

Secretary.

Entered,

To the Resident Commissioner of Public Lands
of the Colony of South Australia.

RECEIVED this *21st* day of *May* 18*39*,
the Land Order of which the above is a Copy.

(Signed)

Sentenced to transportation

THE HULKS ON THE THAMES ... NINETEENTH CENTURY

'*Convict hulks are totally forgotten Places teeming with every Crime that can degenerate a Man.*'

So wrote Henry Adams, a convict held on the *York* and *Antelope* convict hulks for seven years, from 1823 to 1830.

From 1787, when transportation to Australia began, all male prisoners convicted and sentenced to transportation in England, and some in Scotland, were sent to the prison hulks to await transportation. The hulks were decommissioned naval ships that were repurposed as floating prisons, moored on the Thames, off the south coast of England, and overseas in territories such as Bermuda.

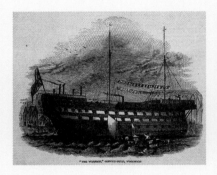

The convict hulk, *Warrior*, moored at Woolwich in 1846.

While many of us are familiar with the convict transportation to Australia that began in the late eighteenth century, the practice was actually much older, as were the convict hulks. In 1717, legislation introduced the sentence of transportation for seven years, fourteen years or life. From 1718 to 1776, convicts were transported to North America, but when war broke out between Great Britain and her colonies this outlet closed and Britain's already overcrowded jails could not accommodate the extra convicts. As a temporary solution, in 1776, Parliament passed '*An Act to authorise, for a limited Time, the Punishment by hard Labour of Offenders who for certain Crimes, are or shall become liable to be transported to any of His Majesty's Colonies and Plantations*'. As a result of this legislation, convicts were imprisoned on two old warships stationed at Woolwich docks for two years, and employed on public works. The hulks were considered an imperfect, emergency, temporary measure, yet they survived in British waters for eighty years, and for longer still in Bermuda and Gibraltar.

The number of hulks and the rules governing their administration changed during these eighty years, but the hulks were universally feared throughout that time. While work was done to retrofit the old warships to accommodate the prisoners, the ships were filthy and overcrowded, disease like typhus and cholera spread quickly and many feared the 'moral contagion' of keeping prisoners together in closely confined quarters.

The *Justitia* hulk moored at Woolwich from 1829 was the largest and most poorly supervised of the hulks, holding 500 convicts with only one warder on board. Convicts typically rose at 5am to wash themselves and the ship, before performing hard labour for eight to nine hours a day on land, working in the naval dockyards on tasks such as loading coal or mending ships, or on public works like river cleansing or road building.

Deck plans for HMC Hulk *Thames* 1850, showing the layout of the main and lower decks. **BELOW**

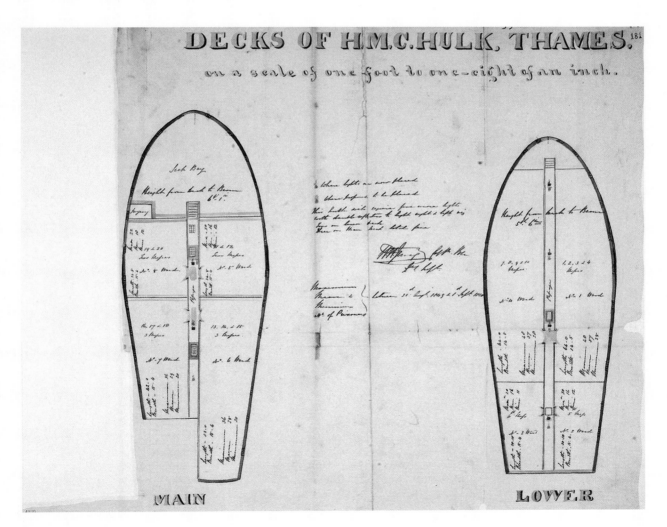

While the hulks were part of the prison establishment and so under the authority of the Home Office, those stationed at Bermuda were staffed by Royal Navy officers and crew. The first hulk, the *Antelope*, arrived at Bermuda in 1824. The convicts on board provided labour in the naval dockyard and in the archipelago's limestone quarries. In his log for the *Antelope* kept between February 1824 and February 1825, Anderson Angus, acting surgeon, reports that the convicts were healthy, well fed and well treated:

'The Prisoners ... the last three months have been in a more healthy state than they ever have since they arrived in Bermuda, the Climate of which seems to have operated beneficially on the most of them as a great many of the Prisoners when they embarked

in the Antelope were much broke down by the irregular [manner] they have been accustomed to live in so that the majority of them had shattered constitutions. The diet of the Prisoners ... is abundant and good, is served out in a most regular [manner], the greatest attention is paid to the Personal cleanliness of the Prisoners, and their clothing, bedding etc. The prisoners are obliged to get up at an early hour in the morning, and are again down at sunset and must be in bed at eight o'clock. During the day they are employed on shore at the various public works on the Island. The Prisons are thoroughly cleaned out [twice] a day after the Prisoners go on shore, and in wet weather they are made to remain under the house till the decks are [clean] and dry. The strictest vigilance is observed by the Officers and Guards to prevent the impudent use of men. The men are never suffered to be exposed to the rain or sun in the hot weather, and when the slightest complaint is made by any prisoner that he is sick or is unable to work he is taken [off] the labor list and retained on board, and treated according to the circumstances of his case... The excellent rules laid down for regulating the discipline of the Ship which are carefully and attentively enforced by the Executive Officers over the Prisoners has been the cause of keeping the Prisoners in so healthy a state during the twelve months.'

This peaceful picture of the Bermuda convict station is shattered elsewhere in Angus's own log where, in his notes on his treatment of Halliday, he reports an attack by one of the convicts on Lieutenant Hire, the hulk overseer, and William Halliday, chief mate, on 28 September 1824:

'While Henry Adams a Prisoner was brought up for to be punished for disorderly conduct, and when he was ordered to strip [to the waist to be flogged] by Lieut. Henry Hire, he drew from his waist one Instrument resembling a carpenters chisel, and made two thrusts at Lieut. Hire with intention to stab. As Hy Hire was protecting himself from the thrusts Mr Halliday closed on Adams in order to disarm him, and put him down, in which act Halliday was stabbed by Adams in the left side with the chisel.'

Halliday survived his injuries and was discharged back to his duties within weeks. Adams, meanwhile, was returned to England for trial. A deposition from Lieutenant Hire to John Henry Capper, Superintendent of Convicts, dated

30 September 1824, describes Adams as a *'turbulent and troublesome character'* who used *'very abusive language and invective'* against Hire and Halliday. Hire also accuses Adams of inciting trouble among other convicts by spreading allegations of abuse on the *Antelope*. It was for this conduct that Adams had been brought before the other convicts to be whipped in September 1824.

Adams, a carpenter, was originally convicted of larceny at the Hampshire Summer Assizes in 1823, and sentenced to seven years' transportation. He spent time on the hulk York at Gosport before he was transported to Bermuda in December 1823. Shortly after his return to England, Adams wrote a series of letters to the Home Secretary Robert Peel, to radical MP John C Hobhouse and to Captain Alexander Lamb, overseer of the *York* hulk, to which he had been transferred. Adams' letters catalogue a series of abuses on the *Antelope* and the *York* which he calls on Peel to investigate and Hobhouse to bring to public consciousness. In his letter to Peel dated 16 January 1826, he writes:

> *'Churches are Built, Bible Societies raised, Gaol Discipline and Slave Emancipation Meetings, yet most strange to tell Convict Hulks are totally forgotten Places teeming with every Crime that can degenerate a Man which loudly calls for inquiry.'*

Adams' account of life on board the *Antelope*, from his letter to Hobhouse dated 31 April 1826, could not be more different to Angus's official report. In the letter, Adams denounces *'the conduct of Keepers and Convicts at Bermuda'*, which he claims:

> *'was of such a disgracefull nature that I wrote a letter to Mr Capper [Superintendent of the Hulks] stating facts. The Overseers informed of what I had done was going to flog me, but refused to tell me my Crime. This I resisted yet offering to submit if I was told any offence. This was refused and [the] Armed Guards was ordered to cut me down, I was attacked, wounded in the head and breast and being seized behind by the mate I wounded him with a Chizle having my tools in my possession at the time. This, Sir, was my offence. Man was going with man. I had dared to make it known. Officers was acting like drunken savages. The Antelope was literally speaking a floating Hell.'*

DOCS. 1 & 2   Henry Adams' letter to MP John C Hobhouse, 16 June 1825.

York Hulk Jan'y 16 - 1825

Sir/
            Finding that Mr Cappes means to wrong
me out of my Tools as well as Money I intends to
Apply to Mr Peel directing my Letter as a private
Letter by that means preventing him from seeing
its contents as if I send it otherwise he will I have
no doubt Suppress it. Mr Cappes conduct Speaks Volumes
he fears to let my Case become public if by wounding
a Villian I done wrong by an exposure I should be
blamed but otherwise is the Case I acted right
he knows it and wish to present they public from
knowing and Judging about it.—

            Mr Cappes said he would detain my Letters will
he dare detain Letters directed to Mr Brougham
and Mr G Bennett.— I shall try his power I am only
a Seven Years Man I scorn all Royal Mercy I wish
to look at they Bay Hulks and I shall Apply to
leave this Country — coming from a warm Climate
I feel the Cold Severely I brought a Bed and Blanket
with me I applied for a Blanket and had a small
Old one given to me more then too Months ago I

Applied for Stockings Nine Weeks I wore a pair with
washing but At length I had an Old p.r given me which
I could get no worsted to Mend if I am not Allow'd
I will Apply to M.r Peel, if I get Wet I must remain
in my wett Cloaths, its impossible to be clean as I am
now Situated and I shall endeavor to lay my Case
before Parliment, I have been Cruelly treated my
Breast and Arms shews indelible proof how I have
suffer'd — and for what — writeing a Letter to M.r
who now proves that —

     Justice with interest never will agree
     Truths a Goddess he'll refuse to see
therefore I shall not waste Breath or Paper during
my Confinement by Applying to him — No I will
at the fountain head and see if he dare prevent me
from doing so I am an Englishman I have a right
to complain and shall maintain that right —

     Against you I have no Complaint I consider you
as a person of Justice and humanity and if I serve
in this Ship any Complaint I have to make shall
be made to you — you Commands — to you alone to
Complain was you aware of many things I firmly

believe they would be Alter'd if I leave as I hope I
shall let others make them Known — if I stay I will
do it allthough I gain enemies elsewhere —

where I now Work there is scarce a tool to use
and what I left at the Dock Yard I have lost often
haveing often been promised that I should go and
get them — Work's expected to be done and no tools
to do it with what Rations I get is Shamefully small
at the Leviathan I had Eighteen pence p. Week
that the humane Mr Capper deprived me of — I would
not Escape when I could with ease so I was removed
and he now hopes in Vain to make me start No I
will not give him a Chance of getting Rid of me for
ge I hope yet to make my foes tremble in spite
of power — I shall meet them if God spares my
life

I remain Sir with respect your
most Obet humble Servant

Hen. Adams

Capt. Lamb

Adams' letters are full of anger at his treatment in Bermuda and in England. He complains that since his transfer back to the *York* he has been kept in double irons and that Capper has been reading his post, preventing him from making his allegations public. His description of life on board the *York* contained in his letter to Captain Lamb, dated 16 January 1826, confirms that Adams continued to find life on the hulks difficult:

> 'Coming from a warm Climate I feel the Cold severely... I applied for a Blanket and had a small old one given to me more than two months ago. I applied for stockings nine weeks I wore a pair without washing but at length I had an Old pair given me which I could get no worsted to mend. If I am not allow'd cloaths I will apply to Mr Peel. If I get Wet I must remain in my wett cloaths, its impossible to be clean as I am now situated and I shall endeavor to lay my case before Parliament. I have been Cruelly treated. My head breast and arms shews indelible proof of how I have suffer'd.'

The Home Office investigated Adams' allegations and, as evidenced by a letter from Robert Peel to John Capper dated 20 April 1827, considered them unfounded. Included with Adams' letters is a letter from the overseer of the *York* hulk, Alexander Lamb, confirming that Adams' experience was typical:

> 'His slops have been issued to him in the usual manner, bearing in mind that no new slops are issued so long as any second hand ones remain in store. He receives 3 ¼ oz of biscuit, three days in the week, the other three one half-penny worth of tobacco and a pint of small beer daily as a ration from the Ordnance. He is at present employed in the carpenter's shop at the Gun Wharf, where he makes himself useful and is attentive, 'tho his language is violent, and I certainly consider him a most mischievous and dangerous character.'

While Adams' allegations were dismissed by the Home Office and the Admiralty, his description of life at the Bermuda convict station is strikingly similar to reports made over twenty years later by George Baxter Grundy, a former convict who had been pardoned and returned home.

Grundy was so disgusted by his experience that he felt compelled to report his concerns to the Home Office in May 1849. His letters were forwarded to the Colonial Office to investigate. In his list of sixteen complaints, he accuses officers of defrauding the public by employing convicts on private matters instead of on public works, of meting out unnecessary and cruel punishments, and of drunkenness, blasphemy and turning a blind eye to prostitution among the convicts. Grundy claims that the setting of such a poor example by naval officers, including Henry Hire, whom he names, prevented the moral reclamation of the convicts:

> 'It is Sir, in consequence of having such men in authority, that drunkenness among the convicts is a common occurrence, and Sir, that vice leads them to commit, (I must speak plainly on this matter), the most unnatural crimes ever heard of. I am positive that were the Government aware of the abominable work carried on in the Hulks they would sink them.'

The Governor of Bermuda was asked to investigate Grundy's allegations, but an enquiry refuted the ex-convict's statements. The Bermuda convict station was so far from home that in many ways it appears to have been out of sight and out of mind. The sharp contrast between official reports of life on the hulks and the testimony of convicts such as Adams, Grundy and others is thought provoking, at the very least. An 1847 Home Office inquiry into the general treatment and conditions on the Woolwich hulks undertaken by Captain William John Williams, Inspector of Prisons, uncovered many administrative failings in the hulk establishment, with particular concerns regarding overall management and supervision of the hulks, diet, punishment and cleanliness. As a result, changes were made to both staff and regulations, but within ten years the era of the hulks came to an end in England, and in 1852 they were retired in Bermuda as well.

List of documents from The National Archives

Index

List of contributors

Introduction
Hester Vaizey

1 EXPLORATION AND DISCOVERY

Spying in the Mediterranean
Timothy Cross

Voyages around the Pacific
Daniel Gilfoyle

Exploring Botany Bay
Emma Down

Expedition to the Northwest Passage
Timothy Cross

Antarctic exploration
Timothy Cross

2 MUTINY AND PIRACY

Pirate or Privateer?
Benjamin Trowbridge

A privateer's commission
Daniel Gilfoyle

The pirate Blackbeard
Gary Thorpe

Mutiny on the *Bounty*
Benjamin Trowbridge

A most savage mutiny
Bruno Pappalardo

3 SCIENCE AND SURGERY

Measuring the Transit of Venus
Timothy Cross & Bruno Pappalardo

Accidents and Disease on board
Bruno Pappalardo

A great naturalist's voyage of discovery
Stephen Twigge

Scurvy on a convict ship
Janet Dempsey

Exotic flora and fauna
Bruno Pappalardo

Cholera on a convict ship
Christopher Day

4 THE NAVY

Life in the Navy
Bruno Pappalardo

The Battle of Quiberon Bay
Benjamin Trowbridge

The Battle of the Nile
Dr Richard Dunley

The Battle of Trafalgar
Bruno Pappalardo

The Battle of Navarino Bay
Dr Richard Dunley

5 EMIGRATION AND TRANSPORTATION

Emigration to the Americas
Roger Kershaw

Convict ships to Australia
Briony Paxman

Emigration to Australasia
Roger Kershaw

Sentenced to transportation
Briony Paxman

Naval consultant:
Bruno Pappalardo

With thanks to:
Paul Carter & Paul Johnson

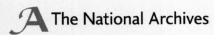 **The National Archives**

The National Archives is the official archives and publisher for the UK Government, and for England and Wales. We work to bring together and secure the future of the public record, both digital and physical, for future generations.

The National Archives is open to all, offering a range of activities and spaces to enjoy, as well as our reading rooms for research. Many of our most popular records are also available online.

nationalarchives.gov.uk
Twitter: @UKNatArchives
Facebook: The National Archives